THE MIDDLE EAST IN THE MIDDLE AGES:
THE EARLY MAMLUK SULTANATE 1250–1382

The Middle East in the middle ages

THE EARLY MAMLUK SULTANATE 1250–1382

Robert Irwin

Southern Illinois University Press
Carbondale and Edwardsville

Southern Illinois University Press, P.O. Box 3697,
Carbondale, Illinois 62901

Library of Congress Cataloging in Publication Data

Irwin, Robert, 1946–
    The Middle East in the Middle Ages.
    Bibliography: p.
    Includes index.
    1. Egypt — History. 2. Mamluks. 3. Islamic
Empire — History — 1258–1517. I. Title.
    DT96.4.I78   1986   909′.097671   85–26102

ISBN 0–8093–1286–7

Printed and bound in Great Britain

CONTENTS

Source: Reproduced with permission from I.M. Lapidus, *Muslim Cities in the Later Middle Ages,* Cambridge University Press.

ABBREVIATIONS

BEO	*Bulletin d'Etudes Orientales*
BSOAS	*Bulletin of the School of Oriental and African Studies*
EI(1)	*Encyclopaedia of Islam* (first edition, 1913–36)
EI(2)	*Encyclopaedia of Islam* (second edition, 1960–)
IJMES	*International Journal of Middle Eastern Studies*
JA	*Journal Asiatique*
JAOS	*Journal of the American Oriental Society*
JESHO	*Journal of the Economic and Social History of the Orient*
JRAS	*Journal of the Royal Asiatic Society*
REI	*Revue des Études Islamiques*
SI	*Studia Islamica*
WZKM	*Wiener Zeitschrift für die Kunde des Morgenlandes*

To Felicity who has spent so much of her time competing with the Mamluks, usually successfully.

INTRODUCTION

'Why another history of the Mamluk Sultanate?' I can (with difficulty) imagine some readers asking. 'Do we not already have Gustav Weil's *Geschichte des Abbasidenchalifats in Egypten?*' Well, yes, but Weil's history was, as its title suggests, unduly preoccupied with the affairs of the shadow caliphate in Egypt at the expense of the Mamluks themselves. Many readers now find the heavy gothic print of the *Geschichte* hard going, and besides the book was written over 120 years ago. The pace of Orientalist scholarship is extremely slow, its fields are broad and few people work in them. Weil's was the first and last history of the period to provide a scholarly apparatus of regular references. Later general surveys of the period, those of William Muir, Gaston Wiet and John Bagot Glubb, have not rendered Weil's scholarship obsolete, nor did they seek to do so. Nevertheless, though the advance of scholarship in this area has been patchy, important and often brilliant work has been done on particular aspects of Mamluk history in recent decades. (Ayalon on armies, Lapidus on towns, Haarmann on sources and folklore and Garcin on provincial life are among the examples that come to mind.) Interest in Mamluk institutions and culture has certainly increased in recent years and, while this book was nearing completion, new studies have appeared, of which I have not been able to take full account.[1] New sources have also come to light and a few of them have even been printed. It is time, after 120 years, for a new work of synthesis.

This work offers a chronological survey of the history of the Bahri Mamluk Sultanate and a narrative framework within which recent research and, perhaps, future research may be understood. In it political events are matched to administrative reforms and both to cultural developments. The notes and bibliography direct the reader's attention to the massive body of primary and secondary materials that bear on the subject. The subject is of some importance. For over two and a half centuries the Mamluk Sultanate was one of the world's great powers. The decisions its sultans took not only affected the fortunes of their subjects — in Egypt, Syria, Tripolitania, the Hejaz, Cilicia and Eastern Turkey — but also the destinies of those in the Crusader principalities, Byzantium, the European trading powers, the sultans of India and the vast Mongol empire. The spice trade which flowed through Egypt and Syria was of crucial importance for the economic development of medieval and renaissance Europe. For a long time the region was a major source of cotton and linen textiles, and the Mamluk period is of the first importance for the history of Islamic architecture, book production and metalwork. Much of what we think of as distinctively Islamic was not really the product of some earlier and rather notional 'Golden Age of Islam', under the first four caliphs, or the Abbasids, or the Fatimids. Rather the shape of such things as the layout of Cairo, the structure and content of the *Arabian Nights* and the development of dervish orders are really products of the Mamluk age.

Moreover, the unique system by which the governing white slave elite was recruited, trained and promoted to the highest positions in the state, is, or should be, of particular interest to students of comparative political science and sociology. The weakness of hereditary principle and the rise of something like a meritocracy reveals in a peculiarly distinct form the factional nature of politics in the Near East. Potentially, the area and the field provide a superb testing ground for theories about faction and feud. The tenure of power at the top was very insecure — at first sight the history of Egypt and Syria is little more than a sequence of sultans, whose often obscure reigns are embellished only by their own assassination, by the spectres of strangled emirs and slaughtered viziers; yet paradoxically the system itself was very stable. Indeed, in many respects, the mamluk system survived the Mamluk regime and lived on in Egypt until the nineteenth century.

The period is peculiarly rich in sources — chronicles, biographical dictionaries, topographical surveys, encomia on individual sultans, chancery encyclopedias, archival material relating to *waqf*s and legal transactions, poetry and popular romances, manuals of instruction on warfare, falconry, etc. Nor are the sources only literary. Epigraphy, archaeology and numismatics have important contributions to make. If I have made almost no use of the latter type of source material, it is only because the literary materials are so rich and so overwhelming in their bulk. Where possible in the text I have given references to secondary sources in European languages which can take the interested reader further. But often this has not been possible and reference has been made to medieval source material, though preferably to published texts, even if those texts are often relatively late compilations. Many of the best sources for the period remain unpublished and doubtless in many cases undiscovered. Those that have been published have often not been edited or read with the attention they deserve. No extended discussion of chronicle and biographical source material is offered here, but since this is one of the areas in which a great deal of interesting work has been done recently, important studies in source criticism are noted at the end of the introduction.[2] Until the publication of all the best sources (among them al-'Ayni, the remaining volumes of al-Safadi, al-Dhahabi's history, al-Nuwayri's encyclopedia, the rest of al-Yunini, etc.) any history of the period will be premature. This history is certainly premature, but since I do not expect to see all or many more of the best sources published in my lifetime, I thought it desirable to bring out this interim report. Many of its hypotheses and conclusions are undoubtedly wrong and will be challenged in time. That was why it was written.

I should like to thank my typists, Fiona Pankhurst and Rosemary Mead. I am also grateful to Helen Irwin and to Doctors Patricia Crone, Martin Hinds, Hugh Kennedy and David Morgan for reading the work in typescript. I have not always heeded their wise suggestions and the errors that remain are, obstinately, my own.

Notes

1. In particular, see E. Ashtor, *Levantine Trade in the Later Middle Ages* (Princeton, 1983); *Muqarnas: An Annual on Islamic Art and Architecture*, vol. 2 (1984); O. Grabar (ed.), The Art of the Mamluks; *Muslim World*, vol. 73 (1983), for articles by Little on religious policy, Petry on patronage, Mackie on silks, and Bijlefeld on medieval European perceptions; P.W. Edbury (ed.), *Crusade and Settlement* (Cardiff, 1985), for articles by Holt and by Irwin on Crusaders and Mamluks, and by Morgan and by Thorau on Mongols and Mamluks.
2. The following sources are especially useful:
Ashtor, E., 'Some Unpublished Sources for the Bahri Period', *Scripta Hierosolymitana*, vol. 9 (1961), pp. 11–30
—— 'Étude sur quelques chroniques mamloukes', *Israel Oriental Studies*, vol. 1 (1971), pp. 272-97
Cahen, C., 'Les Chroniques Arabes concernant la Syrie, l'Égypte et la Mesopotamie de la conquête Arabe à la conquête Ottoman dans les bibliothèques d'Istanbul', *REI*, vol. 10 (1936), pp. 332-62
—— *La Syrie du Nord* (Paris, 1940), esp. pp. 62-89
—— 'Editing Arab Chronicles: A Few Suggestions', *Islamic Studies*, vol. 1 (1962), pp. 1-25
Douglas, F.M., 'Dreams, the Blind and the Semiotics of the Biographical Notice', *SI*, vol. 51 (1980), pp.137-62
Elham, S.M., *Kitbuga und Lagin. Studien zur Mamluken-Geschichte nach Baibars al-Mansuri und an-Nuwairi* (Freiburg, 1977)
Haarmann, U., 'Auflösung und Bewahrung der Klassischen Formen arabischer

Introduction

Geschichtsschreibung in der Zeit der Mamluken', *Zeitschrift der Deutschen Morgenlandischen Gesellschaft,* vol. 121 (1971), pp.46-60

—— *Quellenstudien zür fruhen Mamlukenzeit* (Freiburg, 1970)

—— 'Quellen zu Geschichte des islamischen Agyptens', *Mitteilungen des Deutschen Archaologischen Instituts, Abteilung Kairo,* vol. 38 (1982), pp. 201-10

Kortantamer, S., *Agypten und Syrien zwischen 1317 und 1341 in der Chronik des Mufaddal b. Abi l-Fada'il* (Freiburg, 1973)

Little, D.P., *An Introduction to Mamluk Historiography* (Wiesbaden, 1970)

—— 'The Recovery of a Lost Source for Bahri Mamluk History: al-Yusufi's Nuzhat al-Nasir fi Sirat al-Malik al-Nasir', *JAOS,* vol. 94 (1974), pp. 42-54

—— 'An Analysis of the Relation between Four Mamluk Chronicles for 737-745', *Journal of Semitic Studies,* vol. 19 (1974), pp. 252-68

—— 'Al-Safadi as Biographer of his Contemporaries', in D.P. Little (ed.), *Essays on Islamic Civilization: Presented to Niyazi Berkes* (Leiden, 1976), pp. 190-211

—— 'The Significance of the Haram Documents for the Study of Medieval Islamic History', *Der Islam,* vol. 57 (1980), pp. 189-219

Meinecke-Berg, V. 'Quellen zu Topographie und Baugeschichte in Kairo unter Sultan an-Nasir b. Qala'un', *Zeitschrift der Deutschen Morgenlandischen Gesellschaft,* supp.3 (XIX Deutscher Orientalistentag, 1975) (1977), pp.538-50

Sauvaget, J., *Introduction to the History of the Muslim East* (2nd edn by C. Cahen) (Berkeley and Los Angeles, 1965)

Schäfer, B., *Beiträge zur mamlukischen Historiographie nach dem Tode al-Malik al-Nasirs, mit einem Teiledition der Chronik Sams ad-Din as-Suga'is* (Freiburg, 1971)

1 THE ORIGINS OF THE MAMLUK REGIME

History is for the most part the creation of settled civilisation, of towns and agricultural centres. The nomad and the pastoralist have left little independent record of themselves. It is however impossible to understand the history of the settled regimes in Egypt and Syria in the Later Middle Ages without some knowledge of the history and way of life of the nomadic steppe peoples of Eurasia. It is necessary to begin by abandoning for a while the conventional fixed point of observation located, as it were, above Cairo or Damascus.

The steppe lands — for the most part treeless, grassy plains — extend in a broadly curving swathe across the Eurasian land mass from tne edge of China to the Danube. The steppes are bounded on the north by the Siberian forests and tundra. In the south the steppes peter out either in desert or in the foothills of mountain ranges. The steppes themselves receive relatively little rainfall and within historic times desiccation has turned areas of the steppe into desert or semi-desert. To some extent, doubtless, over-grazing of the grasslands has assisted this process, for from about 3000 BC onwards, when the horse and camel were first domesticated, the Eurasian steppes have been dominated by tribes of nomadic pastoralists. These pastoralists raised herds of horses, sheep, goats and camels. Their mobile encampments were transported on the backs of camels or by ox carts. Their armies were cavalry armies. But though the steppes were dominated by horse-rearing nomads, they were not monopolised by them. Some tribes, particularly on the northern fringes, specialised in forest hunting, while on the western steppes rivercraft and fishing played an important part in the steppe economy. On the southern fringes of the steppe settlements were more frequent and crop growing more important. Moreover, the nomad pastoralists themselves were not all of one type. Apart from linguistic and racial divisions, they differed from one another first in the degree of contact that they had with settled civilisations, such as the Chinese empire, and secondly in the nature of their nomadism. Some nomad tribes were transhumants, following a regular annual pattern of movement between winter pasture and summer pasture, a pattern of existence which allows us to call some of them semi-settled. Others, however, were free-ranging nomads relying on military force to take possession of the pasturage they needed from season to season.

These distinctions in degrees of culture and organisation, though often quite radical, are hard for us to trace from the written records of the past for, to the medieval observers of the nomad invasions in China, the Near East and Eastern Europe, one mounted and predatory barbarian looked very much like another. From prehistoric times until at least the late thirteenth century, wave after wave of nomadic warrior tribes threatened the existence of the settled empires of Asia and Europe — Scythians, Sarmatians, Parthians, Huns, Avars, Alans, Uighurs, Ghuzz, Patzinaks, Kipchaks and Mongols. No conclusive explanation for the formation of such large tribal confederacies and their periodic invasions of China, Russia and the Near East can be offered. It is possible that cyclical desiccation of the grasslands or, alternatively, a high birthrate among the nomads drove them southwards and westwards out of the central steppe area. It is more certain that in periods of Chinese strength the emperors intervened and used military force, diplomacy and bribery to keep the nomads on their frontiers weak and divided, but when the Chinese themselves were weak they were powerless to prevent the formation of great tribal confederacies. As these confederacies extended their power, they drove other tribes westwards before them and these in turn pressed on others who eventually appeared on the eastern and northern fringes of Europe and the Near East in the dual role of refugees and invaders. This westward drift of tribes was rarely, if ever, reversed — partly perhaps because there is a tendency for the grasslands to become lusher in the west because of the rivers that flow into the Caspian and Black Seas.[1]

The first Turkish empire was formed on the steppes north of the Gobi during a period of Chinese weakness in the sixth century. It subsequently divided into two parts and the western empire extended its sway over Turkestan, Transoxiana and the northern fringes of Khorasan. The Turks moving westwards drove the Avars before them into Europe. In the seventh century the eastern empire of the 'Blue Turks' reabsorbed most of the territories of the western empire, but in the early eighth century this empire was in turn overthrown by the Uighur Turks who took possession of the northern and eastern lands of the 'Blue Turks', while Western Turkestan came under Chinese overlordship.

From the seventh century onwards the movement of the Turkish peoples towards the Near Eastern heartlands was matched by the eruption of Arab tribes from the Arabian Peninsula into the territories of the Byzantine and Sassanian empires. At the time of the Prophet Mohammed's death in AD 632, most of the Arabian Peninsula had submitted to Islam. Within the next 30 years Arab armies had gone on to conquer Egypt, Libya, Syria, Iraq, Armenia and Persia. By the mid-eighth century, when the first of the Abbasid caliphs assumed the leadership of the Islamic community, Arab armies had conquered North Africa and Spain in the west, had advanced to the Indus River in the east and, most importantly, advanced north-east from Khorasan into Transoxiana. Transoxiana by the mid-eighth century was extensively settled by Turks and was to become for a long time the most important area from which Turks were recruited into the armies of the Abbasid Caliphate and of the Arab princes and governors. In 751 an Arab army's victory at the Battle of Talas over a combined force of Chinese imperial troops and Turkish tribesmen confirmed the Arabs in the possession of Western Turkestan.

By the late eighth century the advance of Arab armies up to the Caucasus, the Caspian Sea, the Aral Sea and across the Oxus gave the Caliphate a long common frontier (in so far as one can speak of a 'frontier' in this period) with the Turkish tribes and settlements in the steppe and desert land to the north and, from the early ninth century onwards, Turks were playing an increasingly important role in the affairs of the Caliphate and the states which succeeded it or seceded from it — ultimately a dominant role. The Turks entered the Near East in tribal groups seeking pasturage or as individual mercenaries or mamluks employed in the armies of the Arab rulers.[2]

The word 'mamluk' can be translated as 'slave' (the verbal root M–L–K has the sense of 'to possess'). Normally the term 'mamluk' was specifically used to refer to a military slave. However, there are some indications that in the early period of Islam, the term was occasionally used to refer to a free client or devoted follower of a ruler or an emir. More importantly, throughout the medieval and early modern periods the term 'mamluk' was extended to refer to military slaves after their emancipation.[3] In considering the mamluk institution we should avoid giving it associations which the term slavery may have for us. The mamluks were not hewers of wood and drawers of water. They did not serve as bath attendants nor did they labour in the fields. There are other terms in Arabic which can be used for such menial slaves (e.g. *'abd* or *khadim*). The mamluks were first and foremost military slaves. In so far as they performed or could be expected to perform other functions, these were normally of a ceremonial or an administrative nature. Thus we find mamluks acting as the equerries, cup bearers and falconers of the rulers and we find them serving also as provincial governors, major-domos of the royal household or treasurers. Far from degrading him, the 'slavery' of a mamluk was the enviable first stage in a career which opened to him the possibility of occupying the highest offices in the state. In the early centuries of the history of the institution it was relatively unimportant whether the mamluk who rose to high office had been manumitted or not. In general it seems that it was not the rule for the mamluks of the Abbasids and the Seljuk rulers to be freed at any particular stage of their career.

The 'slavery' of a mamluk provided the framework within which a young recruit to an elite formation within the army could be trained and disciplined and could be forced to accept a degree of discipline which the early Islamic rulers had not found it possible to impose on their other free-born household, tribal or client levies. This discipline and long period of training were to be particularly important for elite troops because of the growing reliance on horse archers in the Islamic armies. The skills of the horse archer are not easily taught. Moreover, the Turkish horse archer's short recurved bow, composed of splinted wood, horn and sinew, while it was an extremely effective weapon, superior to the medieval English longbow in range, force and accuracy, made enormous demands on its wielder of both strength and application.[4] The slavery of the mamluk enabled the teaching of such specialised skills and the development of the necessary muscles. Beyond that it enabled the inculcation of loyalty due from a mamluk to his *ustadh* ('master' or 'owner'). The bonds thus formed between the mamluk and his *ustadh* might be very close: the mamluk might refer to his *ustadh* as his father and the *ustadh* might reciprocate by making his slave his heir after death. According to some Islamic juridical texts, moreover, the man who emancipated a slave gave him life and therefore was indeed in a sense his father. The duty owed by a royal mamluk to the sultan who purchased and trained him was in no way diminished by subsequent emancipation. The mamluks were soldiers but they were also members of the household, of the extended family of their master.

A mamluk was often taught other skills beyond the purely

military ones in the early years of his enslavement — in particular mamluks were often taught to speak Arabic and sometimes taught to read and write in Arabic as well. The mamluks who were taught Arabic were for the most part Turks — or at least peoples characterised by their Arab masters as Turks, for the medieval Arabs were even more vague than modern ethnographers and etymologists as to the racial and linguistic bounds of the Turks, and at times Mongol, Persian and Caucasian groupings were labelled 'Turk'.

There are occasional references to the employment of mamluks apparently of Iranian origin under the Umayyads and early Abbasids in the eighth century. However, the employment of mamluks by the caliphs and by provincial dynasties only really became widespread in the ninth century and by then the overwhelming majority of such troops were clearly Turkish in origin. The creation by the Caliph al-Mu'tasim (833–42) of a large regiment of Turkish mamluks was particularly important. These mamluks, converted, presumably nominally, to Islam, were not stationed in the Abbasid capital of Baghdad, but instead were placed in nearby Samarra where they might be isolated from court and provincial intrigues. The young pagan Turks were acquired by the ruler as tribute from the eastern provinces of the Caliphate, or as human booty from campaigns in those regions, or by purchase. On the steppes warfare — the raiding of other tribes' herds of livestock and the taking into captivity of the defeated — formed a crucial part of the nomad economy. The slavers who sold Turks to the Islamic regimes were for the most part themselves Turks. At times of hardship, particularly of drought, families might sell their own children into captivity. Then again it occasionally happened, particularly in later centuries, that a man inspired by ambition might sell himself into captivity.

In the course of the ninth and tenth centuries the employment of Turkish mamluks became widespread in other Muslim principalities, some of which were only in nominal allegiance to the Abbasid Caliphate — most notably the Samanid rulers of Transoxiana (819—1005) and the Ghaznavid rulers of Afghanistan and Eastern Iran (994–1040). Turkish mamluks were even employed in Muslim Spain and North Africa. However, although the schismatic Fatimid caliphs — who were rulers of first North Africa and then of Egypt (909–1171) — made use of regiments of Turkish mamluks, most of their slave soldiers were black Africans.

Nubians, Slavs, Armenians, Iranians (but never Arabs) might be employed as mamluks. However, throughout the Islamic lands generally rulers and emirs preferred to make use of Turks, and this was not simply a matter of their relative availability. The fighting qualities of the Turkish peoples may be reckoned as a literary *topos* in medieval Arabic literature. For instance, in his ninth-century 'Epistle Concerning the Qualities of the Turk', al-Jahiz expatiates on the extraordinary abilities of the Turks as archers and horsemen, and then goes on to remark:

> They care only about raiding, hunting, horsemanship, skir-mishing with rival chieftains, taking booty and invading other countries. Their efforts are all directed towards these activities, and they devote all their energies to these occupations. In this way they have acquired a mastery of these skills, which for them take the place of craftsmanship and commerce and constitute their only pleasure, their glory and the subject of all their conversation. Thus they have become in warfare what the Greeks are in philosophy.[5]

Beyond their martial qualities, the Turks were also esteemed in the Near East for their physical beauty, a consideration of some importance if they were to serve as pages and attendants of the ruler (and occasionally as his bedfellows).

At first sight the advantages of possessing an elite army of white slaves are obvious. As indicated above, their status as slaves in principle made it easy to discipline and train the Turks. Moreover, the training and subsequent employment of mamluks was by no means restricted only to military matters. The Turkish mamluks were often taught languages and literary and administrative skills. Thus Turkish mamluks were trained to occupy administrative posts which the religiously orientated education of Arab civilians poorly equipped them to fill. The slave status of the mamluks also made it easier to isolate them from provincial factions and landed interests. The fact that the mamluks constituted a non-hereditary military caste ensured in principle that promotion from within their ranks would be based on merit rather than blood ties and also hindered them from accumulating lands and fiscal wealth. In practice, however, as we shall see, the mamluks ultimately proved to be no more reliable politically and no less riven by faction than other free-born military groupings. Fairly early on, mamluk regiments in several parts of the Islamic world established themselves as a sort of Praetorian Guard exercising effective power and leaving the nominal ruler only a shadow of his authority and, despite the ethic of loyalty to his purchaser/master with which the mamluk was supposed to have been inculcated, again and again we find mamluk troops deserting their employers to whom they were bound neither by blood nor by any long-term landed interest.

Further, if the employment of mamluks was militarily efficient and politically judicious, it is curious that we do not find more widespread evidence of their use in other areas and other times. Parallels can of course be found — for example in the occasional use of gladiators as soldiers by the Romans, in the Russian use of slave administrators *(qullari)*, and in the German employment of administrators and soldiers of servile status *(ministeriales)*. Most strikingly, the Christian kingdom of Georgia employed slave soldiers of Turkish origin. However, setting medieval Georgia aside, the analogies are only occasional and partial. Given the almost universal employment of slave soldiers by Islamic regimes from Morocco to Muslim India and from roughly the early ninth century to the early nineteenth, the mamluk institution can plausibly be viewed as a peculiarly Islamic phenomenon. It is tempting to go beyond this and argue that the mamluk institution was a response to Islam's failure to legitimate other, more satisfactory, ways of distributing political and military power. It could also be argued that there was an unbridgeable gulf between the Muslims' ideal conception of a unitary Islamic state under the leadership of a caliph or *imam* universally acceptable to the Muslim community and the political reality of deep-running provincial and ideological divisions. The preaching and early history of Islam do not seem to have provided any adequate ideological basis for political participation in a vast empire whose rule could no longer be vested in a narrow tribal elite of Arabs. Islamic ideals underwrote the widespread refusal of the '*ulama*' (the religio-clerical elite) to participate in political decision-making. Arab tribal chiefs were unable to extend the sources of their support far beyond their own tribes and immediate clients. In their place came alien rulers who used alien slave guards to distance and protect them from their subjects. Their subjects, united in Islam but divided in everything else, accepted such government as being better than no government at all.

The sort of argument outlined above, which places great

emphasis on the arbitrary and alien nature of rule by slaves, can hardly furnish a sufficient explanation if only because of the widely differing nature of slave soldier systems in Islamic history. The gulf between the slave soldiers and the rest of the population was not always very marked. Thus, for instance, in Seljuk Anatolia Turkish slaves fought alongside free Turkish cavalry. Then again the Ottoman janissaries were from the sixteenth century onwards closely integrated in the social and economic life of the big cities. They were not in any way distanced from local interest groups and, as will become apparent, the same observation applies to a lesser extent to the mamluks of the Later Middle Ages.

The fact that so many Islamic armies relied for their elite troops on men who were or had been formally slaves of course requires explanation. However, it must be noted that mamluks, after their initial period of training at least, were normally paid, and rather generously paid. Their actual terms of service were not so very different from those of mercenaries and conscripts in Western history. Specialised corps of foreign mercenaries are common enough in the European Middle Ages — for instance, Hungarian cavalry in Italy or Genoese crossbowmen in France. It is tempting to look on mamluks as mercenaries in disguise but there are crucial differences. Individual mamluks, like individual mercenaries in Europe, were sometimes successful in establishing for themselves rule over towns or provinces and in founding new dynasties. But if one compares the mamluks with, say, the mercenary condottiere of fourteenth- and fifteenth-century Italy, what is striking in the Islamic case is the failure of broader groups of mamluks to establish themselves in the countryside as a hereditary landed baronage. To some extent this is to be explained by the impossibility of transmitting mamluk status to one's children (see below). To a greater extent, though, it must be understood in terms of the Middle Eastern environment which was, relatively, highly urbanised and fiscally sophisticated. The urban nature of the mamluks is as striking as their servile status. Mamluks were trained and garrisoned in the towns. They were not directly dependent on the seasons of harvest and pasturage. Such freehold property as they managed to acquire tended to be in the towns. Their children mingled with and became assimilated with the townspeople. Even though the mamluks' income would probably derive from assignments of tax revenue from rural estates or from wages based on taxes levied on the countryside, the mamluks were by that very fact closely dependent on a centralised urban regime's power to determine the taxes due to the state and to channel those revenues to the court and the barracks.

Of course it is unreasonable to tax Islam with failing to prevent the rise to power of secular and foreign usurpers and, having failed to do that, of additionally failing to provide some sacrally based form of legitimation for those usurpers. Such a perfectly functional religion is hard to imagine. Nevertheless, some weight must be given to certain aspects of Islamic law and doctrine in seeking to explain the mamluk phenomenon. Thus if one wished to employ idolatrous Turkish horsemen as a standing corps of paid troops, they would have to be brought into the Islamic lands under the technical guise of slaves, for while Christians, Jews and other 'Peoples of the Book' were protected under the Islamic dispensation, idolators were not tolerated within the *Dar al-Islam* (lands of Islam) except as slaves. Conversely, if one was to employ large numbers of slaves at all, they had to be recruited from outside Islamic society, for by Islamic law Muslims could not be enslaved. It is because of this that the Arabian Peninsula, potentially a reservoir of vigorous nomads and skilled horse archers, could not answer the case — even though in the thirteenth century, for instance, a very large part of the 'mamluk' army on campaign would be provided by free-born Arabs, and trainee mamluks seem to have studied archery under Arab masters.

Again, according to Islamic law, a slave cannot exercise any form of jurisdiction over a freeman; to do so he would have to be manumitted. This injunction was not always heeded and it seems that Abbasid and Seljuk mamluks often remained slaves throughout their career. In Mamluk Egypt and Syria, however (that is from the late thirteenth to early sixteenth centuries), it was the rule for a mamluk to be manumitted before exercising independent discretion in military and civil matters. A precondition of the mamluk's manumission was his instruction in and conversion to Islam. He was then debarred by his conversion and manumission from passing on his mamluk status to his children, if he had any.

It is tempting to emphasise the availability of the Turk, his need to be employed — the need of victorious tribes on the fringes of the Islamic lands to sell their captives; the need of impoverished families and individuals to sell themselves; the need of the Turks in general to find a way of entry and a place for themselves in the Near Eastern lands. Yet if it had merely been such an extrinsic factor which explained the rise of the mamluks we should then still have to ask ourselves some questions. Why did the Chinese not similarly make use of Turkish horse archers? Why did the Byzantines and the Hungarians find other means of accommodating the Turks within their lands? Why did the Christian Russians not use an ethnically distinct slave soldiery? Slavery of other kinds was certainly familiar to the Chinese, the Byzantines and the Russians.

Even from the drastically simplified argument presented above, it must be apparent that there is no simple explanation for the widespread use of slave soldiers in Islamic history. Rather, the appearance and rise to power of the mamluks is to be understood in terms of a complex concatenation of social, religio-legal, military and demographic factors. Islamic law, the urban nature of Near Eastern society, Turkish tribal movements and the particular skill of the horse archer — all these factors are crucial in determining the nature of the mamluk institution.

In the late tenth century a new wave of Turks entered the lands of the Caliphate, this time not as individual slaves, but in large bands of free warriors and conquerors. These Turks, the Seljuks, converted at an early stage to Islam. The causes of the appearance of the Seljuk Turks — first in Transoxiana and then in the heartlands of the Middle East — may be traced back to developments on the Chinese frontier/border in the previous century. The weakness of the Chinese empire after the fall of the Tang dynasty led to the formation of a powerful confederacy of the Tunguz, an Altaic group, on the northern frontiers of China. Their expansion in turn put pressure on a Turkish group of tribes known as the Oghuz to move westwards, so that by the early tenth century the Oghuz had reached the River Jaxartes and the edge of Arab-ruled lands. The Seljuks were a leading clan within the Ghuzz (from the broad grouping of the Ghuzz Turks were to come not only the Seljuks, but in later centuries, the Ottomans, the Aqqoyunlu and Qaraqoyunlu dynasties). The Seljuks entered the service of the Ghaznavid rulers of Transoxiana, then in 1037 they rebelled and seized power for themselves. Within a few decades most of the Seljuks seem to have converted to Islam. In 1055 the Seljuks occupied Baghdad and exercised rule over the heartland of the Caliphate under the nominal authority of the Abbasid caliph. These Seljuks are now known as the Greater Seljuks to distinguish them from another branch of the dynasty, the Lesser Seljuks, who moved on westwards in the course of the eleventh century to conquer the greater part of Asia Minor from the Byzantines. Seljuk sultans continued to rule over Iraq and Western Iran until 1194 and became identified with the defence of Sunni Islam not only from Christian powers such as Byzantium, but also from the threat of Shi'ite Fatimid caliphs in Cairo.[6]

In the course of the eleventh century, the rule of the Seljuk sultans over their western lands weakened considerably and many of the towns and provinces of Syria and Iraq were covertly or openly independent of rule by the sultans, though almost everywhere the rulers and elite troops remained Turkish. Moreover, armies sent by the Egyptian Fatimid caliphs succeeded for a time in occupying Palestine and much of Syria. Thus when the armies of the First Crusade (1096–9) entered Syria, they faced disunited Turkish princelings and armies whose religious allegiances were to the rival Caliphates in Sunni Baghdad and Shi'ite Cairo and who were unable to co-operate against the unexpected Christian threat. The Muslim counter-Crusade, or *jihad*, only really began to get under way some 40 years later under the leadership of the Zengid princes of Mosul and, subsequently, Damascus.

Though Zengi and Nur al-Din were Turks and their armies were predominantly turkish in composition, nevertheless considerable numbers of Kurds served as cavalry, in return for money or *iqta'*. (*Iqta'*, in the strictest sense, was the allocation of tax revenues in money or in kind from a designated area of land or other revenue source for a limited period in return for administrative or military service.) The Kurds are racially and linguistically quite distinct from the Turks and Arabs. In the twelfth century many Kurds migrated from their homelands in the Southern Caucasus and Azerbaijan and entered Syria and Iraq either as soldiers or as pastoralist tribesmen. In 1169 Nur al-Din sent an army under two Kurdish generals to take Egypt from the Fatimids. That army was successful and in 1171 Saladin deposed the last Fatimid caliph of Egypt, thereby formally bringing Egypt once more within the fold of Sunni Islam. Soon afterwards he disbanded the black slave regiments of the Fatimids. Though Saladin for some years maintained the appearance of allegiance to his Zengid overlord in Syria, in 1174 on Nur al-Din's death, he cast off this pretence and advanced out of Egypt to occupy Damascus. In 1187 he inflicted a major defeat on the armies of the Crusader kingdom of Jerusalem, and was able to retake much of Palestine from the Christians. The prestige of Saladin's clan, the Ayyubids, owed much to Saladin's prosecution of the *jihad*. In the first half of the thirteenth century rule over Egypt, Syria, the Yemen and parts of Iraq was shared out among the Ayyubid kinsmen and descendants of Saladin.[7]

As has been remarked above, Saladin disbanded the regiments of black mamluk infantry in Egypt. From the late twelfth century onwards until at least the early sixteenth century, the most important part of the Egyptian armies would be furnished by the cavalry. Naturally, Kurdish officers and soldiers were favoured by the Ayyubid princes. Nevertheless, it seems that in general the majority of the officers and elite troops in the Ayyubid armies were Turkish and mamluk.[8] Moreover, reliance on Turkish mamluks increased markedly under the last of the great Ayyubid princes, al-Salih Ayyub, ruler of Egypt from 1240 and of Damascus from 1245 until his death in 1249. Most of the mamluks purchased by al-Salih Ayyub derived from a Turkish tribe, or rather group of tribes, the Kipchaks, who as far as can be determined had not been employed in significant numbers by any previous ruler of Syria or Egypt.[9] In his struggles against the coastal remnants of the Crusader principalities and against rival members of his family, al-Salih Ayyub also made use of Khwarazmian Turkish freebooters.[10] Later, in the 1250s, Shahrazuri Kurds came to be employed as mercenary auxiliaries.[11] The reason for the new availability as soldiers in the Near East of these peoples — Kipchak, Khwarazmian and Shahrazuri — must be traced back to events on the Eurasian steppe, to the rise of the Mongols on the northern frontiers of China and their westward advance towards Europe and the Near East.

Little is known about the history of the Mongols before the rise of Chingiz Khan. They appear in the early twelfth century to have been a small tribe of pastoralists and forest hunters dwelling in North-east Mongolia between Lake Baikal and the Altai mountains. Although the Mongols were frequently confused with Turks and seen as forming part of one race by medieval Arab and European observers, the consensus of modern scholarship seems to be that in their racial and linguistic origins the Turkish and Mongolian peoples are quite distinct. Inevitably, however, as the Mongols extended their sway there was a great deal of borrowing in language and other areas of culture. Eventually the Mongols were to adopt the Turkish Uighur script as the alphabet for their language.

Chingiz Khan (1167–1227) brought about a union of the related Kerait, Naiman and other tribes under the leadership of the Mongol tribe from whom the whole confederacy took its name. The Chin empire in Northern China was far too weak to break up this new confederacy and was itself eventually conquered by the Mongols. In contrast to other more loosely formed nomadic confederacies, Chingiz Khan and his generals relied for their successes in warfare upon a hierarchically structured and tightly disciplined army. Every adult male Mongol had a place in an army that was organised in ascending decimal units. Apart from specially detached expeditionary forces, the Mongol army on the move was the Mongol people on the move. The warriors travelled with strings of spare mounts, with their families (occasionally the women fought too) and with flocks of sheep and horses. The demands such a force made in the way of pasturage and provisioning forced it to move on fairly regularly and at times dictated the route it would take. As the successful Mongol armies moved westwards across the steppes and deserts of Eurasia, their numbers were further swollen by tributaries and allies, mostly from Turkish tribes. Their numbers were also increased by captives from the defeated, who as slaves served the Mongols particularly as artisans and technical experts. Nevertheless, it must be emphasised that by comparison with most of the armies that confronted them the Mongol armies were not particularly large. The 'horde' relied for its victories on mobility, discipline and the fear that the news of their coming spread in advance of them.[12]

By 1218 the Mongol advance had brought them into conflict with the Khwarazm-Shahs. The Khwarazm-Shah 'Ala al-Din Muhammad ruled over a Turkish Muslim empire that included Transoxiana as well as much of Iran and Afghanistan. Although the aristocracy of this empire was Khwarazmian Turkish, it has been estimated that as much as half the army of the Khwarazm-Shahs was made up of cavalry from another group of Turkish tribes, the Kipchaks, most of whom may have been purchased as slaves.[13] By 1220 the Mongols had defeated and chased 'Ala al-Din Muhammad from his lands and occupied the Khwarazmian capital, Samarqand. Khwarazmian resistance revived, however, in 1224 under 'Ala al-Din's son, Jalal al-Din Mingburnu, who established himself in North-east Iran and Azerbaijan. Jalal al-Din was further successful in establishing his authority in the Southern Caucasus and Anatolia and posed as the leader of Muslim resistance to the pagan Mongols. Nevertheless, Mongol generals in a campaign in 1230–1 were finally successful in defeating and eliminating Jalal al-Din.[14] Jalal al-Din's retreat westwards across Iran, and his campaigns in the Caucasus, as well as the subsequent Mongol pursuit had caused widespread disruption to settled and tribal life in the Near East. After 1231 large bodies of Khwarazmian Turks who had formerly been part of Jalal al-Din's army began to filter down through Iraq and Syria, causing further disruption as freebooters and mercenaries. They were preceded and followed by similar groups of Kurds displaced in these campaigns.

Although the Mongol generals Jebe and Subetey had passed through Northern Iran and Azerbaijan in pursuit of the Khwaraz-mians in 1220–1, they subsequently swept up through the Caucasus and returned to Mongol heartlands via Southern Russia. Further campaigns in the 1230s and 1240s were necessary to bring the Christian kingdoms of Georgia and Cilician Armenia, as well as the Seljuk Sultanate of Anatolia, into a tributary relationship under the Mongol khans, and it was only in 1258 that a Mongol army under Hulegu advanced against the Abbasid caliph in Baghdad. Baghdad was stormed and sacked and Caliph al-Musta'sim slaughtered. Never again would the seat of the pre-eminent authority over the Sunni Islamic world be at Baghdad. Moreover, the Mongol conquest of Iraq led to the almost complete severing of commercial and cultural contacts between it and Egypt and Syria. It also led to an acceleration in the decline of the irrigation system that was crucial to Iraq's agricultural prosperity. The Mongol occupation of Iraq and Iran led to a decline in settled agriculture in many areas and to the increase of nomadic pastoralism.[15] After Hulegu's conquest of Baghdad, he retired to Azerbaijan and began to plan the invasion of Syria which would take place in 1260.

It is likely that by now only the *corps d'élite* of Hulegu's army (and of those other Mongol armies campaigning in Southern Russia and Eastern Europe) actually consisted of Mongols. A very large portion of the Mongol forces was drawn from Kurds, Georgians, Armenians and various Turkish tribes, in particular the Kipchaks. We must now turn to consider the origin and history of the Kipchak race, as they will play a central part in our narrative.[16] In the early eleventh century the Kipchaks were pagan nomads dwelling in the steppes to the north of Turkestan and the Aral Sea. It was to be from their race that most of the sultans of Egypt and Syria between 1259 and 1382 were to be drawn.

Kipchak legends claimed that the race was descended from a boy born from a tree trunk and adopted by Oghuz Khan (the legendary and eponymous ancestor of the Ghuzz Turks). It may be that the intention of this legend is simultaneously to express the Kipchaks' sense of relatedness to and separation from the Ghuzz Turks. Linguistically Kipchak, a dialect of the north-western family of Turkish dialects, is quite distinct from Ghuzz — though a pure form of either dialect is quite rare.[17]

The Kipchak tribes formed a loose confederacy. Unlike the Mongols, they were never to be united and organised under a single strong khan. In the early eleventh century, under pressure perhaps from other Turkish tribes, they began to migrate southwards and westwards. Many, as we have seen, took service under the Khwarazm-Shahs. Others crossed the Volga in the mid-eleventh century and moved into the relatively lush steppe land north of the Caucasus and the Black Sea. As they did so they displaced or assimilated the region's former Patzinak Turk and Bulgar inhabitants. By the 1080s the Kipchaks had crossed the Danube and entered the Balkan lands of the Byzantine Emperor Alexius Comnenus. They feature in Anna Comnena's *Alexiad* alternately as enemies and as allies and *foederati* of the emperor. (The Greeks called the Kipchaks 'Cumans', the Russians called them 'Polovtsians'.)

Most of our knowledge about the medieval Kipchaks comes from Christian observers of their way of life in the Balkans and the Russian steppes. Christian missionaries — at first Eastern Orthodox or Nestorian, increasingly from the thirteenth century onwards Catholic — travelled among the steppe peoples on missions of conversion. Most Kipchaks, like most Mongols and other Ural-Altaic peoples, however, were shamanists and remained thus at least until the last decades of the thirteenth century when many went over to Islam.

Sinor, following Eliade, has argued that 'Shamanism is not a religion', but 'a technique of ecstasy'.[18] The shaman, the seer of the tribe, uses drugs, music or other techniques to achieve ecstasy. His spirit temporarily leaves his body to move about in the invisible world. There he communicates with and receives guidance from the spirits of the ancestral dead and animals. The Kipchaks' spiritual life was not restricted to consulting shamans. According to Robert of Clari, who heard of Kipchak practices from Crusaders in the Balkans at the beginning of the thirteenth century, 'they [the Cumans or Kipchaks] worship the first animal encountered each day'.[19] (It is more likely that they practised divination from such chance encounters.) Kipchak personal names were also chosen on the basis of omens from the natural world. From a reference in John of Piano Carpini, it appears that the Kipchaks shared with the Mongols the worship of the oracular Earth goddess Itugen, though they called her Codar. They probably also worshipped the sky god Tengri.[21]

The Mongol custom of burying a chieftain's best horse with his master was also found among the Kipchaks — a practice clearly implying a belief in the afterlife. (It also seems from the testimony of Joinville's informant — Philippe de Toucy, who had visited the Kipchaks in the Balkans — that they, like the Mongols, sometimes buried alive the servants of a great chieftain with him.)[22] In general the horse was central to the Kipchak way of life. It was customary to eat horseflesh, particularly at wake feasts. Besides the consumption of horsemeat, the horse's blood could be made into black pudding, mare's milk fermented to produce a treacherously alcoholic drink called *qumiz*, and horsehair used in the making of tents. The Kipchaks traded extensively in horses. Ibn Battuta, who visited the Kipchak steppes north of the Black Sea in the 1330s, has described how Kipchak drovers would regularly take herds of thousands of horses from there past the Caspian and then down through Turkestan to sell them eventually in India.[23]

The Kipchaks, as is evident from Western testimony of their prowess in the Balkans, were famed for their horse archery and for their tactical employment of feigned retreat. John of Piano Carpini, speaking of the Mongols, tells us that the only things the men in the camp made were arrows and that children were forced to practise archery from as young as three or four years old.[24] It is probable that such comments should be applied to the Kipchaks also. Mention has already been made above of the employment of Kipchaks in the armies of the Byzantines. Alexius Comnenus settled some Kipchak tribes in the Balkans as *foederati* in the late eleventh century. Later in the 1250s Michael Palaeologus employed Kipchaks as mercenaries.[25] We have also already seen how Kipchaks formed a substantial part of the Khwarazmian and Mongol armies. In the Caucasus Kipchak tribes were settled in the lowland areas by King David of Georgia and used by him and his successors as cavalry. More significantly, the Christian Kings of Georgia also recruited Kipchaks as a pagan slave bodyguard. It is here perhaps that we find the closest parallel with the Muslim mamluk institution.[26] Generally the Kipchaks were so widely employed outside their homeland as soldiers that they may almost be called the Ghurkas of the Middle Ages.

The Kipchaks' military reputation preceded the coming of the Mongols, but the Mongol invasion of the western steppe encouraged a Kipchak diaspora. In 1221–2, as has been mentioned previously, a Mongol army advanced through the Caucasus towards the Kipchak steppes. The Kipchaks deserted a largely Christian confederacy of Caucasian peoples and fought on the side of the victorious Mongols. Subsequently they were themselves betrayed by the Mongols. Some were massacred, others joined the Christian Russian principalities' resistance to the Mongols, others again fled into the Byzantine empire and some of these Kipchaks were eventually resettled by Theodore Lascaris in Asia Minor. Devastating though this Mongol expedition was, it was only a preliminary raid. The actual conquest of the Kipchak steppes began in 1236 under Batu, the Mongol Khan of the Golden Horde — that is, the westernmost of the Mongol appanages formed after the death of Chingiz Khan. By 1240 that conquest was more or less complete and the Mongols had begun an invasion of Eastern Europe.[27] A new wave of Kipchak refugees fled into Bulgaria and Hungary (Kipchak was still spoken in parts of Hungary in the late eighteenth century).

The Kipchak steppes from then on until the 1340s formed the greater part of the territories of the Mongol Khan of the Golden Horde. Though the khans were peripatetic, a capital of sorts was established at Saray on the lower Volga. The Mongol and Kipchak aristocracies intermarried, Kipchak eventually displaced Mongol as the language of the rulers and an indigenous literature much influenced by earlier Khwarazmian models developed.[28] The khan encouraged trade on the Volga and with the Italians in the Crimea. The Kipchaks who were recruited into Egyptian armies in the late thirteenth and early fourteenth centuries came from a region where settled culture and commerce was by no means unknown. The *Codex Cumanicus*, a dictionary compiled by Christian missionaries in the 1330s, testifies indirectly to the variety of crafts and activities pursued in the Kipchak lands.[29]

In the short term, however, the Mongol invasions of the 1220s and 1230s led to tribal displacements, famines and inter-tribal feuding over diminished resources and this in turn led to a cheap and plentiful supply of slaves for interested purchasers like the Sultan al-Salih Ayyub in Egypt and Syria. In 1242–3, for instance, the

Barali tribe of Kipchaks fled into the Crimean Peninsula and put themselves under the protection of the Turkish Awlaq Anas Khan. They were, however, betrayed, attacked and some of their children taken into captivity to be sold eventually as slaves in Aleppo (these Barali children included Baybars and Baysari, of whom we shall hear more).[30]

The history of Egypt, Syria and Mesopotamia under the Ayyubids in the early thirteenth century must be seen in terms of fairly continuous warfare and diplomatic manoeuvring between rival members of the Ayyubid family to secure paramountcy over the territories that they had inherited. Al-Salih Ayyub (eldest son of al-Kamil and ruler in Jazira) had been invited to rule in Egypt in May 1240 after a faction of Kurdish and Turkish emirs had deposed al-Salih's brother, al-'Adil II. Many of the Turkish emirs who took part in the plot had been former mamluks of al-Salih's and al-'Adil's father, al-Kamil (ruler of Egypt from 1218 to 1238). Al-Salih himself had arrived in Egypt with his own force of mamluks which he had built up in the 1230s as protection against his father and brothers. As ruler of Egypt, al-Salih Ayyub proved to be taciturn, ruthless and militaristic.[31] His personality and policies were to provide the model for his mamluks who ruled Egypt as sultans after his death.[32] Al-Salih Ayyub built up a large cavalry army in Egypt. The greater part of this army consisted of freemen, was dispersed in provinces throughout Egypt and was mobilised only for specific campaigns. For reasons that are now mysterious this force, the bulk of the army from the mid-thirteenth century on, was called the *halqa* (literally, the ring), a term which half a century earlier under Saladin seems rather to have been applied to the small elite bodyguard attendant on the person of the ruler.[33] Al-Salih Ayyub also created a new elite corps, the Bahriyya. These were mamluks who derived their name from the fact that they were garrisoned on the island of Rawda on the River Nile (Bahr al-Nil) just outside Cairo. The Bahri mamluks seem to have numbered between 800 and 1,000 men and to have been composed predominantly of Kipchak Turks.[34] To command his armies and guide him in his councils al-Salih Ayyub relied to a greater extent than his Ayyubid predecessors and rivals upon emirs drawn from the ranks of the mamluks. Even so, free Kurdish emirs were still prominent in military and administrative offices.

Once he had consolidated his rule over Egypt, al-Salih Ayyub turned his attention to Syria and Iraq where hostile Ayyubid kinsmen ruled over Damascus, Hama, Homs, Aleppo, Subayba and Diyarbakr. In 1244, seeking additional military support against his rivals, he invited a large army of Khwarazmian horsemen who had taken refuge in Iraq from the Mongols to join his army when it advanced out of Egypt to occupy Palestine and Southern Syria. The Khwarazmian horde under the command of Husam al-Din Berke Khan accepted al-Salih Ayyub's invitation and moved rapidly through Syria and Palestine, looting and killing at random. As a by-blow of their passage they took and sacked Jerusalem, thereby depriving the Crusader principality of its capital. Later that year al-Salih Ayyub and the Khwarazmians at the Battle of Gaza jointly defeated the combined armies of his Ayyubid rival in Damascus and the Franks from the coastal remnant of the kingdom of Jerusalem. Subsequently and with Khwarazmian help, al-Salih Ayyub went on to occupy Damascus in 1245, though he was unable to dislodge his Ayyubid kinsmen elsewhere. Then in 1246, finding his Khwarazmian allies dangerously uncontrollable, he turned on them and defeated them at a battle near Homs.[35] Berke Khan was killed and two of his sons were taken into captivity later to become emirs under the Mamluk regime.[36] The remnants of the Khwarazmian horde dispersed throughout Syria and Palestine.

In the meantime, news of the loss of Jerusalem and the terrible Christian defeat at Gaza had led to the clamour for a new Crusade in Western Europe. In December 1244 Louis IX of France took the cross and assumed the leadership of what was to be a predominantly French Crusade.[37] The Crusaders planned to occupy Egypt or at least the Delta, either permanently or in order to use as a bargaining counter to secure the return of Jerusalem and the hinterland of Palestine. Preparations were elaborate and it was only in June 1249 that the French landed on the coast of the Egyptian Delta. The Kurdish and Arab garrison at Damietta did not distinguish itself and the fortified port rapidly fell to the Crusaders' assault. Then, however, there were delays: the Nile was in full flood in September and October and the French army did not commence its advance down the river until 20 November, as the flood waters receded.

Al-Salih Ayyub had been seriously ill even before the landing of the Crusaders. The strain of directing Egypt's defences still further weakened his health. On 22 November 1249, just as the Crusader advance southwards down the Delta began, he died. Al-Salih Ayyub's death in the middle of a military crisis was the immediate reason for the formation of a junta to take over temporary direction of affairs. Al-Salih Ayyub's son Turanshah had not been trusted by his father and had been kept at a safe distance in Diyar Bakr, where he governed Hisn Kayfa. Faris al-Din Aqtay al-Jamdar, the mamluk *muqaddam* or commander of the Bahri mamluks, was now sent by the junta to urge Turanshah to hurry to Egypt and assume the Sultanate and the leadership of the Muslim armies against the Crusade.

In the meantime, a small circle of al-Salih Ayyub's trusted advisors and generals took over the administration. The dominant figures in this interim junta seem to have been Shajar al-Durr (al-Salih Ayyub's former concubine and queen), Fakhr al-Din ibn al-Shaykh (a member of a prominent clan of Khurasanian Arab origin and commander-in-chief of the Egyptian army), Baha' al-Din ibn Hanna (the vizier) and Jamal al-Din Muhsin (the chief eunuch, with authority over the mamluks). This group attempted to keep al-Salih Ayyub's death secret from the bulk of the army and populace until Turanshah should have arrived in Egypt.[38]

The French began their advance through the Delta towards Cairo in November. Because the Nile's waters were slow to subside, they found progress across the innumerable waterways and irrigation works difficult and suffered considerably from harassment by bedouin skirmishers. By late December they had reached the Ashmun canal and faced the fortified town of Mansura — less than a third of the way from Damietta to Cairo. The main Egyptian army was encamped in and around Mansura and all the fords across the Ashmun canal were guarded. Only on 8 February did a detachment of the French army under the king's brother, Robert of Artois, succeed in making a crossing at one of the less well-defended fords. Having done so, they went on to surprise a selection of the Egyptian army and kill the commander-in-chief, Fakhr al-Din ibn al-Shaykh. Without waiting for reinforcements, Robert of Artois's party rode into Mansura. Though they penetrated the town fairly easily, a belated defence was organised in the town by the Bahri mamluks. Narrow streets were blocked, volleys of arrows were fired from the rooftops and Robert of Artois and many of his following perished in the streets.

Joinville's apparently naive yet eloquent narrative of Louis IX's Crusade has persuaded many that the chief cause of its failure was Robert of Artois's rash behaviour at Mansura and the losses that the French suffered that day. Joinville's chronicle, however, should rather be regarded as an apologia for Louis IX's misjudgements.

Although as a result of the forcing of the ford Louis's army had been able to cross over *en masse* to the south side, his position was hopeless — and had been hopeless from the first. His army was not large enough to drive the Egyptian forces from Mansura and his supply line with Damietta down the Nile was vulnerable to harassment by Muslim river boats. At the end of February Turanshah arrived to take charge of the Muslim army at Mansura, though he came too late to derive much credit from what was to be regarded as essentially a Bahri mamluk defeat of the French army. Only in April did Louis accept the fact that further advance was impossible and order a retreat. As the French army retreated towards Damietta, it began to fall apart; on 6 April Louis was forced to surrender. Louis and most of his army were taken into captivity.

The new Sultan al-Mu'azzam Turanshah began negotiations with his royal captive to secure the surrender of Damietta and a large ransom for the captive French. By the time the terms for the ransom and evacuation of the Crusaders were finally agreed in May, Turanshah was was no longer alive.[39] Though Turanshah had arrived from Hisn Kayfa in February with only a small retinue, he had rapidly set about appointing his own (Mu'azzami) mamluks to key posts. He had also acquired the mamluks and property of Fakhr al-Din ibn al-Shaykh, the former commander-in-chief of the army. This presumably gave him the confidence to disregard the wishes and advice of prominent Kurdish emirs such as Husam al-Din ibn Abi 'Ali and of his father's Bahri mamluks. Particularly shocking to the sensibility of these white slaves was Turanshah's promotion of blacks to positions of power in the palace administration. A black eunuch was made *ustadar* (master of the royal household) and another was made *amir jandar* (master of the royal guard). Arab chroniclers (who wrote later in the Mamluk period and had no interest in presenting Turanshah favourably) described Turanshah's behaviour as unbalanced. According to Sa'd al-Din Juwayni, he was a youth of low intelligence with a nervous twitch which affected his left shoulder and face. On one occasion he set about chopping the tops off candles, shouting provocatively, 'So shall I deal with the Bahris!'[40] But the Bahris struck first. On 2 May 1250 a Bahri mamluk attempted to cut down Turanshah in his tent at Mansura. Since the attempt had been botched, the rest of the Bahris under the leadership of Faris al-Din Aqtay al-Jamdar hunted Turanshah down and killed him. According to Joinville, Faris al-Din Aqtay cut out Turanshah's heart and took it along to show the captive French king, thinking thus to cheer him up.[41]

In the decade up to 1249, a disunited Syria had served as a battlefield for al-Salih Ayyub and those of his kinsmen who resisted him. It was a fertile field for Crusader diplomacy and Frankish raids. It suffered also from demographic pressures caused by invaders. Only some of these new immigrants could be incorporated into the armies of the Syrian principalities. Many of the others roamed around in large tribal or bandit groups. After the murder of Turanshah, al-Nasir Yusuf, the Ayyubid prince of Aleppo, was able to occupy Damascus, while al-Mughith, another Ayyubid, was able to seize Kerak, the Transjordanian fortress where al-Salih Ayyub had sent much of his treasure for safe-keeping during Louis IX's Crusade. During the 1250s these two princes struggled against one another and against the regime in Egypt, and minor Muslim princelings, Isma'ili Assassins, Franks, mamluk groups and mercenaries profited from their struggles.

Egypt was not on the front line until 1249 and was more successful in resisting those strains. It maintained a superficial unity. But the strains were there. In a testamentary letter, dictated in the winter of 1249 by al-Salih Ayyub to Turanshah, who had already been summoned from Diyarbakr, the dying sultan outlined the problems that were then facing Egypt.[42] The immediate problems were of course the presence of the French Crusade in the Nile Delta and the rivalries of the military commanders and courtiers who were trying to organise the defence of the Delta against them.

But there were broader and more deep-seated military problems. Al-Salih blamed many of the difficulties faced by his army on the maladministration of the Copts in the military and financial bureaus. They dispersed the *iqta*'s (the chief source of income for the cavalryman) so widely that the soldiers had difficulty in collecting the revenues that were due to them. They charged exorbitant fees for the issue of *iqta*' diplomas and they also profiteered on the sale of fodder to the army on campaign. The mass of the troops were unmistakably of poor quality. As for the free-born troopers of the *halqa*, 'O my son, most of the army's soldiers come from the common people, from shopkeepers and weavers. All a man has to do is to put on the *qaba*' [the Turkish-style jacket affected by the military], get on a horse and find an emir.' The bedouin employed in the Egyptian army had hardly distinguished themselves in the defence of Damietta and they were not to be relied upon. In future, only those who actually had some idea how to handle a bow and a lance were to be employed. Al-Salih's musings for the benefit of Turanshah included two particularly pertinent pieces of advice. First, to keep off alcohol and, second, to be generous to the Bahri mamluks: 'I strongly recommend them to you . . . I owe everything to them.' As we have seen, Turanshah did not heed the advice. But though the events of 1249 demonstrated that the Bahri mamluks were too powerful to be ignored, the events of the following decade were to show that they were not yet powerful enough to take over al-Salih Ayyub's empire. Kurdish generals, rival Turkish mamluk groupings, courtiers and eunuchs successfully resisted Bahri pretensions. As we shall see, Faris al-Din Aqtay al-Jamdar's attempts to establish a Bahri hegemony only ended in his own assassination in 1254. In the four years that followed, Baybars's efforts to recoup the regiment's fortunes in Syria were similarly fruitless. The shock of the French Crusade was insufficient to install a Bahri Mamluk regime. It would take the Mongol onslaught, ten years later, on Syria and Egypt to establish the mamluks as the necessary defenders of the *Dar al-Islam* against the infidel Mongols and Franks.

Notes

1. For the history and culture of the Eurasian steppes, see G. Hambly, *Central Asia* (London, 1966); T. Talbot Rice, *The Scythians* (London, 1957); D. Sinor, *Inner Asia and its Contacts with Medieval Europe* (London, 1977).
2. On the early history of the Turks, see 'Turks' in *EI(1)*; W. Barthold, *Turkestan Down to the Mongol Invasion* (London, 3rd edn., 1968); C.E. Bosworth, 'The Political and Dynastic History of the Iranian World (A.D. 1000–1217)' in *Cambridge History of Iran*, vol. 5, pp.1–202.
3. For (differing) views on the origins and role of slaves and mamluks in medieval Islam, see for example Ghulam in *EI(2)*; D. Ayalon 'Aspects of the Mamluk Phenomenon: the Importance of the Mamluk Institution' *Der Islam*, vol. 54, no.2 (1976), pp.196–225; C. E. Bosworth, *The Ghaznavids* (Edinburgh, 1963), pp. 98–106; P. Crone, *Slaves on Horses* (Cambridge, 1980), P. G. Forand, 'The Relationship of the Slave and the Client to the Master or Patron in Medieval Islam', *IJMES*, vol.2 (1971), pp.59–66; R. P. Mottahedeh, *Loyalty and Leadership in an Early Islamic Society* (Princeton, 1980), pp.84–9; D. Pipes, *Slave Soldiers and Islam* (New Haven and London, 1981).
4. D. Ayalon, 'Aspects of the Mamluk Phenomenon', pp.218–23; W. F. Paterson, 'The Archers of Islam', *JESHO*, vol.9 (1966), pp.69–87.
5. C. Pellat, *The Life and Works of Jahiz* (Berkeley and Los Angeles, 1969), p.97.
6. On the rise of the Seljuks, see C. Cahen, *Pre-Ottoman Turkey* (London, 1968), pp.19–50.
7. On the Ayyubids, see 'Ayyubids' in *EI(2)*; R. S. Humphreys, *From Saladin to the Mongols* (Albany, 1977); M. C. Lyons and D. E. P. Jackson, *Saladin* (Cambridge 1982).

8. D. Ayalon, 'Aspects of the Mamluk Phenomenon: Ayyubids, Kurds and Turks', *Der Islam*, vol.54, no.1 (1977), pp.1–32; R. S. Humphreys, 'The Emergence of the Mamluk Army' (part 1), *SI*, vol.45 (1977), pp.70, 89–90.

9. Humphreys, *From Saladin to the Mongols*, p.268.

10. D. Ayalon, 'The Wafidiyya in the Mamluk Kingdom', *Islamic Culture*, vol.25 (1951), pp.94–7; R. S. Humphreys, *From Saladin to the Mongols*, pp.262, 274–5.

11. D. Ayalon, 'The Wafidiyya', p.97; R. S. Humphreys, *From Saladin to the Mongols*, p.341.

12. On the Mongol army, see J. Chambers, *The Devil's Horsemen* (London, 1979), pp.51–69; H. D. Martin, 'The Mongol Army', *JRAS* (1943–4), pp.46–85; D. O. Morgan, 'The Mongol Armies in Persia', *Der Islam*, vol.56 (1979), pp.81–96.

13. Cahen, *Pre-Ottoman Turkey*, pp.48–9.

14. 'Khwarazm' and 'Khwarazm-shah' in *EI(2)*.

15. On the effect of the Mongol conquest on Iraq and Iran, see E. Ashtor, *A Social and Economic History of the Near East in the Middle Ages* (London, 1976), pp.249–67; A. K. S. Lambton, *Landlord and Peasant in Persia* (Oxford, 1953), pp.77–104; D. O. Morgan, 'Cassiodorus and Rashid al-Din on Barbarian Rule in Italy and Persia', *BSOAS*, vol.40 (1977), pp.302–20.

16. The following account of the Kipchaks is based on 'Kipcak' in *EI(1)* and *EI(2);* A. B. Boswell, 'The Kipchak Turks', *Slavonic Review*, vol.6 (1927–8), pp.68–85; R. L. Wolff, 'The Second Bulgarian Empire. Its Origin and History to 1204', *Speculum*, vol.24 (1949), pp.198–201.

17. On the Kipchak dialect, see J. Eckman, 'The Mamluk Kipchak Literature', *Central Asiatic Journal*, vol.8 (1963), pp.303–6; O. Pritsak 'Mamluk-Kiptschakisch' in J. Deny *et al.* (eds), *Philologiae Turcicae Fundamenta*, vol.1 (Wiesbaden, 1959), pp.74–81, 85–6.

18. D. Sinor, *Inner Asia History — Civilization — Languages* (Bloomington, 1969), p.241.

19. Robert de Clari, *La Conquête de Constantinople*, P. Lauer (ed.) (Paris, 1974), p.64.

20. C. Dawson, *The Mongol Mission* (London, 1955), p.12; cf. R. A. Skelton, T. Marston and G. D. Painter, *The Vinland Map and the Tatar Relation* (New Haven and London, 1965), p.92 and n.

21. On Eurasian shamanism generally, see J. Aubin, 'Comment Tamerlane prenait les villes', *SI*, vol.19 (1969), pp.84–9; J. A. Boyle, 'Turkish and Mongol Shamanism in the Middle Ages', *Folklore*, vol.8 (1972), pp.177–93; M. Eliade, *Shamanism: Archaic Techniques of Ecstasy* (London, 1964); W. Heissig, *The Religions of Mongolia* (London, 1970).

22. Jean de Joinville, *Histoire de Saint Louis*, N. de Wailly (ed.) (Paris, 1868), p.177–8.

23. Ibn Battuta, *The Travels of Ibn Battuta*, vol.2, H. A. R. Gibb (trans.) (Cambridge, 1962), p.478; cf. Giosofat Barbaro, *Travels to Tana and Persia*, W. Thomas (trans.) (London, 1873), p.20.

24. Dawson, *The Mongol Mission*, p.18.

25. *The Cambridge Medieval History*, vol. 4, *The Byzantine Empire* (Part 1), J. M. Hussey (ed.) (Cambridge, 1966), pp.218, 324–5.

26. 'Kabk' in *EI(2);* 'Kurdj' in *EI(2);* W. E. D. Allen, *A History of the Georgian People* (London, 1932), pp.99, 106, 172–4.

27. R. Grousset, *L'Empire des steppes* (Paris, 1948), pp.306–8, 329–31; J. J. Saunders, *The History of the Mongol Conquests* (London, 1971), pp.59, 80–3.

28. On Mongol-Kipchak cultural assimilation, see A. Bodroglieti, 'A Collection of Turkish Poems from the 14th Century', *Acta Orientalia Academia Scientarum Hungarica*, vol.16 (1963), pp.244–5; B. Grekov and A. Yakoubovski, *La Horde d'or* (Paris, 1939), pp.67–8.

29. *Codex Cumanicus*, G. Kuun (ed.) (Budapest, 1880); cf. now, L. Ligeti, 'Prolegomena to the Codex Cumanicus', *Acta Orientalia Academia Scientarum Hungarica*, vol.35 (1981), pp.1–54.

30. Yunini, *Dhayl Mir'at al-zaman*, vol.3 (Hyderabad, 1960), p.240; cf. Ibn Taghribirdi, *Nujum*, vol.7 (n.d.), pp.95–6.

31. On the reign of al-Salih Ayyub, see C. Cahen, 'Le Testament d'al-Malik al-Salih Ayyub', *BEO*, vol.29 (1977), pp.97–114; Humphreys, *From Saladin to the Mongols*, pp.246–316 (*passim*).

32. D. Ayalon, 'The Great Yasa of Chingiz Khan: A Re-examination' (part C1), *SI*, vol.36 (1972), pp.156–8.

33. Ayalon, 'Aspects of the Mamluk Phenomenon: Ayyubids, Kurds and Turks', pp.15–16; Ayalon, 'Studies on the Structure of the Mamluk Army — II', *BSOAS*, vol.15 (1953), pp.448–9; R. S. Humphreys, 'The Emergence of the Mamluk Army' (part 2), *SI*, vol.46 (1977), pp.147–8.

34. 'Bahriyya' in *EI(2)*; D. Ayalon, 'Le Regiment Bahriya dans l'armée mamelouke', *REI* (1951), pp.133–41; Humphreys, 'The Emergence of the Mamluk Army' (part 1), *Studia Islamica*, vol.45 (1977), pp.94–7.

35. Humphreys, *From Saladin to the Mongols*, pp.274–5, 284–7.

36. A. G. Walls, 'The Turbat Barakat Khan or Khalidi Library', *Levant*, vol.6 (1974), p.45.

37. For a good general account of Louis IX's Crusade, see J. R. Strayer, 'The Crusades of Louis IX', in R. L. Wolff and H. W. Hazard (eds), *A History of the Crusades*, vol.2, *The Later Crusades* (Madison, 1969), pp.487–508.

38. On the leading figures in Egypt at the time of al-Salih Ayyub's death, see Cahen, 'Le Testament d'al-Malik al-Salih Ayyub'; Humphreys, *From Saladin to the Mongols*, pp.301–2; G. Schregle, *Die Sultanin von Ägypten* (Wiesbaden, 1961), pp.48–54.

39. On Turanshah's brief reign, see Schregle, *Die Sultanin von Ägypten*, pp.55–8.

40. C. Cahen, 'Les Mémoires de Sa'd al-Din ibn Hamawiya Djuwayni' in *idem*, *Les Peuples Musulmans dans l'histoire médiévale* (Damascus, 1977), pp.476–7 (also in *Bulletin de la Faculté des Lettres de Strasbourg*, vol.7 (1950)).

41. Jean de Joinville, *Histoire*, p.125.

42. Cahen, 'Le Testament'.

2 THE TURBULENT DECADE

For nine years after the death of Tursanshah a conspiratorial elite manoeuvred for control over Egypt. The distribution of power and its relation to formally exercised authority defies easy analysis and, as we shall see, for the first five years or so it is quite difficult to determine who was supposed to be ruling at any one time. It is conventional to date the beginnings of the Bahri mamluk regime to 1250, but this is debatable. Not one of the five rulers who held the Sultanate between 1250 and 1260 was a Bahri mamluk, and two of those rulers openly opposed the Bahri faction. Moreover, for the first two years at least there was a widespread reluctance among the former emirs and slaves of al-Salih Ayyub to acknowledge that the Ayyubid Sultanate over Egypt had really ended with the murder of Turanshah.

Therefore — somewhat bizarrely — when al-Salih Ayyub's widow Shajar al-Durr became sultana in May 1250, the coins issued in her name proclaimed her *Malikatu' l-Muslimin, Walidatu' l-Malik al Mansur Khalil Amir.* That is to say that she ruled as Queen of the Muslims by virtue of her motherhood of al-Salih Ayyub's son, Prince Khalil; that prince, however, had died in childhood during al-Salih Ayyub's reign.[1] Though Shajar al-Durr was of Turkish or Armenian origin and a former slave, there is no evidence that her assumption of the throne was supported by the Bahris. Indeed, she does not seem to have had any substantial source of support. Moreover, the independent rule of a woman was without precedent in the Muslim Near East. Although the other side of Shajar al-Durr's coins proclaimed Egypt's spiritual allegiance to al-Musta'sim, the Abbasid caliph at Baghdad, her Sultanate was not acceptable to him, nor was it popular in Cairo. Therefore in July 1250 she abdicated, and at the same time she seems to have married a Turkish emir, 'Izz al-Din Aybak al-Turkomani. He now took the throne and assumed the regnal title al-Malik al-Mu'izz. Aybak had a relatively mild and pious temperament and, though he had been formerly a mamluk and al-Salih Ayyub's poison-taster, it would appear that he was not one of the Bahris, but rather a middling-rank mamluk emir who was made sultan by non-mamluks in a deliberate attempt to keep the Bahris from power.[2] This attempt was not entirely successful.

However disciplined the Bahris may have been in battle, in peacetime their indiscipline and riotous behaviour were a permanent menace to the lives and commerce of the citizens of Cairo. Their leader, Faris al-Din Aqtay al-Jamdar, was too powerful to be ignored; on the other hand, he was also too unpopular to take the throne for himself (though his followers used to call him al-Malik (that is, Prince) al-Jawad.[3] Nevertheless, five days after the enthronement of al-Malik al-Mu'izz Aybak, Aqtay and the Bahris did succeed in forcing him to step sideways in favour of an Ayyubid child prince, a grandson of al-Kamil's, Musa. Ostensibly al-Ashraf Musa reigned from 1250 to 1252.[4] In practice his accession marked the sharing out of power between Bahris and anti-Bahris and he was to be the first of many child mock-sultans who fronted juntas of feuding military men in this period.

Though coins were struck in al-Ashraf's name alone,[5] al-Mu'izz Aybak does not seem to have renounced his royal title. Moreover, Aybak continued to exercise a great deal of power as al-Ashraf Musa's *atabak*. Like most military offices and titles in the Mamluk regime, the office of *atabak* can be traced back to Seljuk times. In Seljuk usage the *atabak* was both the guardian of a prince and the commander of his army. In Mamluk times this double sense persisted. Additionally, however, the title *Atabak al-Asakir (Atabak* of the Armies) came to be used of the commander-in-chief of the Sultan's armies even when that sultan was not a minor and had assumed independent rule. The two senses were not distinct and the commander-in-chief of the former sultan could normally expect to become the guardian of the under-age heir. The powers of the *atabak* depended not so much on the definition of the office as on the man who held it and the context in which he held it. In general it was a key office in the Mamluk Sultanate.[6] Often, as we shall see, its tenure was the prelude to usurpation of the throne itself.

Al-Mu'izz Aybak and the non-Bahri emirs were forced to compromise with the Bahris, because of the serious military threats facing the regime in 1250. That year the bedouins of Upper Egypt rebelled, declaring that they would never accept rule by slaves. Only in 1253 was their revolt bloodily put down by Emirs Aqtay al-Jamdar and Aybak al-Afram.[7] The winter of 1250-1 also saw the first of Ayyubid Prince al-Nasir Yusuf's attempts to conquer Egypt from Syria. After the murder of Turanshah, Kurdish emirs in Damascus had invited al-Nasir Yusuf, the ruler of Aleppo, to come and assume power. So al-Nasir Yusuf bloodlessly occupied Damascus. He then attempted the conquest of Egypt. In February 1251, about half-way down the eastern edge of the Nile Delta on the road to Cairo, his army encountered the Egyptians. Battle was joined at Kura, near the Egyptian military base of Abbasa. Though the Syrian forces were initially successful, Faris al-Din Aqtay and the Bahri mamluks played a crucial role in finally defeating them. This attempt by al-Nasir Yusuf to conquer Egypt had not only failed, but also had the long-term effect of strengthening the position of al-Mu'izz Aybak against his Bahri mamluk rivals. In the course of battle between the Syrian and Egyptian forces, al-Nasir Yusuf was deserted by the 'Azizis (that is, the large group of mamluks who had been purchased by al-Nasir Yusuf's father, al-'Aziz of Aleppo). The 'Azizi mamluks were Turks and seem to have been influenced by some feeling of racial or caste solidarity with the mamluks on the Egyptian side. Be that as it may, a section of the powerful and extensive clan of Qaymari Kurds also deserted al-Nasir Yusuf.[8]

In 1254, strengthened not only by the support of the 'Azizis and the Qaymaris but also by his own purchases of mamluks, al-Mu'izz Aybak felt strong enough to move against Aqtay, the Bahris and the Ayyubid child sultan, al-Ashraf Musa, who had been used as their mouthpiece. Aqtay seems to have been unaware of the danger he was in and, indeed, he had been advertising his own pretensions to the Sultanate by negotiating to marry the daughter of the ruler of Mosul. In January 1254 al-Mu'izz Aybak invited Aqtay to a meeting of the Cairo Citadel. Once inside, Aqtay was surrounded by Mu'izz's mamluks and the senior Mu'izzi emir, Sayf al-Din Qutuz, cut him down. Aqtay's head was then thrown down to the suspicious Bahri mamluks who had gathered outside the gates of the citadel.[9] Most of the Bahris now fled Egypt. Many followed Aqtay's deputy, Baybars al-Bunduqdari, who escaped to take service first with al-Nasir Yusuf in Damascus, then with another Ayyubid prince, al-Mughith, who ruled over Kerak in the Transjordan, and later again some followed Baybars back to take service with al-Nasir Yusuf once more. Others fled to the court of the Seljuk sultan in Anatolia. Others again stayed to make their peace with al-Mu'izz Aybak.[10]

Al-Ashraf Musa was now deposed and al-Mu'izz reassumed the throne and, for the first time, struck coins in his own name — or rather, and again somewhat bizarrely, in the name of the very dead al-Salih Ayyub and himself as al-Salih Ayyub's lieutenant.[11] Such tortuous legitimating procedures demonstrate the strength of Ayyubid traditions and of the personal cult of al-Salih Ayyub; they also suggest that there were serious difficulties in making a slave Sultanate acceptable. Even after the purging of the Bahris, al-Mu'izz Aybak's throne was still far from secure.

Shajar al-Durr had heard rumours that al-Mu'izz Aybak was planning to marry a daughter of the ruler of Mosul who would replace her as Aybak's chief wife. In April 1257, therefore, she had him murdered by bath-house slaves whom she had suborned. Having murdered Aybak, she appealed to those Bahri mamluk emirs who had remained in Egypt to come to her support, but not one of them responded. Al-Mu'izz Aybak's supporters rallied and Shajar al-Durr was killed.[12] Chronicles written in the fourteenth and fifteenth centuries relate that Shajar al-Durr fled to the Red Tower in the citadel, where she immured herself and passed several days grinding her jewels to dust so that no woman might wear them after her. Forced by starvation to descend from the tower, she was beaten to death by the clogs of al-Mu'izz Aybak's concubines and her body left for the dogs to eat. However, it has been persuasively argued that the appearance of such romantic folktale elements in the narratives of late medieval chronicles reflect the increasingly literary approach to history writing in that period, rather than access to independent sources of information unavailable to the earlier chroniclers.[13]

Al-Mu'izz Aybak's 15-year-old son 'Ali was enthroned in March 1257 and took the regnal name al-Mansur. However, this youth's reign — which lasted until November 1259 — served only to provide a façade of stable legitimacy, behind which powerful emirs manoeuvred for position. Among them were the young ruler's *atabak,* Sanjar al-Halabi (a former Salihi Bahri mamluk); Sanjar al-Ghatmi, the leader of those Bahris who had remained in Egypt; and Qutuz al-Mu'izzi, al-Mu'izz Aybak's most favoured mamluk and the killer of Aqtay. Within a short time Qutuz succeeded in outmanoeuvring and imprisoning his chief rival, Sanjar al-Halabi, and increasingly the nominal rule of al-Mu'izz's son became a front for the actual rule of al-Mu'izz's former mamluk.

If the sequence of events in Egypt in this decade seems difficult to follow, in Syria it was all far more chaotic. Broadly, the decade represents the twilight of Ayyubid rule in Syria. Nominally at least, Ayyubid princes ruled over most of Syria. The situation was made more complex, however, by the continued existence of the Crusader principalities which still occupied a narrow coastal strip extending roughly from Lattakia in the north of Syria to Jaffa in the south of Palestine. After the negotiations for the ransoming of the French army had been successfully concluded in 1250, Louis IX had taken the remnants of his army to Palestine where he devoted himself to strengthening the fortifications of the coastal cities and to (fairly successful) diplomatic manoeuvres in which he played off al-Nasir Yusuf against the Egyptians.[14] Louis IX stayed in Palestine until 1254.

Al-Nasir Yusuf not only failed in his attempts on Egypt, but he was also prevented by Frankish manoeuvres and by the presence of an Egyptian army at Gaza from establishing any continuous authority over Palestine. Moreover, his authority within the provinces of Aleppo and Damascus was weak. Abu'l-Fida, the later historian and Ayyubid prince of Hama (1273–1331), describes the roads as being unsafe in his reign, banditry as widespread and travellers and merchants as being threatened by bands of soldiers, Turkomans and bedouin.[15] Presumably many of the warbands that contributed to the unsettlement of Syria in this decade, particularly the Turkomans, had entered from Iraq, as an indirect result of the Mongol advance westwards. Groups of masterless mamluks further contributed to the chaos. Despite the urgings of Baybars and his following of Bahri mamluks, al-Nasir Yusuf made no further attempt to invade Egypt. The disappointed Bahri mamluks then deserted al-Nasir Yusuf and took service with a rival Ayyubid prince, al-Mughith of Kerak. Egged on by the Bahris, al-Mughith in his turn made two attempts to conquer Egypt in 1257 and 1258 which both failed.[16] Baybars and a residue of the Bahris then negotiated their re-entry into the service of al-Nasir Yusuf in 1258.[17] In 1258 al-Nasir's forces were also briefly reinforced by the arrival of 3,000 Shahrazuris.[18] These Kurdish tribesmen were fleeing into Syria in advance of Hulegu and the Mongols.

Al-Nasir Yusuf had been in correspondence with the Mongols from as early as 1250 and he had received a document of *aman* (that is, a guarantee of security) from Great Khan Mongke. It may be that al-Nasir Yusuf had hoped to use Mongol assistance against the Egyptians and against al-Mughith of Kerak. In 1258 he sent his son al-'Aziz to negotiate with Hulegu.[19] It was rarely possible to use the Mongols in such ways. Now as Hulegu's armies approached

Northern Syria, it became clear that al-Nasir Yusuf would be tolerated, if at all, only as a vassal. By the time the Mongols reached the edge of Syria, they had a more or less unbroken sequence of victories and conquests to their credit — over the Chinese, the Kara Khitai, Khwarazmian and Kipchak Turks, the Poles, Russians, Hungarians, the Assassin sect at Alamut and the Abbasid Caliphate in Baghdad. The Seljuk sultans of Anatolia and several of the rulers of the towns of Upper Iraq had submitted themselves to the Mongols. So too had the Christian kings David of Georgia and Hethoum of Lesser Armenia. The Mongol army that crossed the Euphrates in September 1259 was enormous — it may have numbered as many as 120,000 men.[20] Many of the cavalry would have been Turks. Large contingents were furnished by the tributary Armenians and Georgians and their kings, Hethoum and David, rode alongside Hulegu. The presence of substantial numbers of Christians in Hulegu's army and the fact that Hulegu, though himself a shamanist with Buddhist leanings, was married to a Nestorian Christian encouraged the native Christian minorities in the Syrian towns to hope that the coming of the Mongols signalled the end of Muslim hegemony in Syria. Moreover, Bohemond the Prince of Antioch and Count of Tripoli, the northernmost of the Crusader principalities, also submitted to the Mongols.[21] (Later, it seems that the Mongol general Kitbugha promised Bohemond the town of Ba'labakk as part of the spoils of conquest.)[22]

Aleppo, the northernmost of the great Syrian towns, fell to the Mongols on 25 January 1260 — though its citadel continued to resist for some weeks more. The city was extensively ravaged. The Armenians burnt the great mosque. Aleppo's fortifications were not to be rebuilt until the 1290s. Al-Nasir Yusuf in Damascus made no move to come to the assistance of his city, though he was vigorously urged to do so by his Qaymari and Bahri emirs. His army was enraged by this 'idle sportfulness'. However, al-Nasir Yusuf seems to have been unable to trust the army he affected to command. Moreover, he had been unsuccessful in getting an unambiguous commitment from Qutuz in Egypt to join him in standing against the Mongols. Since they had failed to persuade al-Nasir Yusuf to go out and meet the Mongols in battle, his emirs now began to desert him in favour of Qutuz.[23] Baybars fled down into Palestine and rested with a large band of Shahrazuri Kurds camped near Gaza (he married one of their women to cement an alliance between them).[24] At Gaza he began negotiations to secure a guarantee of personal safe conduct from his former enemy Qutuz.[25]

Al-Nasir Yusuf had by now lost so many troops through desertion that he would have been unable to defend Damascus even had he been inclined to do so; accordingly, he in his turn fled south. On 2 March a Mongol army under Hulegu's lieutenant Kitbugha entered Damascus. At about the same time Hulegu with the greater part of the Mongol army began to withdraw from Syria. Hulegu had heard of the death of Great Khan Mongke which had occurred in China in August 1259 and returned to Azerbaijan in order to follow more closely the succession dispute over the Great Khanate that he anticipated would ensue and to defend his territories in Iran and the Caucasus from his rival, Berke Khan of the Golden Horde. It may also have been the case that such a large cavalry army could not maintain itself for any great length of time on Syria's pastures. The force that was left behind with Kitbugha in Syria numbered as few as 20,000 or even 10,000 men.[26] Even so, after Hulegu's departure Kitbugha and the diminished Mongol army prepared to invade Egypt and an advance force was sent through Palestine to Gaza.

The *fainéant* ruler of Damascus and Aleppo, al-Nasir Yusuf, having fled into the Sinai Desert, was eventually betrayed by his retinue into the hands of the Mongols (he was sent off to Hulegu in Azerbaijan and probably executed in 1261).[27] A Mongol governor was appointed to Kerak, with the complaisance of al-Mughith.[28] Two other Ayyubid princes, al-Ashraf of Homs and al-Said of Subayba, joined the Mongol forces.[29] From the reign of Saladin onwards the Ayyubids' prosecution of the *jihad* against the infidel had always played an important part in legitimating their rule over Syria and Egypt, but now it was becoming clear that the defence of Islam had passed from the hands of the Ayyubids into those of the mamluks in Egypt.

In Egypt Qutuz had assumed the throne. He had done this in November 1259, soon after the news of the Mongol entry into Syria had reached Egypt.[30] Qutuz had waited until some of the more dangerous of his Salihi and Mu'izzi rivals were out of Cairo before deposing al-Mansur Nur al-Din 'Ali. Qutuz, as we have seen, had been a mamluk of al-Mansur's father, al-Mu'izz Aybak. Not only was Qutuz not a Bahri mamluk, he was particularly hated by the Bahris because of the leading role he had taken in the murder of Aqtay al-Jamdar. Al-Muzaffar Qutuz now sought to justify his usurpation of the throne on the grounds that his master's son was too young to exercise the leadership of the *jihad* that it was now necessary to proclaim against the Mongols. It seems that Qutuz may also have spread about the story that he was descended from a Khwarazmian prince.[31] Thus a descendant of the Khwarazm-Shahs would now avenge their defeat at the hands of the Mongols; Qutuz's claim was certainly romantic even if it may not have been true. In the summer of 1260 a Mongol embassy arrived in Cairo. The ambassadors poured scorn on the slave origins of Qutuz and the mamluk emirs, and they demanded that Egypt submit itself to the ilkhan. Qutuz promptly had the ambassadors killed.[32] (This manner of proceeding became, as we shall see, something of a tradition in Mongol–Mamluk diplomatic exchanges.)

Those who were determined to make a stand against the Mongols rallied round Qutuz in Egypt — among them al-Mansur, the Ayyubid prince of Hama, the Qaymari Kurds who had finally deserted al-Nasir Yusuf, and Baybars and the Bahris from Syria. Qutuz decided to engage the Mongols in Syria. The army that advanced out of Egypt was a large one, which was further swollen by Syrian bedouin forces, and by the time it met the main Mongol force in Syria it may have numbered over 100,000 men. However, it is important to remember that the mamluks were only a small corps of officers and elite troops in an army which mostly consisted of poorly equipped Egyptian troopers (*ajnad*) plus undisciplined bedouin and Turkoman light cavalry. The Egyptian advance guard under Baybars surprised and defeated the Mongol advance guard at Gaza.

When Kitbugha met Frankish envoys at Safed in Northern Palestine they had assured him of their neutrality.[33] In fact, however, they allowed Qutuz and Baybars safe passage through their lands on the coastal strip and furnished supplies for the Mamluk army.[34] The Mamluk advance force under Baybars found Kitbugha's army near Tiberias in Northern Palestine and was swiftly joined by the main army under Qutuz. The Battle of 'Ayn Jalut (Spring of Goliath) was fought on 3 September 1260.[35] The two armies that confronted one another were very similar in that their best troops were horse archers of Turco-Mongol stock, but in both cases this regular cavalry force was swollen by a larger body of men furnished by allies, tributaries, skirmishers and tribesmen fighting for the promise of booty. According to the mamluk Sarim al-Din Uzbak (who witnessed the battle from the Mongol side) the chief commanders of the Egyptian army under Qutuz were Baybars,

Balaban al-Rashidi and Sunqur al-Rumi; Uzbak was able to recognise Balaban's yellow standard and Sunqur's red and white one on the field. One presumes that Mamluk battle standards were used, like Mongol ones, to rally and direct the troops in the fighting.[36] The Mamluks had as points in their favour high ground and the sun rising behind them — both considerable advantages in a battle between horse archers. Despite this and despite the superior numbers of the Egyptian army, the battle was hard fought and the Mongols were initially successful in breaking the Mamluk left wing. Qutuz, however, managed to rally his troops and drive the Mongols on to marshy terrain. After Kitbugha had been killed in the fighting, those Mongols who were able fled from the valley and attempted to make a stand at Baysan where they were once more defeated by Baybars. The victory of 'Ayn Jalut had saved Egypt and Syria for a time, but in the long run the battle had not decided anything and the Mongols were to return to Syria in 1261, 1280, 1299, 1301 and 1303. Nevertheless, the moral effect of 'Ayn Jalut was enormous, for it showed first that it was possible to defeat the Mongols in the field and, second — like the Battle of Mansura — it confirmed the military prestige of the Bahri mamluks.

The Mongols who survived the battle, together with the troops that had been left garrisoning the Syrian towns, now attempted to flee Syria. Many died in the attempt, as Baybars pursued them hotly and Arab and Turkoman tribesmen blocked their way. After his victory Qutuz lingered in Syria. There was a large number of territorial and administrative dispositions to be made. Because of the disappearance of al-Nasir Yusuf and the deaths or arrests of other princelings, much of Syria was now in Qutuz's gift. In order to ensure the acquiescence of Egyptian emirs to his accession and in order to persuade the reluctant emirs to follow him out of Egypt, Qutuz had been generous with his promises. Inevitably in the dispositions that were made there were disappointments. A prominent Mu'izzi emir, Aqush al-Burli, believed that he had been promised Aleppo. More important, Baybars's petition to be given either Aleppo or some sort of governorship over Palestine had been ignored.[37] On 23 October 1260, while Qutuz was encamped near Gaza on his way back to Egypt, he was murdered by a group of mamluk emirs, prominent among whom was Baybars.

Notes

1. P. Balog, *The Coinage of the Mamluk Sultans of Egypt and Syria* (New York, 1964), p.71. On the brief reign of Shajar al-Durr generally, see R. S. Humphreys, *From Saladin to the Mongols* (Albany, 1977), pp.303-4; G. Schregle, *Die Sultanin von Ägypten* (Wiesbaden, 1961).

2. The chief printed sources for the reign of al-Mu'izz Aybak are the following chronicles for the *hijri* years 648-655: al-Yunini, *Dhayl Mir'at al-Zaman*, vol.1 (Hyderabad, 1954); Abu'l-Fida, *al-Mukhtasar fi Akhbar al-Bashar*, vol.3 (Istanbul, 1869-70); Ibn al-Dawadari, *Kanz al-Durar*, U. Haarmann (ed.) (Cairo, 1971); al-Maqrizi, *Kitab al-Suluk*, M. M. Ziada (ed.), vol.1, pt.2 (Cairo, 1936); Ibn Taghribirdi, *al-Nujum al-Zahira* vol.7 (Cairo, n.d); cf. C. Cahen, ' "La Chronique des Ayyoubides" d'al-Makin b. al-'Amid', *BEO*, vol.15 (1955), pp.161-6; Cahen, 'Les Mémoires de Sa'd al-Din ibn Hamawiya Djuwayni' in *idem*, *Les Peuples Musulmans dans l'histoire médiévale* (Damascus, 1977), pp.477-8 (also in *Bulletin de Faculté des Lettres de Strasbourg*, vol.7 (1950)); Humphreys, *From Saladin to the Mongols*, pp.315-20, 323, 326-30; Schregle, *Die Sultanin*, pp.77-95. On the hostility between al-Mu'izz and the Bahris, see in particular Ibn 'Abd al-Zahir, *al-Rawd al-Zahir*, A. Khowaiter (ed.) (Riyad, 1976), pp.51-4.

3. Ibn Taghribirdi, *Nujum*, vol.7, p.10.

4. *Ibid.*, pp.5-6; Schregle *Die Sultanin*, p.77.

5. Balog, *Coinage*, p.73.

6. 'Atabak' in *EI(2)*; D. Ayalon, 'Studies on the Structure of the Mamluk Army' (part 3), *BSOAS*, vol.16 (1953), pp.58-9; P. M. Holt, 'The Structure of Government in the Mamluk Sultanate' in P. M. Holt (ed.), *The Eastern Mediterranean Lands in the Period of the Crusades* (Warminster, 1977), p.54; A. K. S. Lambton, 'The Internal Structure of the Saljuq Empire' in J. A. Boyle (ed.), *The Cambridge History of Iran*, vol.5 (Cambridge, 1968), pp.239-44.

7. J.-C. Garcin, *Un Centre Musulman de la haute Égypte médiévale: Qus* (Cairo, 1976), pp.184-6.

8. Humphreys, *From Saladin to the Mongols*, pp.315-19.

9. Ibn 'Abd al-Zahir, *Rawd*, pp.52-4; C. Cahen, ' "La Chronique des Ayyoubides" ' p.164; Humphreys, *From Saladin to the Mongols*, p. 326.

10. Ibn 'Abd al-Zahir, *Rawd*, pp.54-61; Shafi' ibn 'Ali, *Husn al-Manaqib*, A. Khowaiter (ed.) (Riyad, 1976), pp.28-9; C. Cahen, 'Mamluk bahrites en Asie mineure? Quand la crible était la paille' in N. Boratav (ed.), *Homage à Pertev* (Paris, 1978), pp. 119-23; Humphreys, *From Saladin to the Mongols*, pp.326-8, 330-3, 342-4.

11. Balog, *Coinage*, pp.75-6.

12. Humphreys, *From Saladin to the Mongols*, pp.329-30; Schregle, *Die Sultanin*, pp.84-94.

13. Schregle, *Die Sultanin*, pp.93-5; cf. U. Haarmann, *Quellenstudien zur frühen Mamlukenzeit* (Freiburg, 1970), pp.117, 164-5.

14. Humphreys, *From Saladin to the Mongols*, pp.321-6; J. Prawer, *Histoire du Royaume Latin de Jérusalem*, vol.2 (Paris, 1970), pp.339-52; S. Runciman, *A History of the Crusades*, vol.3 (Cambridge, 1955), pp.274-80.

15. Abu'l-Fida, *Mukhtasar*, vol.3, p.212.

16. Ibn 'Abd al-Zahir, *Rawd*, pp.157-60; Ibn al-Suqa'i, *Tali Kitab Wafayat al-A'yan*, J. Sublet (trans. and ed.) (Damascus, 1974), p.124; Humphreys, *From Saladin to the Mongols*, pp.331-3.

17. Ibn 'Abd al-Zahir, *Rawd*, pp.60-1; Humphreys, *From Saladin to the Mongols*, pp.343-4.

18. D. Ayalon, 'The Wafidiyya in the Mamluk Kingdom', *Islamic Culture*, vol.25 (1951), p.97; Humphreys, *From Saladin to the Mongols*, p.341.

19. Humphreys, *From Saladin to the Mongols*, pp.334-5, 339-40.

20. P. Jackson, 'The Crisis in the Holy Land in 1260', *English Historical Review*, no. 376 (1980), p.492.

21. *Ibid.*, pp.494-5.

22. Yunini, *Dhayl*, vol.3, p.92.

23. Humphreys, *From Saladin to the Mongols*, pp.346-9.

24. Ibn Taghribirdi, *Nujum*, vol.7, p.179.

25. Ibn 'Abd al-Zahir, *Rawd*, pp.62-3; Humphreys, *From Saladin to the Mongols*, pp.347-8.

26, Jackson, 'The Crisis', p.492.

27. Ibn al-Suqa'i, *Tali*, p.196; Humphreys, *From Saladin to the Mongols*, pp.356-8.

28. L. Hambis, 'La Lettre mongole du gouverneur du Karak', *Acta Orientalia Academia Scientarum Hungarica*, vol.15 (1962), pp.143-6; cf. Ibn 'Abd al-Zahir, *Rawd*, pp.122-3, 150; Ibn al-Suqa'i, *Tali*, p.124.

29. C. Cahen, ' "La Chronique des Ayyoubides" ', p.175; Humphreys, *From Saladin to the Mongols*, pp.348, 350, 360.

30. On the reign of al-Muzaffar Qutuz, the chief sources are Ibn 'Abd al-Zahir, *Rawd;* al-Yunini, *Dhayl*, vols 1 and 2; Shafi' ibn 'Ali, *Husn;* Ibn al-Suqa'i, *Tali;* Ibn al-Dawadari, *Kanz;* Maqrizi, *Suluk*, vol.1, pt.2; Ibn Taghribirdi, *Nujum*, vol.7. See also 'Kutuz' in *EI(2)*.

31. Yunini, *Dhayl*, vol.1, p.368.

32. Maqrizi, *Suluk*, vol.1, pt. 2, pp.367-9.

33. Baybars al-Mansuri, 'Zubdat al-fikra fi tarikh al-Hijra', London, British Library MS Or. Add. 23325; cf. al-Makin in C. Cahen, ' "La Chronique des Ayyoubides" ', pp.172-3.

34. Jackson, 'The Crisis', p.502.

35. On the Battle of 'Ayn Jalut, see ' 'Ayn Djalut' in *EI(2)* and the sources listed there. Additionally, see Ibn al-'Abd al-Zahir, *Rawd*, pp.64-5; Ibn al-Dawadari, *Kanz*, pp.49-50; G. Levi della Vida, 'L'invasione dei Tartari in Siria nel 1260 nei ricordi di un testimone oculare', *Orientalia* (new series), vol.4 (1935), pp.365-6, 375-6; J. Chambers, *The Devil's Horsemen* (London, 1979), pp.154-5; J. Prawer, *Histoire du Royaume Latin de Jérusalem*, vol.2 (Paris, 1970), pp.434-5.

36. For Sarim al-Din Uzbak's eye-witness account which was transmitted by Ibn al-Furat, see Levi della Vida, 'L'invasione dei Tartari'.

37. Maqrizi, *Suluk*, vol.1, pt.2, pp.434-5.

3 BAYBARS I, THE MONGOLS AND THE CRUSADERS

Though Baybars and his court chronicler, Muhyi al-Din ibn 'Abd al-Zahir, were subsequently to claim that it was he, Baybars, who actually dealt Qutuz the lethal blow, in fact it seems that Qutuz was killed by an otherwise unknown mamluk, Anas al-Silahdar.[1] Moreover, the emirs and mamluks who were privy to the murder of Qutuz were a heterogeneous group. Apart from Baybars, only one of them, Balaban al-Rashidi, can be identified as a Bahri. Several of the others were Mu'izzis — that is, former mamluks of al-Mu'izz Aybak. It may be that Qutuz was murdered as a revenge for his deposition of Aybak's son al-Mansur Nur al-Din 'Ali.

In any event, it is clear that Baybars was not the undisputed leader of the conspirators. Furthermore, those conspirators were only a minority among the emirs and soldiers encamped at Gaza. It was therefore not at all a foregone conclusion that Baybars would now succeed to the throne. As news of the murder spread, other powerful emirs who had not been involved in the conspiracy assembled in a council tent. A heated debate over the succession followed the arrival of the conspirators. Many of the emirs present, perhaps a majority, wanted Balaban al-Rashidi to take the throne. However, though there are indications that the military and civil elite of the Mamluk period considered the succession to the throne to be in some sense elective, it was not elective in the sense of a simple show of hands. Military backing and wealth made some votes more important than others. In this case Faris al-Din Aqtay al-Musta'ribi cast the deciding vote. Aqtay had been *atabak* of the armies under Aybak's son 'Ali and under Qutuz. He gave his weighted vote for Baybars.[2] According to a later and somewhat hostile chronicler of the life of Baybars, Shafi' ibn 'Ali, Aqtay is alleged to have pronounced: 'He who kills the ruler should himself be ruler, for that is the law of the Turks.'[3] However, since Shafi' specifically identifies Anas al-Silahdar as the killer of Qutuz, perhaps the point of the anecdote is that Baybars should not have become sultan.

As soon as Baybars had been chosen to be sultan, he demanded the *bay'a* (oath of allegiance) from the assembled emirs. They, however, demanded that he should first take an oath to them that he would respect and promote their interests. This was agreed and the

37

two oaths sworn. An advance party under Emir 'Izz al-Din al-Hilli was then despatched to secure the Cairo citadel and shortly afterwards in November 1260, Baybars himself arrived in Cairo.

In Cairo Baybars's first task was to share out the key offices in the royal household and the government of Egypt. This was of course not merely a matter of making administrative dispositions but of buying political support. Aqtay al-Musta'ribi was confirmed as *atabak* of the armies. But this respected Salihi emir in his late fifties was to feature in Baybars's reign less as a military man than as a negotiator and mediator intervening on several occasions with the sultan on behalf of subjects with a grievance.[4] Another senior Salihi emir, Jamal al-Din Aqush al-Najibi, became *ustadar*. The office of *ustadar* (major-domo or master of the royal household) gave its holder power over certain areas of tax control and expenditure, and later in the Mamluk period the financial jurisdiction of this office was to increase as that of the Vizierate declined.[5] A third Salihi emir, 'Izz al-Din Aybak al-Afram, was made *amir jandar*. The *amir jandar* was theoretically responsible for guarding the sultan's tent, but the formal description, set down in chancery manuals, gives a misleading impression of the real function and importance of the emir's responsibilities.[6] Aybak al-Afram's responsibility for guarding the sultan was purely nominal. Until his death in 1295, he acted as master of public works and as senior military engineer for a succession of sultans, supervising the construction and maintenance of buildings, fortifications, siege engines and irrigation works. He also had special responsibilities for Upper Egypt, where he had extensive properties and *iqta*'s. According to Ibn Taghirbirdi, 'he was so wealthy that he could have bought all Egypt'.[7] Other Salihi emirs, similarly wealthy and probably even more powerful — Qalawun al-Alfi, Balaban al-Rashidi, Baysari al-Shamsi and 'Izz al-Din al-Hilli, for instance — were, so to speak, given no ministerial portfolios. Their importance was marked by their right to determine the affairs of state with the sultan in the royal *majlis* (council) and by their right to command in major campaigns. Such emirs had the rank of emirs of a hundred, *muqaddams* of a thousand. This title indicated that they were the possessors of (at least) a hundred mamluks, while on campaign they might expect to command a force of some thousand men. The principal office holders — Aqtay, Aqush and Aybak — also held this rank. Though their numbers fluctuated from reign to reign, there were normally about 24 such officers at the top of the military hierarchy.[8]

At its inception, then, Baybars's regime was a junta dominated by former mamluks of Sultan al-Salih Ayyub. Baybars, however, was successful in placing a few of his personal mamluks in key positions. Though he was young, perhaps only 18, Baybars's favourite mamluk, Bilik al-Khazindar al-Zahiri, was made *Na'ib* (Viceregent) of Egypt.

In the early Bahri period the *na'ib* was, after the sultan, the most important man in Egypt. Together with the vizier he exercised overall supervision of the country's administration and taxation.[9] A little later in 1261 Bilik was also to be given the *ad hoc* post of army administrator; the covert purpose of this appointment seems to have been to undermine Aqtay's position as *atabak* of the armies.[10] Two of Baybars's emirs were also appointed to the office of *dawadar* (pencase bearer) and deputy-*dawadar*. The *dawadar* was the military officer charged with supervising the work of the civilian scribes of the chancery. As such he had responsibility not only for the issue and receipt of official documents, but also, by extension, for the *barid* (state postal service), for foreign affairs and for espionage.[11] One at least of these *dawadar*s, Lajin al-Zahiri, was literate with a good Arabic script.[12] Those mamluks whom Baybars had personally acquired, the Zahiris, were so called from the regnal name Baybars took on assuming the throne, al-Zahir. At the time of his accession, after years of exile in Syria, Baybars can have had relatively few mamluks of his own to promote to high office. It would take years of patient cunning to increase, by purchase, his corps of royal Zahiri mamluks and to use them to displace Salihi emirs from key posts.

Other offices in the palace administration had to be assigned to military men. Some of them should be noted here. The *hajib al-hujjab* (senior chamberlain) was formally the officer in charge of screening and presenting visitors to the sultan — actually he and his subordinate *hajib*s were often entrusted with important diplomatic missions in this period.[13] The *amir silah* (emir of weapons) had charge of the armoury and a section of the sultan's guard.[14] Yet other sections of the royal guards were commanded by the *amir jamdar* and the *ra's nawbat al-nuwab*. The *amir akhur* had charge of the sultan's stables.[15] Beyond the narrow elite of emirs holding office in the household and central administration, there was a much larger body of mamluks who after their emancipation — their graduation, as it were, from the sultan's barracks — received emirates. Though these soldiers were no longer juridically deemed to be slaves, and hence could hold property and exercise authority, still it was customary to refer to them as 'mamluks' and as freedmen they owed no less devotion and service to their royal manumitter than when they had been slaves. Within the Emirate there was a ladder of seniority and promotion. Beneath the emirs of a hundred came the emirs of forty, then the emirs of ten and finally the emirs of five. The emir of forty (who was more commonly known as *amir al-tablakhana* (emir of the military band), from his right to maintain an orchestra to play outside the gate of his house), would be expected to maintain and train 40 mamluks, and similarly down the hierarchy. In times of mobilisation for war the junior emirs, like the emirs of a hundred, would also command somewhat larger bodies of men from the *halqa* (free soldiery).[16]

Although Mamluk government was overwhelmingly dominated by the military, still some of the most important offices were held by Arab civilians. Baybars confirmed Ibn Zubayr, Qutuz's appointee, as vizier for the time being. Under the Fatimid and Ayyubid rulers of Egypt, their viziers had been men of real power and influence. Traditionally the vizier's jurisdiction had extended over almost all the bureaus of the administration. Though the vizier remained an influential official, from the reign of Baybars onwards there was an increasing tendency to restrict his competence to fiscal affairs. A high proportion of the staff of the bureaus (*dawawin;* singular, *diwan*) dealing with finance and taxation were recruited from native Coptic Christians and viziers were frequently drawn from administrators who had converted from Christianity to Islam.[17] The other senior civilian job in the administration was that of senior scribe. Under Baybars this official was known as the *katib al-sirr* (scribe of the secret). From the reign of Qalawun onwards the growing importance of this official — to some extent at the expense of the vizier — was marked by a change of title to that of *sahib al-insha'* (head of the chancery). Just as the vizier worked closely with the Na'ib of Egypt, so the *sahib al-insha'* worked with the *dawadar* and shared with the *dawadar* a broad area of responsibility that extended far beyond the drafting of official documents. There were relatively fewer Copts among the chancery scribes and throughout the first half century of the Mamluk chancery the top jobs were dominated by a scholarly Muslim family, the Banu 'Abd al-Zahir.[18]

The chief *qadi*, at the head of the civilian hierarchy of judges and jurisconsults, was outside the Mamluk administration as narrowly defined. However, the post was in the gift of the sultan and the chief *qadi* would be expected to advise on and underwrite royal decisions. The *qadis* administered justice according to the *shari'a* law of Islam. Mamluk sultans, like their Zengid and Ayyubid predecessors, presided over a form of justice, *siyasa* justice, that rested on discretion of the ruler with regard to affairs of state and matters of life and death, and was not strictly based on the prescriptions of the *shari'a*. However, in practice, the sultan was advised in the administration of *siyasa* justice by the senior *qadis*, while for their part, the *qadis* depended on the sultan and his officers for the enforcement of such penalties as execution, mutilation or imprisonment.[19] The *muhtasib* (market inspector) of Cairo had jurisdiction over markets, commercial weights and measures, the passing of coins, the enforcement of certain urban taxes and the policing of the streets. Since the origins of his office lay in the enforcement of the provisions of the *shari'a* with regard to weights and measures, this officer was nominally under the chief *qadi*, but in practice the *muhtasib* was appointed by the sultan and his policing duties meant that he worked closely with the military.[20]

In many cases Baybars had been obliged to leave Qutuz's appointees in their offices. Qutuz had been a popular if (only because?) short-lived ruler and Baybars found it necessary to keep secret the location of his burial lest it became a place of pilgrimage.[21] Baybars by contrast was not popular with the citizens of Cairo. He was remembered by them as one of the leading officers of the Bahris who had terrorised Cairo in the early 1250s. Baybars found it necessary to buy popularity by abolishing some of the uncanonical taxes that Qutuz had imposed at the time of the Mongol emergency. Even so, it was a couple of months before he dared ride through the city's streets in public procession.

At the time of his accession to the Sultanate Baybars was probably in his early forties. As has been noted above (in Chapter 1), he was one of the Barali Kipchaks who had fled into the Crimea in the 1240s and been enslaved there. Aged about 14, he had then been sold in Aleppo and was eventually acquired by Ala al-Din Aydakin al-Bunduqdar — at the cheap price of 800 dirhems because of a cast in one eye. Sometime in the 1240s Aydakin was disgraced and imprisoned by Sultan al-Salih Ayyub and, as a result, his mamluks — including Baybars — passed into the hands of the sultan. Al-Salih Ayyub put him in the *Jamdariyya*, a guard section of the Bahri mamluks. After the sultan's death, Baybars had played a leading part in the murder of Turanshah. In exile in Syria from 1254 onwards, he had been involved in an unsuccessful plot to murder al-Nasir Yusuf of Damascus in 1258.[22]

Short in stature, broad chested, rarely blinking, ferociously energetic, Baybars governed from the saddle and the military encampment. Opposition from any quarter was dealt with ruthlessly and Baybars did not shrink from the occasional exemplary crucifixion or bisection of his victims. Still he was not addicted to the refinements of cruelty that distinguished some of the later Qalawunid and Circassian sultans. His public appearances were noisily bombastic and decisive. Privately, he slept fitfully, his rest being disturbed by nightmares and his stomach easily upset.[23] The way in which he had advanced his career gave him little reason to trust those around him and not only did he establish an elaborate espionage system under the *dawadar*, he was himself liable to make surprise visits of inspection on his officers and prone to wandering the streets in disguise to discover what was being said about him. In short, he lived on his nerves.

Baybars was neither the first nor the last conspirator and murderer to become Sultan of Egypt. The question cannot be avoided: how could the rule of these usurpers be publicly justified and legitimated? In the first place the sultan ruled because he ruled — by the decree of fate. As Baybars's panegyricist Muhyi al-Din ibn 'Abd al-Zahir put it: 'Fortune [*al-su'ada*] made him king.'[24] A related notion advanced by '*ulama*' who wrote on the nature of political power, was that any rule, no matter how arbitrary its origins, was better than no rule at all. As Badr al-Din ibn Jama'a, writing in the early fourteenth century, put it:

> When the *Imama* [leadership of the Muslim community] is thus contractually assumed by one person by means of force and military supremacy, and thereafter there arises another who overcomes the first by his might and his armies, then the first is deposed and the second becomes Imam, for the reasons of the well-being and unity of the Muslims.[25]

Sultans also claimed to rule by virtue of their natural abilities and actual achievements. It was common for them to commission early on in their reign tracts celebrating their courage, military prowess, acts of justice and piety, etc., and such tracts tended to extend themselves into chronicles of the reign. Thus Muhyi al-Din ibn 'Abd al-Zahir wrote for Baybars, al-'Ayni for al-Mu'ayyad Shaykh and al-Zahir Tatar and Ibn Taghribirdi for Jaqmaq.

Then again it was also held that sultans ruled by virtue of the acclamation of the leading men of the realm. We have already seen how Baybars was elected by the emirs and received the *bay'a* from them. It was also desirable that he be acknowledged by the leading *'ulama'*, in particular the *qadis*. At the time of Baybars's accession the Muslim legal hierarchy in Egypt was headed by the chief *qadi* of the Shafi'ite *madhhab* (law school). In 1265 Baybars created chief *qadi*ships for the other three leading *madhhabs* and a year later was to carry out the same reform in Syria. Presumably the main purpose of this restructuring of the legal hierarchy was to weaken the independent power of the Shafi'ite *qadi*, who now retained only a vague seniority over the others, though an additional motive may have been to advance the Hanafi *madhhab* to which the mamluks and most Turks tended to belong.[26]

Besides being in a sense elected by their subjects, the Mamluk Sultans of Egypt and Syria were also invested with their thrones by the Abbasid caliph, the spiritual leader of the Muslim community. At the time of Baybars's accession there was no Abbasid caliph (the last, al-Musta'sim, had been killed after the Mongol capture of Baghdad in 1258). It was therefore necessary for Baybars to invent one. During Qutuz's brief reign, a man, who claimed that he was an uncle of the last reigning caliph in Baghdad and that he had escaped across the Iraqi–Syrian desert with the bedouin, turned up in Damascus. Baybars had him brought to Cairo and in a series of elaborate ceremonies in 1261 invested him as caliph and then had himself invested as sultan by the man he had elevated. Caliph al-Mustansir proved to be a less pliable tool than Baybars had hoped. Moreover, a number of contemporaries clearly had doubts about the real parentage of al-Mustansir. Therefore, in the autumn of 1261 the caliph was sent off with what may have been a deliberately under-equipped expeditionary force to retake Baghdad from the Mongols. A force of 6,000 Mongols effortlessly slaughtered al-Mustansir and most of his army.[27] A new man who claimed to have made a similar escape from Baghdad was speedily produced and invested as the Abbasid Caliph al-Hakim in 1262. After al-Hakim early on showed an unwelcome inclination to dabble in political intrigue, he (and his successors) were placed under a form of distinguished house arrest in a palace just outside Cairo.[28] Thereafter, with hardly any exceptions, the caliphs were to play a negligible role in Egyptian politics. However, they were regularly brought out on ceremonial occasions and the residence of the Sunni Caliphate in Egypt may have given the Mamluk sultans some prestige elsewhere in the Islamic world — in Arabia, North Africa, Anatolia, and elsewhere.[29]

Baybars also claimed to rule as al-Salih Ayyub's natural heir. According to Ibn 'Abd al-Zahir, Baybars through having been trained and educated by al-Salih Ayyub, had acquired that sultan's nobility of blood and royal virtues — qualities that Turanshah, for instance, had conspicuously failed to inherit. Baybars posed as the maintainer of the good traditions of al-Salih Ayyub. Throughout his reign and those of his successors al-Sa'id Berke Khan and Qalawun, a mamluk who was about to be promoted to the rank of emir swore his oath of loyalty to the sultan over the tomb of al-Salih Ayyub. Finally, and related to the above aspect of Mamluk rule, Baybars and his successors maintained the tradition of the Zengid and Ayyubid sultans as leaders of the *jihad*.[30] Baybars's successes against the infidel Mongols, Crusaders, Armenians and Nubians played a crucial part in the justification of his rule to the public. Plainly, then, there was no lack of legitimatory props for Baybars's Sultanate; yet, equally plainly, if a stronger man armed with a sword came along these props would avail him little.

Indeed Baybars's reign was punctuated by plots — and by alleged plots which gave the sultan opportunities to purge and thin the opposition from his military colleagues. In 1261 there was a purge of some of the key leading Mu'izzi emirs — some of whom, as we have seen, had been involved with Baybars in the plot against Qutuz. In 1263 Balaban al-Rashidi, the emir the Salihis had nearly chosen to succeed Qutuz as sultan, was arrested and imprisoned. A couple of years later the Qaymari Kurdish emirs, Baybars's former allies in Damascus in the 1250s, were similarly dealt with. In 1270–1 there was a major purge of leading Salihi emirs. Baybars, however, never dared move against the most powerful of these — Qalawun, Baysari and Baktash.

Opposition to Baybars and the junta of mamluk emirs came from other quarters. In 1260 the mamluks had to suppress a revolt in Cairo of black slaves and grooms led by a Shi'ite ascetic, al-Kurani.[31] More seriously Upper Egypt, where the bedouin were more powerful and relatively more numerous than in the Delta, had been in endemic revolt since the death of al-Salih Ayyub in 1249. Mamluk control barely extended beyond the garrison towns. In

1262 the bedouin invaded Qus, the capital of Upper Egypt and murdered its governor. The rebels, who declared themselves in favour of the destruction of the mamluk system in Upper Egypt, were bloodily put down by Emir 'Izz al-Din Aybak al-Afram.[32]

Although Baybars's rule was hardly securely established in Egypt, his main preoccupation in the early years, and indeed throughout his reign, would be with the conquest of Syria and the consolidation of his authority there. After the Battle of 'Ayn Jalut Qutuz had appointed a Salihi emir, Sanjar al-Halabi, as Na'ib of Damascus. When Sanjar learnt of Qutuz's murder and Baybars's usurpation, he declared himself independent in Syria and took the title al-Malik al-Mujahid. Sanjar seems to have been popular among the citizens of Damascus, who had in any case no desire to be ruled from Cairo. He was, however, defeated and captured outside Damascus in 1261 by an army sent from Egypt under the command of Baybars's former *ustadh*, Aydakin al-Bunduqdar.[33] From henceforth Damascus and its province would be governed by a *na'ib* appointed by the Egyptian sultan. As a check against the excessive power of the *na'ib* and against the dangers of provincial revolt, a *wali* (governor) was appointed to independent command of the citadel and its garrison. The *wali* reported directly to Cairo. As other Syrian cities came under direct Mamluk control, a similar division of authority was imposed on them.[34]

With Damascus came most of Muslim Palestine and Southern Syria, the southern half of al-Nasir Yusuf's former kingdom. In the fortress of Kerak in Transjordan Baybars's former employer, the Ayyubid prince al-Mughith, continued to resist the Mamluks until in 1263 he was persuaded to emerge for a parley under safe conduct and was then treacherously seized and hastily tried and condemned. However, the charge on which he was found guilty — that he had been involved in collaboration with the Mongols — seems to have been a true one.[35] Al-Mughith was imprisoned and he seems to have been strangled a few months later. Al-Ashraf Musa, the Ayyubid prince of Homs, had actually fought for the Mongols. But since Baybars bore him no old grudges, al-Ashraf Musa was able to make his peace with the new regime. On the latter's death in 1262 he left his principality to Baybars, and Homs was incorporated into the Mamluk empire.[36] In 1272 the lordship of the fortress of Sahyun in Northern Syria similarly passed into the hands of the sultan. Al-Mansur, the ruler of Hama in Northern Syria, had actually fought with Qutuz against the Mongols. Hama was not annexed and directly administered by the Mamluks until 1341. However, its Ayyubid princes were to all intents and purposes provincial governors and courtiers of the Egyptian sultans and Hama's forces part of the armies of the Mamluk empire.[37]

Until he was more securely established in Egypt and the route from Egypt to Damascus via Palestine or Transjordan assured, Baybars was in no position to direct affairs in the north. After 'Ayn Jalut and the flight of the Mongols back across the Euphrates, one of al-Nasir Yusuf's mamluk emirs, Aqush al-Burli, had taken control of Aleppo. Though Aqush sent protestations of loyalty to Baybars, he refused to surrender himself or the city to the sultan and it was not until 1262 that Aqush al-Burli was dislodged and a *na'ib* from Cairo installed.[38] Therefore when the Mongols invaded Syria a second time, crossing the Euphrates in November 1260, Baybars's forces played no part in driving them out. The army that defeated the Mongols at the Battle of Homs on 10 December 1260 was assembled from the forces of Aqush al-Burli and the Princes of Hama and Homs.[39]

Though there were to be no more major encounters with Mongol armies in Syria during Baybars's reign, there were occasional raids by mixed forces of Mongols and Armenians in the north and, almost every year, there was a Mongol scare and rumours of Mongols massing on the other side of the Euphrates. Early in his reign Baybars established a Mamluk forward defence line on the Euphrates with garrisons at Bira and Rahaba which defended the crossing points and which communicated with Cairo via the *barid* (the state courier service).[40] The front-line garrisons were small and, despite the seriousness of the threat in the north, the better part of the Mamluk army was always based in Egypt. Aleppo's fortifications had been destroyed by the Mongols in 1258 and they were not finally rebuilt until the 1290s. Many villages in the northern and eastern hinterland of Aleppo seem to have been abandoned between the 1240s and 1260s as a result of Khwarazmian, Turkoman and Mongol depredations. Turkoman pastoralists replaced settled peasantry in some parts, but generally population seems to have been thinly spread in Northern Syria. When large bodies of Mongols invaded, the Muslims would burn the pasturage behind them as they retreated. So, by accident or design, Northern Syria became a sort of *cordon sanitaire* against the Mongol Ilkhanate and it was to remain so until the early decades of the fourteenth century.

It was because of the persistence of the Mongol threat and the dependence of Syria on Egypt's armies that Muslim Syria was effectively united with Egypt in a way that it had not been since the time of Saladin. Similarly, it was the persistence of the Mongol threat which spurred Baybars and his successors to eliminate the remnants of the Crusader principalities on the coastline of Syria and Palestine. In the first place the best and most direct route for Mamluk armies and the despatch riders of the *barid* travelling between Egypt to Damascus and the north ran through Palestine — via Gaza, Ramla, Jenin, 'Ayn Jalut and Baysan — and most of that route was closely threatened by Crusader strong points. Though there was a large Muslim garrison in Gaza at the beginning of Baybars's reign, the Muslims held none of the Palestinian ports to the north of Gaza, nor were the towns they held in the hinterland of Palestine — in particular Jerusalem, Nablus and Ramla — fortified. Moreover, much of the best agricultural land was held by the Franks on the coast and the Franks were well placed to harass Muslim cultivation of the rest. The Hospitallers' construction of a fortress at Mount Thabor to the north-west of Baysan posed a particular threat to the Mamluk route through Palestine. Therefore it was against Mount Thabor that Baybars first proceeded in 1263 and razed the partially completed fortifications. That same year he also made demonstrations against other Crusader places, including Acre. In 1265 Caesarea, one of the Crusader ports, was overcome. In 1266 Safed, one of the strongest Templar castles, fell after a particularly long and bloody siege; an attempt against the Teutonic Knights' Montfort failed. In 1268 Jaffa and Beaufort were taken and in 1271 Montfort finally fell.[41]

Although the Crusader towns and castles had relatively small garrisons of knights, their capture by the Mamluks was by no means a foregone conclusion. For the garrisons of Franks could be supplemented by levies of native Christians and disaffected hillsmen. For instance, Christian Arabs assisted the Templars at the siege of Safed in 1266.[42] It is also clear that the Mamluks were at first relatively inexperienced at siege warfare. There were also difficulties in obtaining and transporting the wood and iron necessary for the construction of siege engines (and when they had captured a place Mamluk engineers often experienced considerable difficulties in even partially destroying what the Crusaders had built). Therefore Baybars used economic warfare to wear down his prospective victims. Thus the orchards and crops outside the walls of Acre were repeatedly ravaged and pastureland around the Hospitaller fortress of Crac des Chevaliers burnt.[43] Additionally, the presence of Mamluk armies in Palestine was used to put pressure on the Franks to negotiate and Baybars's bluster and sabre-rattling was often successful in securing concessions from the Franks. These included partitions of territory or of revenue to be jointly administered by Franks and Muslims, as in the truces with Jaffa and Beirut (1261), with the Hospitallers and Tyre (1267), with Beirut (1269), with the Hospitallers (1271), with Tripoli and the Templars of Tortosa (1271), and with Acre (1272.[44] In 1271 the arrival of Prince Edward of England in Palestine may have spurred Baybars to launch a naval attack against Cyprus. Possibly this had the aim of deterring the Cypriots from sending aid to Prince Edward in Acre. However, the small fleet was destroyed in a storm off Cyprus.[45] In any event if a large Mamluk army had been mobilised and sent from Egypt to meet a rumoured Mongol offensive and if rumour proved to be false, as often happened, it was obviously convenient to employ the force instead against the Crusader territories.

The offensives against the Franks in the north were similarly related to the persistent Mongol threat. Bohemond VI, Count of Tripoli and Prince of Antioch, had actually allied himself to the Mongols during their invasion of 1258-9, and Frankish knights had similarly joined Armenian tributaries of the Mongols in raiding Muslim territories in Northern Syria. In general during the early part of Baybars's reign the Franks were stronger in the north than in Palestine. The Hospitallers based at Crac des Chevaliers levied tribute over a large part of the Muslim hinterland, and as late as 1265 Bohemond launched an offensive against Homs. An early attempt by a Mamluk army to capture Antioch in 1262 failed disastrously; it was said that the emir in command, Taybars al-Waziri, had been bribed to withdraw.[46] In 1268 a Mamluk army under the personal command of Baybars did succeed in taking Antioch. The immense amount of booty taken in the victory was distributed between the sultan, his emirs, mamluks and *halqa* troops and among auxiliary Arabs and Turkomans levied in Syria and volunteers for the *jihad* from the large Muslim towns. One presumes that the profits of war provided an additional stimulus to the campaigns against the Crusaders. After a series of softening-up raids in previous years, Crac des Chevaliers was captured in 1271.

An attempt to take Maraclea and assassinate its lord was botched that same year.

Mamluk armies operating against Crusader strong points east of the Orontes were also hindered by the fact that the heretical Isma'ili Assassin sect held a number of fortresses in the Jabal al-Ansariyya. In the early 1260s the Assassins payed tribute to the Hospitallers and received supplies from them. In a series of campaigns from 1265 to 1271 Baybars's generals took over their castles and made the Isma'ilis the sultan's subjects. Thereafter Baybars and his successors seem to have occasionally employed them on assassination missions.[47]

It must be understood that the 'Muslim' Syria that Baybars and Qalawun defended against the Mongols and the Crusaders was confessionally and ethnically divided. Much of Syria was inhabited by turbulent communities whose allegiance to the Mamluk Sultanate or to Sunni Islam was either unreliable or non-existent. The inhabitants of the larger towns — Aleppo, Hama, Homs and Damascus — were predominantly Sunni Muslim Arabs. But the highlands north of the Isma'ili castles were inhabited by Nusayri heretics and Greek Orthodox Christians. Equally, the Lebanese highlands to the south were settled by warlike Druze and Maronite tribesmen. Both groups at times co-operated with the Franks. In general, neither the Mamluks nor the Ottomans after them ever succeeded in establishing anything more than a very nominal control over the coastal mountain ranges of Northern Syria and the Lebanon. In highland Galilee, too, there were Christian and Nusayri villages. Across the Jordan the Mamluk governors of Kerak had to deal with Christian Arabs and rebellious Kurdish tribesmen. Although the paramount shaykhs and emirs of the Banu Fadl Arabs paid formal homage to the sultans of Egypt, it was they and not the sultans who were the real rulers of the Badiya al-Sham (the desert extending eastwards from Damascus up to the Euphrates). Even in regions of Palestine and Syria where there were strong Mamluk garrisons, as at Gaza and Damascus, there is plentiful evidence of nomads and villagers being involved in banditry and in the sale of weapons, Muslim captives and intelligence to the Franks in the late thirteenth century.

Baybars's campaigns against the Shi'ite Isma'ilis, no less than those against the Crusaders, were presented as part of the *jihad* of Sunni Islam. Later in the thirteenth century, as we shall see,

Nusayris and the Druze of the Jabal al-Ansariyya on Mount Lebanon became the victims of the preaching and the armies of the *jihad*. The notion of the *jihad* extended to cover not only wars against the heterodox in arms but the struggle against all forms of immorality — prostitution, hashish eating, beer drinking, the wearing of immodest or over-luxurious dress, Christian and Jewish functionaries lording it over Muslims. At times, particularly at times when God's displeasure had been manifested in the form of pestilence or drought, the sultan would bow to '*ulama*' and popular pressure and enforce decrees against such things. (In their laxer moments, however, the sultans preferred to tax such abuses.)

Volunteers for the *jihad*, who fought in the hope of booty or martyrdom, swelled the professional Mamluk armies who fought in Syria. Bedouin and Turkoman horsemen were also recruited for specific campaigns. They presumably fought for booty, as well as receiving subventions from the sultan. Some of these tribes in any case received regular payment or *iqta's* in return for patrolling the roads and desert areas. The most important part of the army, if not necessarily the most numerous part, was however provided by the sultan's mamluks, the emirs' mamluks and the Egyptian and Syrian *halqa*s. The royal mamluks in the army normally received largesse at the beginning and end of campaigns.

Some of the newly conquered land in Syria was made into *waqf* land — that is, set aside to provide revenue for the maintenance of religious endowments. Most of it, though, was distributed as *iqta's* to emirs. In the early years of Baybars's reign a few of the newly conquered areas were assigned as *milk* (freehold property capable of being transmitted to one's descendants) to those same emirs. There are indications that in this early period, Baybars's colleagues among the emirs expected to be able to transmit their status and wealth to their children. Had they done so, the Mamluk regime would have come to resemble much more closely the feudal regimes of the Christian West. Such hopes, however, were not to be fulfilled save in a few exceptional cases.[48]

Instead, those children of mamluks ('*awlad al-nas*' means 'children of the people' — children of people who matter, that is) who wished to pursue a military career were placed in the *halqa*, the broad body of troops of free birth. As members of the *halqa* they might rise to hold Emirates and *iqta's*, but generally the uppermost levels of the army and the administration were reserved for the mamluks. The *awlad al-nas* were of course only a small minority in the large body of free troopers of the *halqa*. In Egypt the *halqa*, a cavalry force, was officered almost entirely by mamluk emirs. Much of the Syrian *halqa* was also commanded by mamluk emirs, but in Syria quite a large part of the *halqa* was mustered and officered by free-born hereditary emirs — Arabs, Kurds and Turks who were the headmen and landed gentry of their localities. Much of the Mamluk army's infantry came from Syria, the infantry of Ba'labakk being especially famous.[49]

Wafidiyya were also placed in the *halqa*. *Wafidiyya* was the term used to refer to large bodies of cavalry of Turkish, Kurdish or Mongol origin who came as immigrants into Mamluk lands from Iraq, Anatolia and elsewhere to seek protection and employment from the sultan. Particularly important among such *Wafidiyya* were the thousands of Mongols and Turks who came over to Baybars in waves in the years 1262–4 and again in 1266–7.[50] Many of those Mongols and Turks did so under instruction from Berke the Mongol Khan of the Golden Horde. Berke Khan ruled over the Mongol conquests in South Russia from 1257 to 1261. In 1262 he became involved in a war with Hulegu, the Ilkhan of Mongol Persia. The cause of their conflict is not clear: it may have had to do with their support for rival candidates for succession to the Great Khanate in Mongolia and China from 1260 onwards, or it may have been because of Berke's and Hulegu's conflicting claims to rule over the Caucasus and Azerbaijan. An alliance between Baybars and Berke was therefore natural, though it proved impossible to co-ordinate their military campaigns against Hulegu, because of the time it took embassies to pass between Cairo and Saray, the Golden Horde capital on the lower Volga. A letter from Baybars carried by an Alan merchant first reached Berke in 1261, and subsequently there were more formal exchanges of embassies in 1262–3 and 1264. These exchanges continued with Berke's successor, Mongke Temur (1267–80).

Baybars and Berke were drawn together by more than a common hostility to the Ilkhanate of Persia. Though most of Mongol and Turkish subjects of the Khans of the Golden Horde were still pagan, Berke and some of his family had converted to Islam around the year 1260. Berke may have wished to have his rule confirmed by the Abbasid caliph in Cairo and was keen also to receive instruction and advice from '*ulama*' and Sufis sent by the Mamluk sultan. Commercial ties between the lands of the Golden Horde and Egypt and Syria were at least as important. Archaeological evidence shows that Egypt sent textiles and ceramics to Southern Russia, but the balance of the trade would certainly have been in favour of the Golden Horde, for from there came not only furs, but wood (which was a strategic material very scarce in Egypt) and, most crucially, slaves.[51] The continuing supply of Kipchak slaves to Egypt could only be assured through the complaisance of the Khan of the Golden Horde. (It was necessary also to secure the agreement of the Byzantine emperor to the safe passage of ambassadors and commerce from the Golden Horde through the Bosphorus; hence the embassy sent by Baybars to Michael VIII in 1261–2.) In the early years of Baybars's reign the ships bringing slaves to Egypt may have been Muslim, but some time between 1261 and 1265 the Genoese established a trading colony at Caffa on the Crimean Peninsula and from then on, though the sultans maintained merchants and agents at Caffa, the carrying trade was mainly in the hands of the Genoese.[52]

According to the fifteenth-century historian Ibn Taghribirdi, Baybars was responsible for introducing Mongol institutions and customs to Egypt. The Mongol law code, the *yasa*, replaced the *shari'a* as the code of the military class. Such offices as the *amir akhur* (emir of the stables) and the *hajib* (chamberlain) were first introduced to Egypt in the reign of Baybars and were inspired by the equivalent offices in the Mongol hierarchy. Al-Maqrizi, also a fifteenth-century historian, similarly asserted that Baybars introduced the *yasa* to the detriment of Islamic *shari'a* law. Such assertions have a certain *prima facie* plausibility. Mongol influences might have come through diplomatic and commercial contacts with the Golden Horde, or through the influx of Mongol *Wafidiyya* into Egypt and Syria, or indeed through respectful imitation of the Mamluks most dangerous enemies, the Mongols of the Ilkhanate in Iran.

However, though there are a few indications of Mongol influence on such relatively trivial areas as the procedure for retiring service officers and on hairstyle and dress, the notion that Baybars imposed a Mongol pattern of organisation on the Egyptian court and army must be regarded as a fifteenth-century myth. For there is now considerable doubt as to whether the *yasa*, even among the Mongols themselves, ever existed as a written code with the force of law. Secondly, there is no direct evidence at all for the application of the *yasa* in the Mamluk lands in the thirteenth or early fourteenth centuries. Thirdly, as far as can be determined, rank and entitulature under the Mamluk sultans derived from less outlandish prototypes. Such offices as *amir akhur* and *hajib* had been borrowed from the Turko-Iranian entitulature of such earlier Islamic regimes as the Seljuks, the Khwarazmians and the Ayyubids. It is true that the chiefs of the Mongol *Wafidiyya* enjoyed great prestige. Some of them joined the mamluk emirs in the deliberations of the sultan's *majlis* and Baybars, Qalawun and other leading mamluks married the daughters of *Wafidi* emirs. The warriors that these chiefs brought with them, however, were less well trained than the mamluks and correspondingly less well rewarded.[53]

Moreover, potential influence of these initially pagan Turco-Mongol warrior bands was more than counterbalanced by the concurrent immigration of Muslims into Egypt and Syria, in particular of prominent refugees from Abbasid Baghdad, Seljuk Konya and the former lands of the Khwarazm-Shahs. Such refugees had formerly been minor princes, viziers, household officers and generals in the lands that were now under Mongol suzerainty.[54] If there were innovations in protocol and administration in late-thirteenth-century Egypt (and this is not altogether clear), then it is to the defunct regimes of Baghdad, Konya and Samarqand that one must look first for sources of inspiration.

The refugees coming from Iraq and Anatolia were not all courtiers, soldiers and tribesmen. Theologians, scholars and Sufis came looking for employment in Cairo and Damascus. Ibn Taymiyya, for instance, one of the most famous and influential religious and political thinkers of the Late Middle Ages, was born in Harran in 1263. His family fled before the Mongols in 1269 and Ibn Taymiyya was to make his career in Damascus.[55] We can further deduce from changes in themes and style in the art of the period that metalworkers, glass blowers and book illuminators moved from Mosul into the Mamluk lands in this period – and the stream of skilled refugees was also swollen by artisans, doctors, astrologers, etc. It is scarcely an exaggeration to claim that, under the Mamluks, Egypt and Syria became a sort of Noah's Ark for an older Eastern Islamic culture.

Another prominent immigrant who was to exercise considerable influence over Baybars, Shaykh Khadir al-Mihrani, had fled into the Mamluk lands from Upper Iraq for a more disreputable reason. Had he lingered in Jazirat ibn Umar, he would have been castrated for sleeping with the daughter of one of the emirs there. In Aleppo he got himself into the same sort of trouble and moved on down to Damascus. In Damascus in the 1250s he established himself as a Sufi shaykh and was successful in securing the patronage of a prominent Qaymari Kurdish emir. A *zawiya* (a Sufi hospice) was built for him in Damascus and it was later claimed that Baybars, when still an emir, encountered Khadir there and that Khadir prophesied that Baybars would one day become sultan. However, such prophetic tales were commonly attached to the early careers of sultans; for instance, a sand diviner prophesied the accession of Qutuz and a later astrologer that of Barquq. This *topos* in royal biographies must be seen not simply as a tale of wonder, but as an indication that the rulers concerned came to power by the decree of the stars, that their royal nature could be divined from marks on their faces or in the sand — an additional way of legitimating their rule.

It is certain, however, that when Baybars did become sultan, Khadir became the sultan's spiritual counsellor. The shaykh and the sultan did the Sufi *dhikr* (recitation) together. Baybars built Khadir a new *zawiya* and relied on his advice and predictions. Khadir was said to have correctly predicted the fall of the Crusader town of Arsuf in 1265 and of Safed in 1266. (A contemporary competitor, Shaykh 'Ali al-Majnun — the Mad — was present at the sieges of Arsuf and of Caesarea and was observed to enter into a trance state so as to employ a form of spiritual warfare against the Crusader fortifications. Both 'Ali al-Majnun and Khadir received valuable *waqf* land after the fall of Safed.) Assured of Baybars's protection, Shaykh Khadir led pogroms and riots against the Jewish and Christian subjects of the sultan and organised the destruction and looting of synagogues and churches — an activity which was certainly materially profitable, even if the more orthodox *'ulama'* were dubious about its spiritual benefits.

Shaykh Khadir resembled Rasputin not only in the occult sources of his authority over the sultan, but in his sexual appetite — that is if all the stories are to be believed. He also sought to divert money and gifts coming to the sultan into his own pocket. Therefore in 1273 a coalition including some of the most powerful men in Egypt was formed to press for his trial and execution. This coalition was headed by Baybars's favourite, Bilik al-Khazindar (Na'ib of Egypt) and Baha' al-Din ibn Hanna (Vizier of Egypt from 1261 until his death in 1278). The coalition also included such powerful Salihi emirs as Qalawun and Baysari. They accused Khadir of peculation, fornication with the wives and daughters of emirs, and sodomy. Though they pressed for the death penalty, arguing that Khadir possessed too many state secrets to live, Khadir was alleged to have saved himself by prophesying that the sultan's death would certainly follow shortly upon his own. However, Khadir was closely imprisoned in the Cairo citadel until his death in 1271.[56]

Bilik al-Khazindar, the leader of Shaykh Khadir's accusers, had been the first of Baybars's mamluks to be advanced during the sultan's reign. Not only was he made *na'ib al-saltana* and given some jurisdiction over the army, but the sultan treated his favourite mamluk as if he were his own son. Bilik was married to a princess of the royal house of Mosul and given the castles of Banyas and Subayba to hold as *milk* (a freehold appanage).[57]

Throughout his reign a large part of Baybars's income was set aside for the purchase of more mamluks — mainly of Kipchak stock from the lands of the Golden Horde. By the end of his reign the sultan was said to have more than 4,000 mamluks.[58] Naturally the powerful and wealthy Salihi emirs—Qalawun, Aybak al-Afram, Baysari and Baktash al-Fakhri— sought to maintain their positions by increasing their mamluk retinues and by establishing households which mirrored on a smaller scale the hierarchy of the royal household. Despite all their efforts, the control of the Salihis over the affairs of the realm was being eroded from year to year. In the last years of Baybars's reign, trusted Zahiri mamluks had been successfully installed in key posts. Besides Bilik as *na'ib al-saltana,* and Balaban al-Rumi as *dawadar,* Baybars was eventually able to place Shams al-Din Aqsunqur al-Fariqani in the post of *ustadar* some time in the 1260s. During the sultan's frequent absences from Egypt, Aqsunqur acted for him and held the title of *na'ib al-ghayba.*[59] Outside Egypt the most important office, the post of na'ib of Damascus, was held by Aydamur al-Zahiri from 1271 onwards. Hisn al-Akrad (the former Hospitaller fortress of Crac des Chevaliers) was held by Aybak al-Mosuli, another of Baybars's Zahiri mamluks, but he was murdered in mysterious circumstances in 1277. (Aleppo in the decades immediately following the Mongol occupation of 1260 was of little importance, a semi-inhabited ruin, left under the governorship of Nur al-Din 'Ali ibn Majalli, a mamluk of the former Ayyubid ruler al-Nasir Yusuf.)[60]

The need for Baybars to have mamluks he could rely on absolutely, particularly in the administration of Egypt, becomes more apparent if we consider the extraordinary sequence of campaigns and tours of inspection the sultan made in the course of his 17-year reign. In AD 1261 (AH 659) Baybars made a military demonstration against Crusader-held places in Palestine and visited

Damascus. In 1263 (AH 661) he appeared in Palestine again, forced John Lord of Jaffa to recognise his suzerainty, raided the suburbs of Acre, visited Jerusalem and winkled al-Mughith out of the fortress of Kerak. In 1265 (AH 663) he advanced out of Cairo because of an abortive Mongol scare, but then turned to take Caesarea and Arsuf from the Franks. In 1266 (AH 664–5) he ravaged Palestine, captured Safed and visited Damascus. Subsequently in 1266–7 (AH 665) he returned to Cairo and then returned to Palestine to raid Acre and to organise the administration and supplying of Safed. In 1268 (AH 666) he captured Jaffa and Beaufort and went on for the first time to the north. In the north he raided Tripoli, visited Hama and Homs, captured Antioch, and threatened the Assassin leaders. He then returned to Cairo via Damascus. In 1269 (AH 667) he inspected places now held by the Mamluks in Palestine, returned to Cairo briefly for a surprise visit of inspection, returned to Palestine and threatened Tyre to force Margaret, Lady of Tyre, to make a truce with them. Then he went to Mecca and Medina on pilgrimage. His visit had a political as well as a spiritual purpose, for while there he received the submission of the Sharif of Mecca. It was, therefore, from this year that a form of suzerainty, however vague, was established over the Hejaz.[61] From the Hejaz he returned to Kerak. He was at Kerak at the beginning of 1269–70 (AH 668) and proceeded from there to Damascus, on to Aleppo, back to Damascus, then on to Jerusalem, Hebron and Gaza before returning a little later, in the winter of 1269 (AH 668), to Cairo. He subsequently re-emerged to visit Damascus and Safed, before proceeding to threaten the Hospitaller fortress of Margat and the Isma'ili castles in the north, and finally to raid the vicinity of Hisn al-Akrad (Crac des Chevaliers). In the late summer of 1270 (beginning of AH 669) he was in Damascus. From there he returned to Cairo. Then towards the end of winter he passed through Damascus on his way to threaten Tripoli before going on to caputre Hisn al-Akrad, Safita and Hisn 'Akkar. Afterwards, he returned to Egypt via Damascus, threatening Montfort and Acre as he passed. In the summer of 1271 (beginning of AH 670) he was successively at Kerak, Damascus, Hama, Homs, Hisn al-Akrad, Hisn Akkar, Damascus, Aleppo, Damascus, the hinterland of Acre, Cairo, Caesarea, Damascus, and Hisn al-Akrad. In 1272–3 (AH 671) he took an army up to Bira on the eastern side of the Euphrates to ensure that a Mongol threat to that fortress was fended off. In 1273–4 (AH 672) he was in Cairo, Damascus and Cairo. In 1274–5

(AH 673) he left Cairo in the summer to visit the fortresses east of the Dead Sea. Then he returned to Cairo before setting out again in midwinter for Northern Syria. From there he invaded Cilician Armenia and successfully sacked its main towns before returning to Damascus. The following year, 1275–6 (AH 674), was relatively quiet; Baybars spent it in Damascus, Cairo and Kerak. The first half of 1276–7 (AH 675) was spent in Kerak, Damascus, Aleppo and Cairo.

The energy of the sultan is astounding: no less so is the readiness of his army to fight winter and summer campaigns. Their most ambitious campaign, however, was yet to come. Early on in his reign, Baybars had entertained hopes of intervening in Anatolia on behalf of 'Izz al-Din Kaykaus, one of the claimants to the Seljuk throne. Anatolian lands were optimistically distributed to Egyptian emirs as *iqta'* and subsidies were sent to Kaykaus to foster resistance to the Mongols. But the Mongol candidate, Rukn al-Din Kaykhusrau, triumphed and the status of Seljuk Anatolia as a Mongol tributary was confirmed. Subsequently, *Wafidiyya* from the Seljuk court of Konya came to Egypt and doubtless urged Baybars to intervene there, but the pro-Mongol Christian kingdom of Cilician Armenia lay across the most direct route to Konya. Only in 1275, urged on both by the *pervaneh*, the politically ambiguous chief minister of the Seljuk court, and by the Qaramanli Turkoman tribesmen who were in revolt against the Mongols in the mountainous Taurus region lying between Konya and the Cilician plain, did the Mamluks plan an invasion of Anatolia. The projected invasion of 1276 had to be aborted because of the appearance of a strong Mongol army in Anatolia.

In the spring of 1276, however, Baybars led a large Mamluk army through Eastern Turkey, avoiding the Cilician Armenian strongholds, and encountered and defeated a Mongol army in the vicinity of Albistan on 16 April 1277. Subsequently, he swung west and occupied Kayseri. There he had himself crowned sultan and coins struck in his name — an indication of his intention to extend his rule as not only the heir of the Ayyubids but also of the Seljuks. However, the approach of a second Mongol army, the failure of the *pervaneh* to come over unambiguously to Baybars's side and the difficulty of liaising with the rebellious Turkoman tribesmen forced Baybars to retreat.[62]

Doubtless he intended to return to Anatolia, but this was his last campaign. In June 1277 he was back in Damascus. There he was taken sick, apparently after drinking qumiz while watching a polo match. Inevitably there were rumours of poison. Qumiz, though, is a treacherous drink, potentially lethal if it is allowed to go off. Baybars died on 20 June 1277.[63]

Notes

1. Shafi' ibn 'Ali, *Husn al-Manaqib*, A. Khowaiter (ed.) (Riyad, 1976)), p.31; cf. Ibn 'Abd al-Zahir, *al-Rawd al-Zahir*, A. Khowaiter (ed.) (Riyad, 1976), p.68.
2. On the murder of Qutuz and its immediate aftermath, in addition to the two sources listed above, see al-Yunini, *Dhayl Mir' at al-Zaman* (Hyderabad, 1954–5), vol.1, pp.370–1, vol.2, pp.1–2; Abu'l-Fida, *al-Mukhtasar fi Akhbar al-Bashar*, vol.3 (Istanbul, 1869-70), p.207-8; Ibn al-Dawadari, *Kanz al-Durar*, U. Haarmann (ed.) (Cairo, 1971), pp.61-2; al-Maqrizi, *Kitab al-Suluk*, M. M. Ziada (ed.), vol.1, pt.2 (Cairo, 1936), pp.434-5; Ibn Taghribirdi, *al-Nujum al-Zahira*, vol.7 (Cairo, n.d.), pp.83-4, 101-2.
3. Shafi' ibn 'Ali, *Husn*, p.32.
4. See, for instance, Ibn 'Abd al-Zahir, *Rawd*, pp.150, 181, 256, 262, 393-4; Shafi' ibn 'Ali, *Husn*, pp.110, 127; Maqrizi, *Suluk*, vol.1, pt.2, pp.447, 535, 545.
5. On the *ustadar*, see D. Ayalon, 'Studies on the Structure of the Mamluk Army' (part 3), *BSOAS*, vol.16 (1953), pp.61-2; *idem*, 'The System of Payment in Mamluk Military Society', *JESHO*, vol.1, (1957-8), pp.283-6; M. Gaudefroy-Demombynes, *La Syrie à l'époque des Mamelouks* (Paris, 1923), pp.1x-1xii; P. M. Holt, 'The Structure of Government in the Mamluk Sultanate' in P. M. Holt (ed.), *The Eastern Mediterranean Lands in the Period of the Crusades* (Warminster, 1977), p.56.
6. On the formal functions of the *emir jandar*, see Ayalon 'Studies' (part 3), pp.63-4; Gaudefroy-Demombynes, *La Syrie*, pp. lix-lx; R. S. Humphreys, *From Saladin to the Mongols* (Albany, 1977), p.456n.
7. Ibn Taghribirdi, *Nujum*, vol. 8, p.81; on his career, see in particular Ibn al-Suqa'i, *Tali Kitab Wafayat al-A'yan*, J. Sublet (trans. and ed.) (Damascus, 1974), pp.19-20; J.-C. Garcin, 'Le Caire et la province: constructions au Caire et à Qus sous les Mameluks Bahrides', *Annales Islamologiques*, vol.8 (1969), pp.48-51.
8. On emirs of a hundred see Ayalon, 'Studies' (part 1), pp.467-9; R. S. Humphreys, 'The Emergence of the Mamluk Army' (part 2), *SI*, vol.46 (1977), pp.169–73.
9. On the *na'ib al-saltana*, see Ayalon, 'Studies' (part 3), pp.57–8; Gaudefroy-Demombynes, *La Syrie*, pp.lv-lvi; Holt, 'The Structure', p.53.
10. On the acquisition of military responsibilities by Bilik, see Ibn 'Abd al-Zahir, *Rawd*, p.86; Ibn al-Suqa'i, *Tali*, p.68; Yunini, *Dhayl*, vol.1, p.483.
11. On the *dawadar*, see Ayalon, 'Studies' (part 3), pp.62-3; Gaudefroy-Demombynes, *La Syrie*, pp.lvii-lviii; Holt, 'The Structure', p.56; S. M. Stern, 'Petitions from the Ayyubid Period', *BSOAS*, vol.27 (1964), pp.17–18; *idem*, 'Petitions from the Mamluk Period', *BSOAS*, vol.29 (1966), pp.251–2, 268; 'Dawadar' in *EI(2)*.
12. Al-Yunini, *Dhayl mir'at al-zaman*, vol.3 (Hyderabad, 1960), pp.67-8.
13. On the nominal and formal functions of the *hajib*, see Ayalon, 'Studies' (part 3), p.60; Gaudefroy-Demombynes, *La Syrie*, p.lviii; Humphreys, *From Saladin to the Mongols*, pp.468–9; 'Hadjib' in *EI(2)*. On his diplomatic activities, see R. Irwin, 'Real and Fictitious Authority under the Early Bahri Mamluk Sultans' (unpublished conference paper).

14. Ayalon, 'Studies' (part 3), p.60.

15. Ayalon, 'Studies' (part 3), p.63; Gaudefroy-Demombynes, *La Syrie*, p.lviii.

16. The ranked hierarchy of emir of one hunded, emir of forty and emir of ten seems to have evolved and crystallised during the early decades of Bahri Mamluk rule. See Humphreys, 'The Emergence of the Mamluk Army' (part 2), pp.167–73; Ayalon, 'Studies' (part 2), pp.467–75.

17. A. 'Abd al-Raziq, 'Le Vizirat et les vizirs d'Égypte au temps des Mamluks', *Annales Islamologiques*, vol.16 (1960), pp.183–240; R. Chapoutot-Remadi, 'Le Vizirat sous les premiers mamluks', *Acts du XXIX Congrès International des Orientalistes (Études Arabes et Islamiques)*, vol.1, pt.2 (1975), pp.58–62; Holt, 'The Structure', p.58; H. Rabie, *The Financial System of Egypt A. H. 564–741/A.D. 1169–1341* (London, 1972), pp.138–42.

18. W. Björkmann, *Beiträge zur Geschichte des Staatskanzlei im islamischen Ägypten* (Hamburg, 1928), pp.36–55; J. H. Escovitz, 'Vocational Patterns of the Scribes of the Mamluk Chancery', *Arabica*, vol.23 (1976), pp.42–64; 'Ibn 'Abd al-Zahir' in *EI(2)*; 'Insha' in *EI(2)*.

19. N. J. Coulson, *A History of Islamic Law* (Edinburgh, 1964), pp.122, 128, 132, 144; R. Irwin, 'Real and Fictitious Authority'; J. N. Nielsen, 'Mazalim and Dar al-'Adl under the Early Mamluks', *Muslim World*, vol.66 (1976), pp.114–32; E. Tyan, *Histoire de l'organisation judiciaire en pays de l'Islam*, 2 vols (Paris, 1938–43), vol.2, pp.141–288 (especially pp.248–54).

20. A. 'Abd al-Raziq, 'Les Muhtasibs de Fustat au temps des Mamluks', *Annales Islamologiques*, vol.14 (1978), pp.127–46; I. M. Lapidus, *Muslim Cities in the Later Middle Ages* (Cambridge, Mass., 1967), pp.98–101; 'Hisb' in *EI(2)*.

21. Shafi', *Husn*, p.31.

22. The chief published sources covering the life and reign of Baybars, are: Ibn 'Abd al-Zahir, *al-Rawd*, partially translated by F. S. Sadeque as *Baybars I of Egypt* (Dacca, 1956); Izz al-Din Ibn Shaddad, *Tarikh al-Malik al-Zahir*, A. Hutait (ed.) (Wiesbaden, 1983); Shafi' ibn 'Ali, *Husn;* Ibn al-Suqa'i, *Tali*; Yunini, *Dhayl*, vols 1–3; Abu'l-Fida, *al-Mukhtasar*, vols 3–4; Ibn al-Dawadari, *Kanz;* Ibn al-Furat, *Tarikh al-duwal wa'l-muluk*, vol.7, Q. Zurayq (ed.), (Beirut, 1942) partially translated by U. and M. C. Lyons and J. Riley-Smith as *Ayyubids, Mamluks and Crusaders*, 2 vols (Cambridge, 1971); Maqrizi, *Suluk*, vol.1, pt. 2; Ibn Taghribirdi, *Nujum*, vol.7. See also, A. A. Khowaiter, *Baybars the First: His Endeavours and Achievements* (London, 1978); 'Baybars I' in *EI(2)*.

23. On Baybars's temperament and constitution, see the remarkable account by his doctor, Ibn al-Nafis, *The Theologus Autodidactus of Ibn al-Nafis*, M. Meyerhof and J. Schacht (eds) Oxford, 1968), pp. 33–4, 68–70.

24. Lyons and Riley-Smith, *Ayyubids*, vol.1, p.79, vol.2, p.99.

25. H. A. R. Gibb, *Studies on the Civilization of Islam*, (Boston, 1962), p.143.

26. J. H. Escovitz, 'The Establishment of Four Chief Judgeships in the Mamluk Empire', *JAOS*, vol.102 (1982), pp.529–31.

27. Ibn 'Abd al-Zahir, *Rawd*, pp.99–112; Sadeque, *Baybars I*, pp.123–34; Shafi'i, *Husn*, pp.37–46.

28. Ibn 'Abd al-Zahir, *Rawd*, pp.141–8; Sadeque, *Baybars I*, pp.158–64; Shafi', *Husn*, pp.51–5.

29. On the Abbasid Caliphate in Cairo generally, M. Chapoutot-Remadi, 'Une Institution mal connue: le Khalifat abbaside du Caire', *Cahiers de Tunisie*, vol.20 (1972), pp.11–23; J.-C. Garcin, 'Histoire, opposition politique et pietisme traditionaliste', *Annales Islamologiques*, vol.7 (1967), pp.33–89; A. Schimmel, 'Kalif und Kadi im Spätmittelalterlichen Ägypten', *Die Welt des Islams*, vol.24 (1942), pp.1–26.

30. On the Mamluks and *jihad*, see E. Sivan, *L'Islam et la Croisade* (Paris, 1968), pp.165–89.

31. Maqrizi, *Suluk*, vol.1, pt.2, p.440; Lapidus, *Muslim Cities*, p.171.

32. J.-C. Garcin, *Un Centre Musulman de la haute Égypte: Qus* (Cairo, 1976). pp.189–90.

33. Ibn al-Dawadari, *Kanz*, pp.63–4, 69–70; Maqrizi, *Suluk*, vol.1, pt.2, pp.438–9, 444–5. In the winter of 1260 Sanjar struck coins in both his name and Baybars's. However, he also struck coins in his name alone. See Ibn al-Dawadari, *Kanz*, p.64; A. Berman, 'The Turbulent Events in Syria in 658–9 A.H./1260AD Reflected by Three Hitherto Unpublished Dirhems', *Numismatic Circular*, vol.84 (1976), pp.315–16.

34. Gaudefroy-Demombynes, *La Syrie*, pp.cviii-cx.

35. Ibn 'Abd al-Zahir, *Rawd*, pp.148–51; Sadeque, *Baybars I*, pp.164–6, Shafi' ibn 'Ali, *Husn*, pp.55–7.

36. Ibn 'Abd al-Zahir, *Rawd*, p.185; Sadeque *Baybars I*, pp.202–3; 'Hims' in *EI(2)*.

37. 'Hama' in *EI(2)*); 'Sahyun' in *EI(1)*.

38. Ibn 'Abd al-Zahir, *Rawd*, pp.133–5.

39. *Ibid.*, pp.96–7; Maqrizi, *Suluk*, vol.1, pt.2, p.442; J. A. Boyle, 'Dynastic and Political History of the Ilkhans' in J. A. Boyle (ed.), *The Cambridge History of Iran*, vol.5 (Cambridge, 1968), p.352.

40. On the *barid*, see J. Sauvaget, *La Poste aux chevaux dans l'empire des Mamelouks* (Paris, 1941).

41. On Baybars's campaigns against the Crusader principalities, see Khowaiter, *Baybars*, pp.77–118; S. Runciman, *A History of the Crusades*, vol.3 (Cambridge, 1955), pp.315–48.

42. Ibn 'Abd al-Zahir, *Rawd*, p.260.

43. 'Harb' in *EI(2)*; 'Hisar' in *EI(2)*.

44. On Mamluk–Crusader treaties, see P. M. Holt, 'The Treaties of the Early Mamluk Sultans with the Frankish States', *BSOAS*, vol. 43 (1980), pp.67–76; R. Irwin, 'The Supply of Money and the Direction of Trade in Thirteenth Century Syria' in *Coinage in the Latin East: The Fourth Oxford Symposium on Coinage and Monetary History*, P. W. Edbury and D. M. Metcalf (eds), *British Archaeological Reports International Series*, vol.77 (1980), pp.79–81.

45. Ibn 'Abd al-Zahir, *Rawd*, pp.386–8; G. Hill, *A History of Cyprus*, vol.2 (Cambridge, 1948), p.167.

46. Ibn 'Abd al-Zahir, *Rawd*, p.245; Ibn Wasil, 'Mufarrij al-Kurub', Paris, Bibliothèque Nationale MS 1703 f. 40b.

47. On the campaign against the Syrian Assassins, see B. Lewis, *The Assassins* (London, 1967), pp.121–3.

48. R. Irwin, 'Iqta' and the End of the Crusader States' in P. M. Holt (ed.), *The Eastern Mediterranean Lands in the Period of the Crusades* (Warminster, 1977), pp.62–77.

49. Ayalon, 'Studies in the Structure' (part 2), pp.448–59; Humphreys, 'The Emergence of the Mamluk Army' (part 2), pp.148, 162-5; R. Irwin, 'Iqta' and the End of the Crusader States', p.71; 'Halka' in *EI(2)*.

50. D. Ayalon, 'The Wafidiyya in the Mamluk Kingdom', *Islamic Culture*, vol.25 (1951), pp.81–104.

51. On Mamluk relations with the Golden Horde, see B. Grekov and A. Yakoubovski, *La Horde d'Or* (Paris, 1939), pp.79–81.

52. A. Ehrenkreutz, 'Strategic Implications of the Slave Trade between Genoa and Mamluk Egypt in the Second Half of the Thirteenth Century' in A. L. Udovitch (ed.), *The Islamic Middle East* (Princeton, 1981), pp.335–45.

53. On possible Mongol influences on the Mamluks, D. Ayalon, 'The Great Yasa of Chingiz Khan: A Re-examination', *Studia Islamica*, vol.33 (1971), pp.97–140 (part A), vol.34 (1971), pp.151–80 (part B), vol.36 (1972), pp.113–58 (part C1), vol.38 (1973), pp.107–56 (part C2); D. P. Little, *An Introduction to Mamluk Historiography* (Wiesbaden, 1970), pp.126–8; D. P. Little, 'Notes on Aitamis, a

Mongol Mamluk' in U. Haarmann and P. Bachmann (eds), *Die Islamische Welt zwischen Mittelalter und Neuzeit* (Beirut, 1979), pp.198–229; J. M. Rogers, 'Evidence for Mamluk-Mongol Relations 1260–1360' in *Colloque international sur l'histoire du Caire* (Cairo, 1969), pp.385–404.

54. For an extensive list of all prominent *Wafidiyya*, see Ibn Shaddad, *Tarikh*, pp.329–38.

55. 'Ibn Taymiyya' in *EI(2)*; and see below pp.96–8.

56. E. (Ashtor)-Strauss, 'Scheich Hidr, ein Beitrag zur Geschichte der Juden in Damascus', *WZKM*, vol.44 (1937), pp.237–40; P. M. Holt, 'An Early Source on Shaykh Khadir al-Mihrani', *BSOAS*, vol.46 (1983), pp.33–9; E. Sivan, *L'Islam et la Croisade*, pp.180, 182; L. Pouzet, 'Hadir Ibn Abi Bakr al-Mihrani (m.7 muh. 676/11 Juin 1277), Sayh du Sultan mamelouk Al-Malik az-Zahir Baibars', *BEO*, vol.30 (1978), pp.173–83.

57. Ibn 'Abd al-Zahir, *Rawd*, pp.86–7; Sadeque, *Baybars*, p.111.

58. Ibn Shaddad, *Tarikh*, p.244; Ibn Taghribirdi, *Nujum*, vol.7, p.179.

59. Ibn al-Suqa'i, *Tali*, p.18; Ibn Taghribirdi, *Nujum*, vol.7, p.280.

60. Humphreys, 'The Emergence of the Mamluk Army' (part 2), pp.155–6.

61. On Baybars in the Hejaz, Ibn 'Abd al-Zahir, *Rawd*, pp.354–7, where Ibn 'Abd al-Zahir claims that Baybars's visit to the Hejaz was at least partially motivated by the need to forestall a Mongol expeditionary force.

62. C. Cahen, *Pre-Ottoman Turkey* (London, 1968), pp.284–90.

63. On the circumstances of Baybars's death and obsequies, see Ibn 'Abd al-Zahir, *Rawd*, pp.473–5; Ibn Shaddad, *Tarikh*, pp.222–6; Ibn al-Suqa'i, *Tali*, p.66; Yunini, *Dhayl*, vol.3, pp.245–8.

4   THE RISE OF THE QALAWUNIDS

Al-Sa'id Nasir al-Din Berke Khan, Baybars's son and heir, had been born in Egypt in 1260. His mother was a daughter of a prominent Khwarazmian *Wafidi* and the grand-daughter of Husam al-Din Berke Khan, the man who had led the Khwarazmians into Syria to assist al-Salih Ayyub and had subsequently been killed by him. Al-Sa'id Berke Khan's Khwarazmian mother and her brother, Emir Badr al-Din Muhammad, were to be influential at Berke's court.[1]

Baybars had done everything possible to ensure his son's succession. In 1264, shortly before the ceremonies attendant on his circumcision, Berke Khan was named sultan and the army took an oath of loyalty to him.[2] In 1267 the oath to him as sultan was renewed and Bilik was appointed to watch over his education and household.[3] In 1276 Berke Khan was betrothed to Ghaziya Khatun, daughter of Qalawun[4] (by then Qalawun's ascendancy over the rest of the Salihi emirs was apparent). In 1277 while Baybars was away in Anatolia and Syria, Berke Khan was, nominally at least, governing Egypt, acting under the advice of Bilik, the na'ib, and Baha' al-Din ibn Hanna, the vizier.

Bilik kept Baybars's death secret until the sultan's body had been brought back to Cairo and the unopposed accession of Berke could be assured. Berke Khan was alleged to have been delighted by the news of his father's unexpected death. He shared his father's ruthless attitudes, but not the latter's energy or ability.[5] Bilik was confirmed as na'ib of Egypt, but Berke Khan and his mother seem to have resented Bilik's tutelage. Bilik died suddenly in August 1277, very likely from poison.[6] He was replaced as na'ib by Aqsunqur al-Farqani, who proved to be insufficiently pliable and was in turn replaced by Sunqur al-Alfi al-Salihi and then by Kunduk al-Zahiri. Aqsunqur al-Farqani was imprisoned, as were several of the senior Salihi emirs, including Sunqur al-Ashqar and Baysari. Kunduk al-Zahiri was of Mongol birth. He was one of the favoured young mamluks whom Baybars had chosen to be educated with his son. He was now in 1278 appointed from the ranks of the *Khassakiyya* to the office of *na'ib*. The *Khassakiyya* were a select corps of young mamluks who had successfully completed their training in the Cairo barracks, had been formally emancipated and who then served in the citadel as the bodyguard, equerries and pages of the sultan pending their eventual promotion to the rank of emir and the assignment of *iqta'* and more responsible jobs.[7]

Kunduk's appointment was an indication of Berke's determination to favour *les jeunes* at court at the expense both of the old guard of grand Salihi emirs and of the new guard of Zahiri emirs. This determination was so obvious that there was very nearly a Salihi revolt that year, near the beginning of Berke Khan's reign. However, some of the Salihi emirs recently arrested were released on the advice of Berke's uncle, Badr al-Din, and the revolt was narrowly averted. Then, on the advice of the *Khassakiyya,* Berke Khan ordered the mounting of an expedition against Cilician Armenia. The expedition was 1,000-strong and under the command of Qalawun and Baysari, the two Salihi generals who posed the greatest danger to Berke Khan's throne. The expedition may have had a valid military purpose; it may have been intended to bring aid and comfort to the Qaramanli Turkomans who were resisting the Mongols in the Taurus region. However, the widespread contemporary understanding was that the expedition had no other purpose than to order some political nuisances out of Egypt. Qalawun and Baysari took their army slowly up through Syria to Damascus and beyond. In the meantime, Kunduk showed unwelcome signs of wishing to take his administrative responsibilities seriously and of trying to curb the extravagance of the *Khassakiyya.* The *Khassakiyya* attempted his assassination and though they failed, Berke Khan took this as a sign that Kunduk should be deposed. Out of office, Kunduk began to correspond with the Salihis who were inconclusively raiding Cilicia. Berke went up to Damascus to oversee things there. Qalawun's army returned secretly from Cilicia and, skirting Damascus, hurried on to Cairo where they joined Kunduk and a rapidly growing body of emirs and mamluks in revolt against Berke Khan. Berke Khan hurried back to Cairo and managed to slip into the citadel. What support he had, however, rapidly fell away: the citadel was surrounded and the best that his mother's negotiations could secure for him was that he should abdicate and be assigned the castle of Kerak to rule as a semi-independent appanage. Berke abdicated in August 1279.

The rebel confederacy of emirs replaced Berke with his brother, Salamish, who took the regnal title al-'Adil. Salamish was seven years old and his brief tenure of the throne gave the emirs time to consider who they really wanted to rule them. This took some three and a half months after which, in December 1279, Salamish was deposed and sent to join his brother at Kerak. Berke Khan died at Kerak in 1280 as a result of a fever which developed after he had fallen from a polo pony. Sayf al-Din Qalawun al-Alfi had acted as Salamish's *atabak al-'asakir* and it was Qalawun who emerged, after months of manoeuvring and conferring, as the emirs' choice to be sultan.[8]

Qalawun was a Kipchak of the Burj Oghlu tribe. He seems to have been born around 1220. He was therefore approaching 60 when he came to the throne and, though he was to prove a firm and vigorous ruler, his career as sultan does not display quite the same frenetic energy as Baybars's. He had also been relatively old when he was enslaved and brought to Egypt and, unlike most Mamluk sultans, he never learned to speak Arabic fluently. He passed from the hands of an emir into the ranks of al-Salih Ayyub's Bahris in 1249. His nickname, 'al-Alfi' (the thousander), refers to the fact that because of his extreme good looks he fetched the remarkably high price of 1,000 dinars. By the time Baybars came to the throne, Qalawun was already recognised as one of the leading Salihis. For instance, he was one of the four leading emirs to be given control of the Rawda fortress where the Bahris were garrisoned. Later on, in 1265, he was one of only two emirs to whom Baybars confided the disturbing news that the Mongols had attacked Bira, and, as we have seen, his daughter married Baybars's son and heir. Qalawun was an experienced soldier and had taken part in many campaigns against the Crusaders. He had also commanded major expeditions against Cilician Armenia in 1266 and again in 1275.

Qalawun was to reign from 1280 to 1290. He took the regnal title al-Mansur and his mamluks were therefore known as Mansuris. There are many similarities between the reigns of Baybars and Qalawun. Both were Salihi Bahris of Kipchak origin. As we shall see, both had to deal with the attempted revolt of a Salihi emir in Damascus and with Mongol invasions two years running at the beginning of their reigns. Both campaigned patiently to erode the Crusader presence in Syria and Palestine. Both sent similar expeditions against the Cilician Armenians and the Nubians. A rump of Salihi emirs who had been powerful in Baybars's reign remained so under Qalawun — only increasingly wealthy and increasingly elderly.

Though Qalawun was successful in getting most of the emirs to back him, he does not seem at first to have been particularly popular with the people at large. On his accession, Qalawun abolished certain (mainly commercial) taxes known as *mukus* (singular, *maks*), which were taxes that were held to have no sanction in *shari'a* law.[9] Despite this, it was some months before Qalawun dared ride through the streets of Cairo in public procession — and when he did so he was pelted with offal.

In Syria resistance took a more determined form. During what was in effect the interregnum of Salamish's Sultanate, Emir Sunqur al-Ashqar had been assigned the governorship of Damascus. Sunqur al-Ashqar was a Salihi emir, but he had been closer to Baybars than most of his Salihi *khushdashiyya*. (A mamluk's *khushdash* was one who had been acquired, trained and manumitted by the same master: *khushdashiyya* as a group were conventionally held together not only by service of the same master, but even afterwards by loyalty to their former companions in servitude. Sometimes this sentiment of group solidarity was a factor in politics but, as we shall see, it could not be counted upon.)[10] Sunqur al-Ashqar had been the last important emir to abandon the cause of Berke Khan and it seems likely that he was offered Damascus as the price of his acquiescence in Berke Khan's deposition. When in April he heard of Qalawun's accession to the Sultanate in Egypt, Sunqur declared himself ruler in Damascus and had coins struck for himself as al-Malik al-Kamil.[11] His cause seems to have been popular in Damascus, where the citizens still had not resigned themselves to being ruled from Cairo. Sunqur al-Ashqar was further successful in rallying a formidable body of support in Syria as a whole. Sunqur was backed by Baybars's children Salamish and Khidr at Kerak, by al-Mansur of Hama (according to Bar Hebraeus, the effective governor of Syria during the reign of Berke Khan),[12] by the Mamluk governors of Aleppo, Safed, Hisn al-Akrad and Sahyun, by Sharaf al-Din 'Isa ibn Muhanna the shaykh of the paramount clan of Fadl bedouin, and by the infantry of Ba'labakk.

Nevertheless, in a battle at Jasura south of Damascus on 21 June 1280, Sunqur's army was defeated by an Egyptian army under the command of Aybak al-Afram. Qalawun named Sanjar al-Halabi, who had been the popular leader of the Damascan revolt some 17 years earlier, as the new Na'ib of Damascus. When in 1281 Qalawun entered Damascus, he was at pains to be heard declaring 'Baybars hated the citizens of Damascus, but I like them'.[13] However, it does not seem that this sentiment was reciprocated; Qalawun was never really popular in Damascus.

Sunqur al-Ashqar and those who still followed him fled northwards to install themselves in the fortress of Sahyun and from there Sunqur continued to control a great deal of Northern Syria. After being ousted from Damascus, Sunqur allegedly appealed to Abaqa (the Mongol Ilkhan of Persia from 1265 to 1282), for assistance in resisting Qalawun. This is not improbable for Sunqur al-Ashqar had spent the early years of Baybars's reign as a prisoner first of Hulegu and then of Abaqa; while in honourable captivity he had married a Mongol girl. Moreover, his allies Sharaf al-Din Isa and the Fadl bedouin ranged freely between Syria and Iraq, and while the Fadl generally professed loyalty to the Mamluk sultans, they were always tempted to play off the Mongols against the Mamluks and to act as intermediaries, spies and smugglers between the two.[14]

In September 1280 a Mongol force entered Syria and plundered defenceless Aleppo before withdrawing. But this was only a preliminary foray and they would return. The Mongols counted on Sunqur's support or at least neutrality. As on previous and subsequent occasions, the Mongol intervention was timed to coincide with Muslim disarray. Just as there were always Mongol renegades at the Mamluk court, so there was always some support for the Mongols in Syria. However, on this occasion before the Mongols could reappear, Qalawun and Sunqur al-Ashqar came to terms. In a pact of May 1281, Sunqur acknowledged Qalawun's Sultanate and was in return confirmed as the lord of Sahyun, Balatunus, Apamea, Antioch, Lattakia, Hisn'Akkar and other places in North-West Syria.[15] Qalawun had also secured his northern flank in Syria by negotiating fairly generous truces with the Hospitallers of Margat in May 1281 and with the Count of Tripoli in the following month.[16]

The main Mongol invasion force entered Syria in the autumn of 1281. It was commanded by Mongke-Temur, brother of the Ilkhan Abaqa, and consisted of perhaps as many as 50,000 Mongols supplemented by 30,000 confederate Armenians, Georgians and Anatolian Turks. There may also have been a few Frankish knights from the north who did not feel themselves to be bound by Bohemond of Tripoli's treaty with Qalawun, as well as a few disaffected Syrian Muslims. The overall size of the Mamluk army which met the Mongols outside Homs on 29 October 1281 is impossible to estimate. Qalawun had brought a trained elite of 800 royal mamluks from Egypt as well as 4,000 *halqa* troops. To this one must add the mamluks of the Egyptian emirs as well as levies from the Syrian towns, plus small armies under the command of the Prince of Hama and Sunqur al-Ashqar and, most importantly, it seems that the greater part of the army consisted of Syrian bedouin and Turkoman light horsemen. The bedouin in particular played a crucial role in the eventual Mamluk victory. Both armies put their best troops in the centre and their auxiliaries in the wings. The right wing of the Mamluk army triumphed over the left wing of the Mongol army, and the Mongol right wing triumphed over the Mamluk left wing. Large parts of both armies believed that they had lost the battle and indeed this was not so very far from the truth, for although, after prolonged and confused fighting, Mongke-Temur was wounded and the Mongols fled back across the Euphrates, the losses on the Muslim side had been very heavy – so heavy that according to Hayton of Armenia their victory practically amounted to a defeat. Certainly, many senior emirs are listed in the obituary collections as having died at the Battle of Homs. In so far as the Mamluks held the field, their victory seems largely to have been due to the leading role played by the Syrian bedouin in the battle.[17]

Abaqa was furious at his brother's defeat and planned another expedition for the following summer, but, before this could be launched, he died in April 1282. The Mongol *quriltay* (deliberative council) chose his older brother Teguder Ahmad to succeed him, setting aside the claims of Abaqa's son Arghun. As the second, Arabic, part of his name implies, Teguder Ahmad had converted to Islam. Acting on the advice of Persian Muslims in the administration, the new ilkhan sent two embassies in 1282 and 1283 to Qalawun in Egypt, proposing peace and the opening of frontiers to trade. The reply drafted by Qalawun's chancery was non-committal, verging on hostile. Mongol insinuations about Mamluk spies in Iraq were matched by claims that Mongol spies disguised as traders had been arrested in Syria.[18] Moreover, it is probable that Qalawun was not prepared to make peace on the Euphrates front so long as the Mongols were conducting a vigorous campaign against Muslim Turkoman tribesmen in Anatolia. On the other side Teguder Ahmad's peace policy had not been popular among the

Mongol generals and its rebuff doomed him. In 1284 he was deposed and killed. Arghun, who was neither a Muslim nor inclined to peace with the Mamluks, became the new ilkhan.

After the Battle of Homs, Sunqur al-Ashqar and his followers returned to Northern Syria; Qalawun was in no position to detain him. Similarly, Qalawun was in no position to mount new assaults against the Crusader strongholds. It would be necessary to rebuild the Mamluk army first. Indeed, in Northern Syria in the early years of Qalawun's reign the Hospitallers of Margat were on the offensive raiding Muslim lands and an early attempt in 1280 to seize Margat, undertaken on the initiative of Balaban al-Tabakhi, the Na'ib of Hisn al-Akrad, had ended in a humiliating defeat for his army.[19] There were problems, too, in Palestine. The movement of the Egyptian army through Palestine in the spring and summer of 1281 on its way to encounter the Mongols had necessitated the displacement of Arab tribesmen (*al-'urban wa'l-'ushran*) from their customary pasture ground. The pastoralists thus affected were threatened with famine and it is not surprising that in October or November 1281 the tribesmen rebelled. They sacked Nablus and Gaza and an army had to be sent from Egypt to suppress the revolt.[20] Therefore Qalawun's relations with the Crusader cities on the coast were peaceful in the years that immediately followed the Battle of Homs.[21] On 16 April 1282 a new peace was concluded with the Templars of Tortosa and on 3 June 1283 a truce with Acre was made. In both cases there were detailed stipulations covering the partition of revenues and authority in border areas.[22]

When the Mamluks were ready to mount a campaign, they chose an easier target than the Mongols or the Crusaders. In 1283 the Na'ib of Aleppo (no longer a venerable Kurdish emir but one of Qalawun's most favoured mamluks, Qarasunqur al-Mansuri) led a major expedition into Cilician Armenia and sacked Ayas and the next year there was a smaller follow-up raid. The Mongols under Ilkhan Ahmad do not seem to have been able or inclined to offer the Armenians protection and the kingdom was also weakened by Qaramanli Turkomans raiding from the Taurus highlands. The Armenians were of course being punished for their presence on the right wing of the Mongol army at the Battle of Homs, as well as for assistance that they had given the Franks of Antioch and Tripoli in earlier years. But more than this, it was Cilicia's wealth that attracted the Mamluk armies. The region was rich in wood and iron, two commodities that were always in short supply in Egypt and

Syria. Furthermore, since the Mongols did not possess their own port on the Mediterranean, the Armenian port of Ayas was the most important outlet for the transmission of goods coming from the Mongol lands to Europe.

As a result of the Mamluk campaigns of 1283 and 1284 the Armenian king Leon II sued for peace in 1285. Qalawun's price was high. In return for a truce that was supposed to last ten years, ten months and ten weeks, Leon agreed to pay an annual tribute of silver coin equivalent to the value of 250,000 dirhams and 250,000 dirhams-worth of livestock and other goods in kind. There were other clauses in the truce document guaranteeing among other things the secure passage of subjects and allies of the sultan through Armenian lands. It appears from the truce document that a major concern of Qalawun's was that Muslim merchants and *Wafidiyya* should be able to reach the Mamluk lands via Cilicia. It was also stipulated in the truce document that Leon was to put no obstacles in the way of slavers bringing young mamluks and slave girls to the sultan.[23] That Ayas was an important port for the slave trade is apparent from Genoese notarial documents registered at Ayas in the 1270s.[24] Presumably many of the slaves that were shipped to Egypt or Europe from Ayas had been shipped from Caffa or Tana to Trebizond and then brought overland to Ayas. In a treaty concluded with the Byzantine emperor Michael VIII in 1281 Qalawun's negotiators had shown a similar concern with securing the free passage of slavers and their human cargo through the Byzantine lands.[25]

By the end of his reign Qalawun had an enormous corps of royal mamluks in his service. Estimates vary between 6,000 and 12,000. Certainly it was far more than Baybars in a longer reign had been able to acquire and more than any sultan subsequently was to possess. With the broad body of royal mamluks a smaller group with higher prestige, consisting of 300 emirs and 3,000 mamluks, was selected and stationed within the citadel. Because they were stationed in the citadel they were known as Burjis ('of the tower').[26] Most of the rest of the royal mamluks were billeted in Cairo — the fortress of Rawda had been destroyed, probably because it was seen as a potential security threat.

As we have seen, it was not until the middle years of Baybars's reign that a regular sea-borne trade in slaves was organised by the Genoese. They brought to Egypt slaves whom the sultan's agents in the Crimea had selected, plus presumably additional slaves that they would sell for themselves in Egypt. The white slaves who had been purchased in the Crimea had been brought there usually by Turkish and Mongol slavers. They were acquired as a result of inter-tribal warfare on the South Russian steppes and the Caucasus, or because impoverished parents had decided to sell their children or because they had been kidnapped. Much of the trade passed through the Bosphorus. Besides Ayas, other ports on the south coast of Turkey — Satalia and Candelore, for example — also handled slaves.

Whereas al-Salih Ayyub and presumably Baybars had restricted recruitment largely to Kipchaks, Qalawun made his purchases from a wide variety of races. He acquired Turks, Mongols, Circassians, Abkhazes, Georgians, Greeks and other Europeans as mamluks. The Circassian element was particularly prominent in the Burji regiment.

Not only did Qalawun acquire a lot of mamluks, he trained them thoroughly and promoted them slowly. Unlike Baybars, Qalawun had had time to acquire a large and experienced mamluk household before he became sultan. Thus Turuntay, the *ustadar* of Emir Qalawun's household, became *na'ib al-saltana* when Qalawun became sultan. Lajin, a mamluk of Prussian or Greek origin who had been a page and then a *silahdar* (arms bearer) in the emir's later household, served the sultan as *na'ib* in Damascus. Kitbugha al-Mansuri, a Mongol who as a youth had been captured at the first Battle of Homs in 1260 and then been acquired by Qalawun as a mamluk, was to serve Qalawun as *na'ib al-ghayba* during the sultan's absences from Egypt. Baybars al-Mansuri, a Turkish mamluk who had been part of Qalawun's retinue from as early as 1265, became *dawadar* on the sultan's accession. Qarasunqur al-Mansuri, a Circassian, was one of the batch of Qalawun's mamluks made emirs of a hundred on the sultan's accession and he was to become na'ib of Hama and later of Aleppo. Sanjar al-Shuja'i was another mamluk made emir of a hundred at the beginning of the reign and he was to become vizier in 1283. (Under Qalawun the Vizierate was for the first time assigned to mamluk emirs.) Other Mansuri mamluks who rose to become powerful emirs under the sultan included Balaban al-Tabakhi, who became *na'ib* first of Hisn al-Akrad and then of Tripoli; Baydara, who became *amir majlis* (amir of the council) and later *ustadar* and vizier; and Salar, an Oirat Mongol captured during the expedition to Anatolia in 1277.

The variety in origins of the mamluks listed above is striking. So too is the fact that at least three of them — Baybars al-Mansuri, San-jar al-Shuja'i and Baydara — were literate in Arabic.[27] With a large and experienced household in his service, Qalawun was able to fill almost all the key offices with men devoted to him. Baybars as sultan had not succeeded in advancing his position much beyond that of *primus inter pares* among his Salihi Bahri colleagues; Qalawun's rule was more absolute. Not that Qalawun directly challenged the position of the ageing and dwindling body of Salihi emirs. Emirs like Aybak al-Afram continued to be honoured and consulted. (Incidentally, a knowledge of Arabic culture was not a monopoly of the Mansuris; Aybak al-Afram had been instructed in *hadith* — that is, traditions concerning the Prophet — while Baysari was famous for his taste for cultivated literature and his great library.) Turuntay, Qalawun's *na'ib* in Egypt, indeed complained that Qalawun treated the children of the Salihis too generously — presumably in allowing them to inherit at least some portion of their fathers' wealth and status in the military hierarchy.[28] Nevertheless, Qalawun was able to play off the Salihis against Baybars's Zahiris. He treated the Zahiris with a mixture of harshness and generosity. Some Zahiri mamluks were actually promoted emirs when Qalawun came to the throne, others were dispersed to small-time jobs in provincial garrisons, others again were purged. The main purge took place early on in the reign. Kunduk al-Zahiri, whose accession to the side of the Salihis had played such a large part in the overthrow of al-Sa'id Berke Khan, had drawn a large number of conspirators together in a plot to assassinate Qalawun. Some of his supporters were Zahiris like himself, others were Mongol *Wafidiyya* or Mongol mamluks who supported Kunduk because he was of Mongol birth. Kunduk relied also on the support of the great Salihi emir Baysari, but in the event Baysari betrayed the plot to Qalawun. Kunduk was executed by drowning and many Zahiris fled abroad.[29] As the reign progressed other plots were discovered and individual opponents picked off. Though Qalawun was to be presented by historians of the Qalawunid period as a more benevolent figure than Baybars, it is doubtful whether this picture reflects anything more than partisan bias.

In Syria Qalawun moved his *na'ib*s from post to post at relatively frequent intervals, thus preventing the potentially over-ambitious emirs from establishing independent power bases in the provinces. When Qalawun was himself in Syria, Egypt was governed for him by his son al-Salih 'Ali acting in consultation with the *na'ib al-ghayba*.

Al-Malik al-Salih 'Ali seems to have been in his early twenties at the time of Qalawun's accession. He was a capable and respected prince with a substantial household of his own. The problems Qalawun and his son faced in keeping Egypt peaceful are spelt out in detail in a memorandum prepared by the scribes of the chancery for al-Salih 'Ali's guidance during one of Qalawun's absences from Egypt early on in the reign.

In this document great stress is placed on the importance of maintaining vigilant patrols around the Cairo citadel and also on the need for intensive policing of the city. The *wali*s (local governors) were to ensure that people only travelled by day in Egypt. Close contact with Syria had to be maintained by pigeon post. Troops slow in leaving Egypt to join Qalawun's expedition were to be chased up and, when they were ready to leave, they had to be issued with *laisser-passer* documents. The bedouin of the Delta provinces were to be forced to provide horses for the *barid* and patrols on the roads maintained. Special attention had to be paid to the Delta ports, both because they were vulnerable to sea-borne raids by the Crusaders and because the ports were sources of intelligence about what was happening abroad. The Western merchants in Alexandria were to be handled fairly in commercial transactions, since much of Egypt's prosperity depended on them. On the other hand, they were not to be trusted and they were to be locked up in their caravanserais every night and at midday on Fridays (to prevent a surprise coup while almost every Muslim in the town was at the Friday prayer). For the patrolling of the coast the mamluk governors were heavily dependent on bedouin. On the other hand, the bedouin were not felt to be entirely reliable. A close watch on the bedouin had to be kept, especially at the oases where they gathered, in order to prevent them massing in numbers that could not be controlled. Kurdish tribesmen, particularly Shahrazuri Kurds, presented a similar problem. A lot of Shahrazuri Kurds had settled on the pastures in the Giza region not far from Cairo. The *iqta*'s and incomes of soldiers away on campaign had to be protected by royal officials. Significantly, a large part of the memorandum is concerned with irrigation — the maintenance of irrigation channels, the fair allocation of water rights, the timing of the breaking of the dikes, and the provision of watchmen to guard over the irrigation channels.[30] Generally, one gets the impression from this document that, though banditry of all sorts was indeed widespread, still Egypt under Sultan Qalawun aspired to the condition of a centrally directed police state.

Qalawun's chancery issued other documents besides the above which provide evidence of the concern of the administration with the encouragement of international commerce. In 1288 a general proclamation of *aman* (safe conduct) was issued for merchants coming from foreign parts — from China, India, Persia, Iraq and the Mediterranean lands — assuring them of security for themselves and their merchandise and promising good trading terms. The document, which was really directed at potentially obstructive officials at the ports and elsewhere, particularly stressed the sultan's desire to increase the import of slaves.[31]

As is clear from the memorandum prepared for the guidance of al-Malik al-Salih 'Ali, the presence of Italian merchants in Alexandria and the other Delta ports was regarded with great suspicion. In the Ayyubid period Italian merchants had been allowed to travel freely throughout Egypt; in the early Bahri period the European merchants were confined to the Delta ports. It is likely that in the years immediately following Louis IX's Crusade against Egypt the Italian merchants were expelled from their trading colonies in Alexandria. It seems that the Venetians re-established their colony in Alexandria and received various concessions relating to customs dues and the import of bullion by a treaty which they concluded with Sultan al-Mu'izz Aybak in 1254. The Genoese, however, had been more closely involved in the funding of Louis's Crusade and it seems probable that they did not re-establish themselves in Egypt until 1263 when they sent an embassy to Baybars (another embassy followed in 1275), but the details of those negotiations are not known. Venice subsequently negotiated a treaty in 1288 to secure the position of its merchants travelling in the Muslim hinterland of Syria. The presence of Italian commercial colonies in Egypt, although potentially a security risk, was nevertheless welcome to the sultan not only for commercial reasons but because those colonies were hostages for the good behaviour of the Italian trading republics. If Genoese or Venetian citizens involved themselves in Crusading expeditions or acts of piracy, then the persons and goods of their compatriots in Alexandria could be seized by the sultan.

Though there are indications that Egypt did possess a merchant marine it was certinly very small. Essentially, the Mamluk sultans were dependent on Genoa for the import of Kipchak and Circassian slaves. They were dependent also on both Genoa and Venice to purchase the spices which came to Egypt from India, China and the East Indies via the Red Sea. Venetian, Genoese and, to a lesser extent, French and Spanish merchants distributed the spices to European markets. The duties they paid not only on the spices they exported but also on the textiles, bullion and other commodities they imported provided the sultan with an important part of his income.[32]

Though much less is known about it, there is no reason to think that the other side of this commercial equation — that is, the trade with India, China and the Indies — was any the less profitable for the sultan. Not only were tolls levied on goods as they entered the Red Sea ports controlled by the sultan, but, unlike trade in the Mediterranean, a great deal of the Indies carrying trade was handled by Muslim subjects of the sultan. The wealthy merchants specialising in the spice trade with the East formed a loose corporation and were known as the Karimi merchants. The fortunes of these merchants were vulnerable to the sultan. In cases of need the sultan could and did levy forced loans on them. The interest Qalawun's administration had in fostering trade with the East is shown by the commercial treaty concluded with Ceylon in 1285. While Egypt received spices from the East and sold most of what it received to the West, it also imported copper from Europe and re-exported it to India.[33]

As we shall see, Qalawun's relations with Genoa were complicated by the political ambitions of Genoese adventurers in the Eastern Mediterranean and in particular in the Crusader county of Tripoli. Bohemond VII, Count of Tripoli from 1275 until 1287, was also Prince of what remained of the principality of Antioch to the north. Margat and Maraclea in the principality of Antioch were to be the victims of Qalawun's first major offensive against the Franks. As has been noted already, a Mamluk army had been humiliatingly defeated by the Hospitallers of Margat earlier in Qalawun's reign. Additionally, Bartholomew of Maraclea had long been a determined enemy of the Muslims and for a while, during the latter part of Baybars's reign, had been a refugee at the Mongol court in Tabriz. However, the impending sieges of Margat and Maraclea furnished Qalawun with a pretext for bringing a large army into North-West Syria with which to threaten Sunqur al-Ashqar's semi-independent principality. Since Sunqur's return to his base at Sahyun in 1281, his position had actually been strengthened by the flight to him of many of the Salihis and Zahiris who had been implicated in Kunduk's plot.

In the spring of 1285 Qalawun invested the fortress of Margat and, after an arduous siege, the Hospitallers surrendered. Qalawun lacked the fleet with which to establish an effective blockade of Maraclea, so he threatened the Count of Tripoli, who in turn bribed Bartholomew of Maraclea to surrender his castle. That summer Qalawun also negotiated truces with Beirut and Tyre. The following year an earthquake also rendered the port of Lattakia open to Mamluk occupation. In 1287 Sunqur al-Ashqar surrendered himself and his castle to Husam al-Din Turuntay al-Mansuri.

The city of Tripoli could no longer now expect any assistance from strongholds in the north. In 1283, moreover, the Christian Maronite communities in the highlands to the south of Tripoli had been ravaged by a Mamluk army. Qalawun's decision to move against Tripoli in the year 1288, however, may not have been a product of a long-term strategy for the reduction of Crusader principality but rather a campaign that was forced on him to pre-empt a Genoese attempt to take over the city and the danger of Tripoli becoming part of a Genoese empire in the Levant. In 1287 the effective government of Tripoli was taken over by a Crusader lord of Genoese descent, Bartholomew of Embriaco, acting in concert with a Genoese merchant prince, Benito Zaccaria. In 1288 the Egyptian army was mobilised outside Cairo ready to march against Tripoli, but the expedition was called off because of the sudden sickness and death of Qalawun's son, al-Salih 'Ali. The following year Qalawun did lead an army against Tripoli and in April 1289 the city fell to his army.[34] The booty was immense and the corresponding enthusiasm of his army for the enterprise may have encouraged Qalawun to set about immediately preparing for a siege of Acre — commissioning the construction of siege engines and sending *shadd*s (military inspectors) to inspect the supplies stored in his Syrian fortresses. The pretext for the breaking of the ten-year truce with Acre, a massacre of Muslim merchants, only came to hand in the following year.

In the meantime, Benito Zaccaria, who had made his escape from Tripoli before it fell, began a campaign of piracy against Alexandria's shipping. Qalawun took retaliatory measures against the Genoese community in Alexandria and thereby was successful in bringing pressure to bear on the Genoese republic which in turn succeeded in forcing Zaccaria to abandon his piratical activities. A new treaty with Genoa, which seems actually to have extended their privileges and allowed them freedom of movement in Egypt, was concluded in May 1290.[35] Qalawun was preoccupied throughout most of the year with the elaborate preparations necessary for the siege of Acre; he died, aged about 70, in November 1290 before the expedition could set out.

Throughout most of Qalawun's reign al-Salih 'Ali had been recognised as co-ruler and it had been taken for granted that he would succeed Qalawun. However, Al-Malik al-Salih 'Ali had died first — in 1288 — and, though Qalawun seems to have been reluctant to make formal acknowledgement of it, al-Salih 'Ali's younger and less popular brother, Khalil, then became the heir apparent. Those who had worked closely with al-Salih 'Ali and had attached themselves to his fortunes — among them the *na'ib al-saltana,* Husam al-Din Turuntay al-Mansuri — faced imminent ruin (so of course did the mamluks assigned to al-Salih 'Ali's household, such as Sayf al-Din Salar whom we shall hear more of shortly). It was too late for Turuntay to change course and he spent the last year of Qalawun's reign feuding with Khalil. In particular, he was instrumental in getting the supervisor of the prince's household finances, Shams al-Din ibn Sal'us, flogged and exiled.

Nevertheless, though Khalil had powerful enemies even before he came to the throne, his accession in September 1290 was unopposed.[36] Khalil, who was 27 at the time of his accession, took the regnal title al-Ashraf. Although there are certain superficial similarities between the brief reign of Qalawun's son and that of Baybars's son, Khalil was in fact a very different character from Berke. Berke had been indolent, fond of drink and of having a good time with the young men of the *Khassakiyya.* Al-Ashraf Khalil, on the other hand, proved to be a vigorous ruler accustomed to lead his armies in person. Khalil was particularly respected for his *furusiyya* — that is, his skill in horsemanship, archery and the related military arts. Unlike his father, he spoke Arabic and had a good script. Rather than relying on inexperienced personal mamluks, Khalil in the early part of his reign depended on the cultured and wealthy Emir Baydara al-Mansuri. Baydara had been one of Qalawun's most respected emirs. He had held the offices of *amir majlis* and vizier and possessed enormous estates (and influence) in Upper Egypt. He now became al-Ashraf Khalil's *na'ib al-saltana.* Similarly when later in 1291 the sultan was in a strong enough position to depose Husam al-Din Lajin al-Mansuri from the governorship of Damascus, it was the experienced, pious, cultured (and greedy) Alam al-Din Sanjar al-Shuja'i who became the new *na'ib*.

With the support of these emirs al-Ashraf Khalil was able to arrest Turuntay, who was occupying the post of *na'ib al-saltana* at the time of Qalawun's death. Turuntay's estate was confiscated and Turuntay himself tortured in prison to reveal the whereabouts of other assets. These proceedings raised 1,400,000 dinars for the new sultan and he distributed most of this among emirs and mamluks to buy further political support. Turuntay died a few days after being released from prison, in November 1290. Ibn Sal'us, Turuntay's old arch enemy, was summoned back from exile in the Hejaz and appointed vizier. Ibn Sal'us was a Palestinian Arab from a merchant family. Before becoming head of the financial administration of Khalil's household towards the end of Qalawun's reign, he had combined a career in the Syrian administration with a profitable trade in silks and fabrics. Now Ibn Sal'us seems to have become the most influential figure at the new sultan's court and with the sultan's confidence came greatly expanded opportunities to increase his fortune.[37]

It may be a reflection of Ibn Sal'us's influence that throughout his brief reign al-Ashraf Khalil was to be mainly preoccupied with the consolidation of Mamluk rule in Syria and with dreams of extending that rule to Iraq. The first major campaign of al-Ashraf Khalil's reign had been determined for him in advance. As has been noted above, Qalawun had begun serious planning for the siege of Acre in the previous year. During the winter of 1290–1 siege engines, presumably constructed from Lebanese cedar wood, had been transported from Ba'labakk to Damascus from where they would be taken to Palestine. The size of the engines and heavy snowfalls made this a difficult operation and a number of lives were lost. The siege of Acre began in March 1291. Acre was the Franks' main port on the coast, it was heavily garrisoned and its fall was by no means a foregone conclusion. For a long time the Franks kept the gates of the city open and fought outside its walls. On the Muslim side the army was weakened by intense mistrust between al-Ashraf Khalil and Husam al-Din Lajin al-Mansuri, na'ib of Damascus. Lajin, who was married to a daughter of Qalawun and who had governed most of Syria for some eleven years, was an obvious threat to the sultan; Lajin attempted to flee the siege of Acre and was arrested and briefly imprisoned. Had Acre not fallen, al-Ashraf Khalil could have been in considerable danger from allies of Lajin and of Turuntay, the former *na'ib*, among the emirs and would almost certainly have paid for his failure with his life. After a hard-fought siege of 80 days, however, Acre did fall on 18 May. Antioch and Tripoli had yielded a great deal of booty to the Mamluk conquerors, but the citizens of Acre had had ample warning of the coming onslaught and there are no such reports of plunder in 1291. In the weeks that followed, the remaining towns and strongholds still in Frankish possession — Tyre, Beirut, Athlith, Tortosa and Jebail — were demoralised, and easily occupied by a section of the Mamluk army under Shuja'i.[38] After the successful completion of this operation, Shuja'i became na'ib of Damascus, replacing Lajin.

When, more than a century earlier, Saladin had taken Jerusalem and Acre, their capture had provoked the preaching of the Third Crusade and those Crusaders, having landed at Tyre, had gone on to retake Acre. Al-Ashraf Khalil, fearing a similar resurgence of crusading enthusiasm in the West, ordered the preventative destruction of the Frankish towns and fortresses on the coast.

With the final removal of the Crusader presence from Mamluk Syria, one might have expected a slackening in propaganda for the *jihad*. In fact the reverse happened. On Khalil's return to Cairo early in 1292, Caliph al-Hakim was brought out from the house arrest he had effectively been under since the early years of Baybars's reign. The caliph publicly gave the *khutba* for al-Ashraf — that is, he pronounced the name of the sultan during the invocation of the Friday prayer. The main purpose of the public exhibition of the caliph seems to have been to use him as a mouthpiece for the preaching of the *jihad*. The declared victims of the *jihad* that was then proclaimed were to be the Mongols; al-Ashraf Khalil was also talking about retaking Baghdad for the caliph. However, the actual victims of Mamluk offensives were first the Christian kingdom of Cilician Armenia and, second, Muslim schismatics dwelling in the Lebanese highlands.

In the spring of 1292 Khalil led an army against Qal'at al-Rum (Hromgla), an Armenian fortress on the Euphrates to the north of Bira. As at Acre, the Mamluks made much use of mangonels and after intensive bombardment Qal'at al-Rum was taken by assault in May.[39] A Mongol force sent to assist the Armenians arrived too late and withdrew. The Ilkhanate at this time was in fact in some disarray. Arghun had died in March 1291 and the new Ilkhan Geikhatu was not securely established on his throne. It may have been news of Mongol dissensions that led al-Ashraf Khalil to entertain serious hopes of retaking Baghdad for Islam.

During the summer, while al-Ashraf Khalil rested in Damascus, the *na'ib al-saltana,* Baydara, led an expedition against the Mamluks' second target, the hillsmen of Kasrawan. Kasrawan was an extensive highland area to the north-east of Beirut. The hillsmen (*jabaliyyun*) of the area seem to have been mostly Nusayris, though they may also have been assisted by the Druze and Maronite Christians and others in resisting the Mamluks. The Nusayris, who believed in the divine status of the Prophet's nephew 'Ali, were not regarded as true Muslims by the citizens of Cairo and Damascus. Most of the tribal chiefs in the Lebanese highlands had never accepted Mamluk suzerainty and some groups of hillsmen had fought for the Franks in previous years. Baydara's expedition against Kasrawan was a disaster. His army was ambushed and harassed and in the end he was obliged to negotiate its withdrawal from Kasrawan. The failure of this expedition caused consternation in Damascus and some emirs spread rumours that Baydara had been bribed by the people of Kasrawan not to prosecute the campaign energetically. Baydara excused himself to the sultan, claiming that he had been and was still ill.[40] Al-Ashraf Khalil accepted his excuses and did not remove him from his high office. However, it is possible that from this disaster can be dated the beginnings of the estrangement between the sultan and his deputy.

Al-Ashraf Khalil had a band of *Khassakiyya* on whom he relied for protection and company. The *Khassakiyya* may have influenced royal policy — for example, they successfully urged the sultan to protect the Copts from Muslim agitation against them.[41] But on the whole, the sultan did not advance them to replace his father's emirs. With the exception of Ibn Sal'us, the vizier, the ruling elite consisted of Mansuri emirs. What they all had in common — Ibn Sal'us and the favoured emirs such as Baydara, Sanjar al-Shuja'i and Sunqur al-A'sar — was that they had all been involved in some capacity or another in the financial administration of Egypt or Syria and they had all become very wealthy men.

Khalil's reign, like those of his predecessors, was punctuated by the deposition of emirs and administrators from office, their arrest, the sequestration of their goods, their eventual release or occasional execution (though Khalil's reign was not excessively bloody). It is difficult to determine what lay behind the risings and fallings of the great. The sources are reticent about the political motives — if any

— behind them and the aims of their factions — if any. In part the reticence of the sources reflects the fact that they were written by outsiders, civilians in Damascus or relatively junior military men. In part the caution of the chroniclers must be ascribed to the fact that most of the sources for Khalil's reign were written during the three reigns of Khalil's brother and successor, al-Nasir Muhammad, at a time when it would not have been politic either to disparage the sultan's brother or to laud him excessively, since al-Nasir Muhammad first came to the throne by virtue of Khalil's murder. One other factor must be borne in mind — and this applies to the whole Mamluk period — and that is that contemporary chroniclers and biographers were on the whole reluctant to discuss the role of women and family bonds in the affairs of state. This lay outside the conventions of Arabic history writing. However, despite the meagre amount of evidence available, it is clear that marriage alliances counted for something in the politics of this period. When, for instance, Sunqur al-A'sar, who had occupied the post of *shadd al-dawawin* (financial supervisor) in Damascus from 1283–4 onwards, was deposed in 1290, he was able to save his career and regain his post by agreeing to marry the daughter of Ibn Sal'us. On the other hand, when in 1292 Rukn al-Din Tuqsu was arrested and condemned for treason, Husam al-Din Lajin fell under suspicion and was arrested once more, because he was the former's son-in-law. The mamluk officers and viziers Sanjar al Shuja'i and Baydara al-Mansuri were linked by marriage, for according to Ibn al-Suqa'i, al-Shuja'i had married Baydara's mother — an odd piece of information in that the mamluks were, like Peter Pan's lost boys, not supposed to have mothers.[42]

Disgraced emirs and officials were commonly accused of treason or maladministration. Often, however, one has the impression that it was Khalil's and Ibn Sal'us's need for money that led them to proceed against the individuals concerned. As we have seen, the confiscation of the Na'ib Turuntay's estate at the beginning of the reign had proved very profitable. After Sunqur al-A'sar's deposition in 1290 his reinstatement and marriage to Ibn Sal'us's daughter involved him in agreeing to pay 1,500 dinars as the 'nuptial gift'. Balaban al-Tabakhi secured the deposition of Qarasunqur al-Mansuri from the governorship of Aleppo and his own appointment to it by promising Ibn Sal'us ten million dirhams.[43] Aybak al-Afram, the venerable Salihi emir in charge of fortification and engineering works, had been involved in policy clashes with Khalil, most notably over al-Afram's reluctance to obey the sultan's orders to demolish the fortress of Shawbak in the Transjordan. However, the prospect of sequestrating Aybak's vast estates in Upper Egypt and elsewhere must have provided the sultan with a powerful incentive for arresting Aybak in 1292.[44]

In the light of the above, it is natural that from the summer of 1292 onwards Baydara, the *na'ib al-saltana*, should have begun to feel increasingly insecure. When in 1292 the sultan visited Upper Egypt, he complained that Baydara's granaries were better stocked than the royal ones. Subsequently, the two men became involved in a row about their respective shares of the customs revenue of Alexandria.[45] Baydara began to cast about for potential supporters against the sultan. This was not difficult. In the space of only a few years a number of prominent men had been arrested and some had died while under arrest. Survivors and retainers of the deceased bore grudges against the sultan and still more against the vizier, Ibn Sal'us. In December 1292 six emirs were brought before al-Ashraf Khalil to be strangled in his presence. Three of them — Badr al-Din Baktut, Rukn al-Din Tuqsu and Sunqur al-Ashqar (the former semi-independent ruler of Northern Syria) — had been with Baydara on the disastrous expedition against Kasrawan earlier that year. One of the six, Husam al-Din Lajin the former Na'ib of Damascus, was saved from the bowstring by the intercession of Baydara. The sultan surrendered Lajin to Baydara, stipulating that the disgraced emir should from henceforth serve Baydara as his mamluk — a fatal mistake, as it turned out. The following year Husam al-Din Muhanna ibn 'Isa was treacherously arrested and deposed from his position as leader of the Fadl clan and paramount emir of the Syrian bedouin. Even more indignation was caused by the arrest of the widely respected Emir Aybak al-Afram that same year.

It is possible also that the aggressively ambitious nature of the sultan's schemes gave rise to misgivings in some circles. In the spring of 1293 Khalil had planned a second expedition against Cilician Armenia, an attack which was called off when the Armenian king surrendered three frontier fortresses to the Mamluks. Khalil continued to talk of an offensive against Mongol-held Iraq. He threatened Ilkhan Geikhatu that he would make Baghdad his capital. Having had a fleet constructed to defend the coast of Syria from Frankish piracy, he began to talk of invading Cyprus. He was said to be planning a *rawk* (that is, a survey and redistribution of agricultural lands and the revenues that they yielded), a scheme in which the redistribution of *iqta*'s would presumably have been to his benefit and to the detriment of his rivals among the powerful emirs. In Damascus many houses in the vicinity of the citadel had been demolished to make way for a *maydan* and for Ashrafi foundations, buildings which as it turned out were not to be constructed.

Had Khalil been a less energetic man and a more decadent ruler he might have lived longer. In December 1293 the sultan left Cairo to go hunting. A few days earlier he and Baydara had clashed over the division of revenues in Alexandria. Ibn Sal'us, who was investigating affairs in Alexandria, urged Baydara's deposition. Baydara struck first. On 14 December when Khalil went out hunting without a proper escort he was ambushed by Baydara, Lajin and a small band of Baydara's supporters. Lajin struck the fatal blow, shouting: 'Let he who would rule Egypt and Syria strike a blow like this!'

Notes

1. On Berke Sa'id's mother and her Khwarazmian clan, see A. 'Abd al-Raziq, *La Femme au temps des Mamelouks en Égypte* (Cairo, 1973), p.288; D. Ayalon, 'The Great Yasa of Chingiz Khan: A Re-examination' (Part C1), *SI*, vol.36 (1972), p.144; D. Ayalon, 'The Wafidiyya in the Mamluk Kingdom', *Islamic Culture*, vol.25 (1951), pp.94–7.

2. Ibn 'Abd al-Zahir, *al-Rawd al-Zahir*, A. Khowaiter (ed.) (Riyad, 1976), pp.203–9, 214.

3. Ibn 'Abd al-Zahir, *Rawd*, p.338; Maqrizi, *Kitab al-Suluk*, vol.1, pt.2 (Cairo, 1936), p.573.

4. 'Abd al-Raziq, *La Femme*, p.284 and the references cited there.

5. For a convenient, though late summary and assessment of the reign of Sultan al-Sa'id Berke Khan, see Ibn Taghribirdi, *al-Nujum al-Zahira*, vol.7 (Cairo, 1938), pp.259–74.

6. Ibn al-Suqa'i, *Tali Kitab Wafayat al-A'yan*, J. Sublet (ed.) (Damascus, 1974), pp.67–8.

7. On the *Khassakiyya*, see D. Ayalon, 'Studies on the Structure of the Mamluk Army', BSOAS, vol.15 (1953), pp.213–16.

8. On the reign of Qalawun, see Ibn 'Abd al-Zahir, *Tashrif al-Ayyam wa al-'usur fi sirat al-Malik al-Mansur*, M. Kamil (ed.) (Cairo, 1961); Shafi' ibn 'Ali, 'al-Fadl al-Ma'thur min sirat al-Sultan al-Malik al-Mansur', Oxford, Bodleian Library MS Marsh 424; Ibn al-Suqa'i, *Tali*; Yunini, *Dhayl Mir'at al-Zaman*, vol.4 (Hyderabad, 1961); Baybars al-Mansuri, 'Zubdat al-fikra', London, British Library MS or, Add, 23325; Abu al-Fida, *al-Mukhtasar fi akhbar al-bashar*, vol.4 (Istanbul, 1869–70); Ibn al-Dawadari, *Kanz al-Durar*, U. Haarmann (ed.) (Cairo, 1971); Ibn al-Furat, *Tarikh al Duwal wa al-Muluk*, vols 7–8, Q. Zurayq and N. 'Izz al-Din (eds) (Beirut, 1939–42); Ibn Taghribirdi, *Nujum*, vol.7; 'Kalawun' in *EI(2)*.

9. On *mukus*, see R. Levy, *The Social Structure of Islam* (Cambridge, 1969), p.322.

10. On *khushdashiyya*, see D. Ayalon, *L'Esclavage du Mamlouk* (Jerusalem, 1951), pp.29–31.

11. P. Balog, 'Un Fals d'al-Kamil Shams al-Din Sunqor, Sultan Mamelouk rebelle de Damas', *Revue Numismatique* (6th series) vol.11 (1969), pp.296–9.

12. Bar Hebraeus, *The Chronography of Gregory Abu'l-Faraj*, E. A. Wallis Budge (ed.) (London, 1932), vol.1, pp.458–9.

13. Mufaddal ibn Abi al-Fada'il, *Kitab al-Nahj al-Sadid*, E. Blochet (ed. and trans.) in *Patrologia Orientalis*, vol.14 (1920), p.488.

14. On the tribe of Banu Fadl, see A. S. Tritton, 'Tribes of Syria in the Fourteenth and Fifteenth Centuries', *BSOAS*, vol.12 (1948), pp. 567–74; "Isa B. Muhanna' in *EI(2)*.

15. Maqrizi, *Suluk*, vol.1, pt. 3, pp.687–8.

16. Ibn al-Furat, *Duwal*, vol.7, pp.204–6; Maqrizi, *Suluk*, vol.1, pt.3, p.685.

17. On the Mongol invasions of Syria in 1280 and 1282, see J. A. Boyle, 'Dynastic and Political History of the Ilkhans' in J. A. Boyle (ed.), *The Cambridge History of Iran*, vol.5 (Cambridge, 1968), p.363; J. J. Saunders, *The History of the Mongol Conquests* (London, 1971), p.131; 'Hims' in *EI(2)*.

18. Ibn 'Abd al-Zahir, *Tashrif*, pp.4–17, 43, 48–50; Ibn al-Fuwati, *Al-Hawadith al-Jami'a wa al-Tajarib*, M. Jawwad and M. R. Shabili (eds) (Baghdad, 1934), pp.424–5; Boyle, 'History of the Ilkhans', p.365.

19. Maqrizi, *Suluk*, vol.1, pt.3, p.684.

20. Ibn al-Furat, *Duwal*, vol.7, pp.212, 225–6; Maqrizi, *Suluk*, vol.1, pt.3, pp.689-90, 699; E. Ashtor, *A Social and Economic History of the Near East in the Middle Ages* (London, 1976), p.287.

21. On Qalawun's dealings with the Crusader principalities, generally, see S. Runciman, *A History of the Crusades*, vol.3 (Cambridge, 1955), pp.387–412.

22. Ibn 'Abd al-Zahir, *Tashrif*, pp.20–2, 34–43; Ibn al-Furat, *Duwal*, vol.7, pp.252, 262–70; Al-Qalqashandi, *Subh al-A'sha*, vol.14 (Cairo, 1922), pp.51–63; P. M. Holt, 'Qalawun's Treaty with Acre in 1283', *English Historical Review*, vol.91 (1976), pp.802–12.

23. On Qalawun's dealings with Cilician Armenia, see Ibn 'Abd al-Zahir, *Tashrif*, pp.30–2, 92–103; P. Z. Bedoukian, *Coinage of Cilician Armenia* (New York, 1962), pp.12–13; M. Canard, 'Le Royaume d'Armenie — Cilicie et les Mamelouks jusqu'au traité de 1285', *Revue des Études Armeniennes*, vol.4 (1967), pp.244–59.

24. C. Desimoni, 'Actes passés en 1271, 1274 et 1279 à l'Aias (Petit Armenie) et à Beyrouth par devant des notaires genois', *Archives de l'Orient Latin*, vol.1 (1881), pp.434–534.

25. Qalqashandi, *Subh al-A'sha*, vol.14, pp.72–8; M. Canard, 'Le Traité de 1281 entre Michel Paleologue et le Sultan Qala'un', *Byzantion*, vol.10 (1935), pp.669–80.

26. D. Ayalon, 'Studies on the Structure of the Mamluk Army' (part 1), *BSOAS*, vol.15 (1953), p.223; 'Burdjiyya' in *EI(2)*.

27. On the literary culture of Mamluk emirs in this period, see for instance, Ibn al-Suqa'i, *Tali*, pp.75–6, 114–5; J. -C. Garcin, 'Le Caire et la province', *Annales Islamologiques*, vol.8 (1969), p.51; U. Haarmann, 'Aitun Han und Cingiz Han bei den ägyptischen Mamluken', *Der Islam*, vol.51 (1974), pp.5–6.

28. Ibn al-Dawadari, *Kanz*, vol.8, p.303.

29. Ibn al-Furat, *Duwal*, vol.7, pp.206–8; Maqrizi, *Suluk*, vol.1, pt.3, p.685.

30. A. Moberg, 'Regierungspromemoria eines egyptischens Sultans', G. Weil (ed.), *Festscrift Sachau* (Berlin, 1915), pp.406–21.

31. Ibn al-Furat, *Duwal*, vol.8, pp.65–7; Qalqashandi, *Subh al-A'sha*, vol.13, pp.340–1; S. Y. Labib, *Handelsgeschichte Ägyptens im Spätmittelalter*, (Wiesbaden, 1964), pp.85–6.

32. On Egyptian trade with Europe in the late thirteenth century, see W. Heyd, *Histoire du commerce du Levant au moyen age*, vol.1 (Leipzig, 1923), pp.410, 425;

Labib, *Handelsgeschichte,* pp.32–4; E. Ashtor, *Levant Trade in the Later Middle Ages* (Princeton, 1983), pp.3–44.

33. On trade with the Indies, see S. Digby, 'The Broach Coin — Hoard as Evidence of the Import of Valuta across the Arabian Sea during the 13th and 14th Centuries', *JRAS* (1980), pp.129–38; Labib, *Handelsgeschichte,* pp. 82–4, 90–4.

34. On the background to the conquest of Maraclea and Tripoli, see R. Irwin, 'The Mamluk Conquest of the County of Tripoli' in P. W. Edbury (ed.), *Crusade and Settlement* (Cardiff, forthcoming).

35. Ibn 'Abd al-Zahir, *Tashrif,* pp.165–9; P. M. Holt, 'Qalawun's Treaty with Genoa in 1290', *Der Islam,* vol.57 (1980), pp.101–8.

36. For the reign of al-Ashraf Khalil, see in particular the fragmentary chronicle by Ibn 'Abd al-Zahir, *al-Altaf al-Khafiyya,* A. Moberg (ed.) (Lund, 1902); also the sources listed in the excellent summary of his reign by U. Haarmann in *EI(2) sv* 'Khalil'.

37. On Ibn Sal'us, see in particular Ibn al-Suqa'i, *Tali,* pp.179–82; Ibn Taghribirdi, *Nujum,* vol.8, pp.53–4.

38. On al-Ashraf's campaign against the remnant of the Crusader states, see Runciman, *History of the Crusades,* vol.3, pp.412–22.

39. S. Der Nersessian, 'The Kingdom of Cilician Armenia' in R. L. Wolff and J. W. Hazard (eds), *A History of the Crusades,* vol.2 (Madison, 1969), p.656.

40. H. Laoust, 'Remarques sur les expeditions de Kasrawan sous les premiers Mamluks', *Bulletin du Musée de Beyrouth,* vol.4 (1940), pp.99–101; K. S. Salibi, *Maronite Historians of Mediaeval Lebanon* (Beirut, 1959), pp.115–16.

41. D. P. Little, 'Coptic Conversion to Islam under the Bahri Mamluks, 692–755/1293–1354', *BSOAS,* vol.39 (1976), p.553.

42. Ibn al-Suqa'i, *Tali,* pp.75, 111–12; Maqrizi, *Suluk,* vol.1, pt.3, pp.692, 777.

43. Ibn al-Suqa'i, *Tali,* pp. 72–3.

44. Ibn al-Furat, *Duwal,* vol.8. pp.156, 157. On Aybak's wealth, see J.-C. Garcin, 'Le Caire et la province', pp.47–51.

45. Maqrizi, *Suluk,* vol.1, pt.3, pp.782–3; 'Khalil' in *EI(2).*

5   THE OPERATION OF FACTION, 1293–1310

The fortunes of the ruling elite in the 17 turbulent years that followed the murder of al-Ashraf Khalil may swiftly be summarised as follows.[1] Despite Lajin's boast, it was Baydara who took the royal title al-Malik al-Qahir. His 'reign' lasted a couple of days, before Zayn al-Din Kitbugha al-Mansuri (a favourite emir of Qalawun and then of Khalil), leading a band of Ashrafi loyalists, caught up with Baydara and killed him. Emir Baktimur al-Silahdar cut Baydara's liver out and ate it raw. Baydara's supporters had their hands cut off and were paraded, crucified, on the backs of camels. Lajin, however, escaped. Khalil's eight-year-old brother Muhammad was raised to the Sultanate, taking the regnal name al-Nasir in December 1293. Once again the convention of rule by a child sultan was employed to mask the manoevrings of a father's emirs to seize real power.

The unpopular vizier, Ibn Sal'us, was arrested in Alexandria and died under torture designed to extract from him the whereabouts of the hidden parts of his fortune. He was replaced as vizier by his rival, the former *ustadar* 'Alam al-Din Sanjar al-Shuja'i. Kitbugha, who had not held office under al-Ashraf Khalil, now became *na'ib al-saltana* and Shuja'i's opponent in the struggle for the Sultanate. In 1294, after an abortive attempt by Shuja'i on Kitbugha's life, there was fighting in Cairo which ended with Shuja'i's death. At the end of the year, after a purge of Ashrafi mamluks, Kitbugha deposed al-Nasir Muhammad and declared himself al-Malik al-'Adil. Lajin had emerged from hiding after the death of Shuja'i, and Kitbugha, in order to broaden the basis of support for his Sultanate, made Lajin his *na'ib al-saltana*. In 1296, after Lajin had made an attempt on his life, Kitbugha was persuaded to go into distinguished retirement in Syria. Lajin now became sultan, taking the regnal name al-Malik al-Mansur. In 1298 al-Mansur Lajin was murdered, while at prayer in the citadel. The assassins, relatively junior emirs, were executed soon afterwards. The young prince al-Nasir Muhammad was recalled from his exile at Kerak to front rivalry between two new contenders for the Sultanate, Rukn al-Din Baybars al-Jashnakir and Sayf al-Din Salar. In 1308 al-Nasir Muhammad, finding his position untenable fled back to Kerak. Baybars eventually got the upper hand over Salar in 1309 and was declared sultan. However, al-Nasir Muhammad emerged from Kerak in 1310 and, with the support of some loyalist Mansuri emirs and Syrian bedouin, he was successful in occupying Cairo. For the third time he assumed the throne. Baybars II was strangled and Salar was starved to death, ending up allegedly eating his own excrement.

The third reign of al-Nasir was to usher in a period of relative stability, but after his death in 1340, there were to be many similar periods of prolonged disruption during which street-fighting and assassination determined the distribution of political power. What will make sense of this endless sequence of decapitated viceroys and strangled viziers? This will be discussed in more depth in the concluding chapter, but some tentative early remarks are offered here.

First, the penalties for failure could indeed be strikingly vicious. When publicly enforced, such spectacular punishments as crucifixion and bisection lengthways or sideways gave Cairo and Damascus their street theatres of cruelty. Crucifixion and the cutting off of limbs were familiar retribution in the Arab Islamic world. Some of the forms of execution, however, seem to derive from Turco-Mongol practice and may have been introduced by the Mamluks. Bisection was practised by the Ghuzz Turks of the Volga region in the early tenth century. It was also used later by the Mongol Ilkhans of Iran. For instance, Abu Said had his minister Rashid al-Din executed in this fashion, and later Ghazan dealt similarly with his minister Nauruz. Death by strangulation or hanging was considered an honourable form of execution among the Mongols, more honourable than beheading (where the victim suffered the disgrace of having his blood shed). Later the Ottomans, too, had distinguished opponents disposed of by strangulation with the bow string.[2]

Trials of deposed sultans or defeated emirs before execution were the exception rather than the rule. Yet if any of the *qadi*s or others among the *'ulama'* thought that political murder was not in accordance with the law of Islam they kept quiet about it. Equally striking is the feebleness of the oath bond in Mamluk society. It was normal practice for sultans assuming the throne to take a *bay'a* (oath of allegiance) from emirs and the army. Often, too, we read of beleaguered rebel emirs surrendering to *aman* (an oath of safe conduct), but sultans and emirs were frequently disappointed in the sworn assurances that they had received. More generally, considerations of honour played little part in the ordering of Mamluk feuds. The thing was to catch one's opponent off his guard, while hunting or at prayer or as a guest at one's dinner table. Moreover, Mamluk feuds were rarely about anything other than the acquisition and the distribution of political power. Among the bedouin tribes or again among the households of the *beys* in Ottoman Egypt, the desire to avenge an injury to the household could result in a vendetta lasting many generations and ultimate success might be celebrated in a poem or panegyric chronicle. The non-hereditary nature of the Mamluk elite did not allow this to happen. The mamluks of a deceased *ustadh* quietly transferred their support elsewhere, and they looked for a new coalition to advance their interests. The spectacular nature of some of the executions does not seem to have had a deterrent effect (for there was never a lack of contenders for supreme power). Therefore such demonstrations seem to have been simply celebrations of political triumph. Of course cruelty could have a function at other times. It was not uncommon for viziers and others suspected of being wealthy to die under torture designed to extract the whereabouts of the concealed parts of that wealth.

However, while it may appear excessive by comparison with, for example, the Ayyubid regime which preceded it, Mamluk violence was not without parallels elsewhere in the medieval world. Fifteenth-century England, for instance, was as turbulent as Mamluk Egypt in any century, its casualties from civil strife probably higher and John Tiptoft as cruel an executioner as Emir Sarghitmish. Moreover, in the Mamluk lands imprisonment or the enforced temporary retirement of emirs was more common than their execution. Biographical dictionaries of the period furnish plenty of examples of emirs who were both politically active and long lived. For example, Sanjar al-Halabi was arrested by Qutuz during the reign of al-Mansur Ali in 1257. Subsequently released, he led the Damascan revolt against Baybars, but after his defeat was honourably received in Egypt. Later, in 1271, he was arrested by Baybars for conspiracy. Released for a second time, he was again arrested by Qalawun who was alarmed by signs of a revival of Sanjar's popularity in Damascus. On gaining freedom, probably in the reign of al-Ashraf Khalil, he had his *iqta*'s restored and died in his bed in 1293.[3] To take two further examples: Baysari al-Shamsi, one of Baybars's closest *khushdash*, was imprisoned by al-Sa'id Berke Kh n, offered the throne after the latter's deposition and, having refused, was later imprisoned by Qalawun, freed by al-Ashraf Khalil, offered the throne again after the latter's murder, rearrested in al-Mansur Lajin's reign and died in prison in 1298 during the second reign of al-Nasir Muhammad.[4] The last surviving Salihi emir of the first rank, Baktash al-Fakhri, died in his bed in 1306 during the third reign of al-Nasir Muhammad. He had lived a free man ever since 1259, when al-Mughith had handed him over in chains to the Ayyubid prince al-Nasir Yusuf![5]

One contributory factor to the turbulence of the years 1293–1310 was the size of emirs' retinues. In this period, Qarasunqur al-Mansuri, Na'ib of Aleppo, was reckoned to have 600 mamluks; Asandamur, Na'ib of Tripoli, possessed 500.[6] In part the size of the retinues of mamluk emirs may have been a product of what was happening in the steppe lands of the Golden Horde at this time. In the 1290s civil war had broken out between Khan Toqtu and his general, Nogay — something which the Genoese merchants in the area were able to profit from. When Toqtu finally defeated Nogay's rebels in 1299, according to the soldier and chronicler Baybars al-Mansuri, there was a big influx of slaves on to the market. Therefore, Baybars II, Salar and al-Nasir Muhammad were able to benefit from the cheap availability of slaves. In addition Arabic chroniclers tell us that there was a drought on the steppes in the years 1300–3 accompanied by an epidemic that killed off horses and sheep. As a result the impoverished pastoralists were eager to sell their children to the slave traders.[7]

Although these decades were turbulent and violent at the top, such conflicts scarcely spread more widely. It would be a mistake to envisage the Mamluk lands in this period as being riven by civil war. There were street-fights in Cairo and Damascus occasionally, but usually not even that. Large armies did not face one another in the field, urban fortifications were not destroyed, crops were not ravaged. Egypt's political system was in a sense acutely unstable, but the economic damage stemming from this was negligible.

Khushdashiyya has been seen by some writers as the key to Mamluk politics. It has been seen as the cement that bound mamluk factions together — factions which alternately combined together or fought against one another to promote the interests of their members. A *khushdash* of an emir or a mamluk was one who had been owned by the same *ustadh* (master) as that emir or mamluk. A particularly close bond was supposed to exist between mamluks who had been emancipated by the same *ustadh* at the same time.

Mamluks educated together and inculcated with a common loyalty to the same master were presumed to feel a common bond (*khushdashiyya*) — a bond which was held to survive the emancipation of the mamluks and their subsequent promotion and even the death of their common master. Zahiri should stick with Zahiri, Mansuri with Mansuri, Ashrafi with Ashrafi.[8]

At the end of the fourteenth century the great North African historical thinker, Ibn Khaldun, was to write at length about the phenomenon of *'asabiyya* — that is, the sense of tribal solidarity or clannishness which he believed was particularly strong among nomadic peoples — and to argue that the rise of new dynasties was closely dependent upon the *'asabiyya* of their armies. He went on to propose that the decline of the regimes thus established followed on from the decline of that originally vigorous tribal *'asabiyya*.[9] It is tempting to see *khushdashiyya* as a sort of *'asabiyya*, artificially generated and artificially renewed from generation to generation of masters and mamluks. But the temptation to see *khushdashiyya* as the inevitable expression of a tribalism inherent in Middle Eastern politics must be resisted. *Khushdashiyya* was not an expression of bedouinism nor of Islam thwarted, but of something much more fundamental and widespread in politics.

Close analogies for *khushdashiyya* may be found in Western societies — for instance, in the *amicitia*, which was an important element in the formation of factions in the later Roman republic. Many of Sir Ronald Syme's observations about *amicitia* may be applied without reservation to *khushdashiyya*. For example: 'From ambition or for safety, politicians formed compacts. *Amicitia* was a weapon of politics, not a sentiment based upon congeniality.' Or:

> Roman political factions were welded together, less by unity of principle than by mutual interest and by mutual services (*officia*), either between social equals as an alliance, or from inferior to superior, in a traditional and almost feudal form of clientship: on a favourable estimate the bond was called *amicitia*, otherwise *factio*.[10]

K. B. McFarlane's remarks on political rivalries in the fourteenth and fifteenth centuries are also instructive:

> The 'affinity' had little in common with the modern party; but it did, it seems to me, in many ways resemble the eighteenth

century 'connection' so fully anatomised by Professor Namier.
There was the same element of voluntary interdependence, the
same competition for 'place' and the same absence of any
separate fund of political principle.[11]

Though an awareness of the role of *khushdashiyya* is an aid in
charting political developments in the Mamluk period, it did not
constrain those developments. It was invoked more often in the
breach than the observance. For instance, Sultan al-'Adil Kitbugha
al-Mansuri spent most of his brief reign feuding with his *na'ib*,
Husam al-Din Lajin al-Mansuri. On being driven off the throne by
Lajin's threats in 1297, he is said to have remarked of Lajin that 'he
is my *khushdash*', doubtless seeking with these words faint
reassurance that his life was not in danger.[12] (Subsequently, in 1299,
Husami mamluks took the leading role in the murder of Husam
al-Din Lajin.) We have already seen how, earlier in 1260, Baybars,
a Salihi, combined with Mu'izzi emirs against al-Muzaffar Qutuz, a
Mu'izzi, who was ruling with the assistance of allies among the Salihi
emirs.

Moreover, like so many words in this period, the terms
khushdash and *khushdashiyya* were used somewhat loosely —
sometimes only meaning generation peer. Frequently we shall find
khushdashiyya loyalties being cut and cross-cut by other forms of
loyalty — young, unplaced mamluks against old, rich mamluks;
those garrisoned in Syria against those garrisoned in Egypt, etc. In
any case, an awareness of the role of *khushdashiyya* is of only
limited importance in interpreting the period 1293–1310, since the
overwhelming majority of leading emirs in Cairo and Damascus in
that period were Mansuris.

Since the history of this period must be understood in terms of
struggles for power within the successful Mansuri group, it is
necessary to consider the interest groups and the issues which led to
the formation of factions within the Mansuri elite. In particular, we
must consider the range of support for the various factions. Not only
was *khushdashiyya* not the prime determinant in forming the
mamluk factions, but support for Mamluk factions was not
restricted to mamluks only.

At the end of the thirteenth century a particularly important part
in the struggles for power was played by the non-mamluk sections of
the army — the *Wafidiyya*, the *awlad al-nas* and the *halqa* in
general. Sultan al-'Adil Zayn al-Din Kitbugha (1295–7), in

particular, tried to base his power on groups outside the innermost elite of Mansuri emirs. His rival Husam al-Din Lajin was assured of the suppport of most of the Mansuri-Burji elite. The broader coalition of groups supporting Kitbugha included not only many emirs and mamluks from the declining generation of Zahiris, but also *halqa* troopers, Kurdish auxiliaries and *Wafidiyya*.[13] The *Wafidiyya* were particularly important. Since the early years of Baybars's reign large and small groups of *Wafidiyya* had entered the lands of the Sultanate at irregular intervals and had been granted positions in the army or areas in which to graze their herds. The al-Husayniyya quarter of Cairo, which had expanded considerably since Baybars had founded his mosque there, was particularly an area of settlement for the *Wafidiyya* military and other refugees. A particularly large wave of Mongol *Wafidiyya* entered the Mamluk lands during the reign of Kitbugha in 1296. These were Mongol Oirats who had previously pastured their flocks in Diyarbakr. Presumably they were fleeing the disorders that had overtaken the Ilkhanate since 1295, when Baidu had deposed and murdered Ilkhan Geikhatu, only to be overthrown and killed himself by Ghazan. Ghazan in turn had to put down a revolt by Prince Suge in 1296. The pagan Oirats may also have been fleeing from the effects of Ghazan's declared conversion to Sunni Islam in 1295. This had resulted in the persecution of Christians, Buddhists and others in the Ilkhanate. Sultan Kitbugha was himself a Mongol, and allegedly an Oirat. He was therefore well placed to appeal to the loyalties of this new wave of *Wafidiyya*.[14]

There were other Mongols besides Kitbugha among the Egyptian emirs and mamluks and they too tended to give their loyalty to Kitbugha. For instance, a plot by Sanjar al-Shuja'i against Kitbugha was betrayed to Kitbugha by one of Sanjar's Mongol mamluks, Qunuq al-Tatari.[15] Here racial affinity took precedence over loyalty to the *ustadh*. Again one of the pillars of Kitbugha's government was the Na'ib of Damascus, Sayf al-Din Qibjaq, an emir of Mongol origin (his father had been a *silahdar* of the ilkhans). It was Qibjaq who introduced the Mongol Mamluk Aytamish al-Muhammadi to Kitbugha. Aytamish was a great expert on Mongol history and customs and we shall be hearing more of him. Finally when Kitbugha was overthrown, it was to the court of the Mongol ilkhans that Emir Qibjaq and others of the Mongol mamluks fled.[16]

Yet if Kitbugha had been able to count on the support of the

Mongol mamluks, Lajin's Burji faction included a very strong Circassian element. The struggle between Kitbugha and Lajin was to be echoed later on in the struggle between Salar and Baybars al-Jashnakir. Salar's support was relatively broadly based and included the backing of many of the ageing Salihi and Zahiri emirs, as well as Mongols who favoured Salar because he was a Mongol. Baybars al-Jashnakir, on the other hand, was a Burji emir and a Circassian and it was on Qalawun's former picked elite of Circassian Burjis that he primarily depended for support. So sentiments of racial solidarity were inextricably involved in the struggle for political power between what may be termed the inner and the outer elites of the Mamluk armies.

It is against the background of a struggle between the inner and outer military elites that the Husami *rawk* of 1298 must be understood. This survey of lands and their yields in terms of crops and the ensuing redistrubtion of *iqta*'s took place in Egypt only. The Syrian provinces were excluded. Lajin's main aim in ordering the *rawk* seems to have been to alter the economic basis of politico-military power in his favour. However, we shall consider the subsidiary purposes and incidental changes before coming to the main point of the reform.[17]

First, there was undoubtedly a real need for more accurate information about the relative sizes of royal property (*khass*), emirs' *iqta*'s, *halqa iqta*'s and estates held under other forms of tenure. Officials needed to determine not only the size of the estates, but also the ratio of cultivatable land to waste land within them, the quality of the soil and the tax value of the crops. Slight shifts in the course of the Nile and land improvements — or, alternatively, a local breakdown of the irrigation system — could alter the yield of the land considerably and the last such survey in Egypt had been made under Saladin in 1176.

Second, Lajin wished to put an end to abuses arising from the practice of *himaya*. Although *himaya* is commonly translated as 'protection' and thus for English readers may have overtones of 'protection money', the practice of *himaya* was not intrinsically abusive. What it entailed was the administration of the *iqta*'s of lesser emirs and *halqa* soldiers and the collection of revenues on their behalf by the financial *diwan*s of the greater emirs — or even by the sultan's own officials, in which case overall supervision was in the hands of the *ustadar*. Given that soldiers often had to be absent from their *iqta*'s at the time when their revenue in kind was due to be collected, that their *iqta*'s might be quite widely dispersed, and that the poorer soldiers and emirs could not afford to maintain their own *diwans* of officials competent enough and influential enough to prevent the *muqta*'s being cheated by the peasants on their *iqta*'s, the practice of *himaya* was inevitable. It was almost equally inevitable, however, that the *diwan*s of the great emirs would take for themselves a significant part of the revenues thus collected as payment for services rendered. In extreme cases this could lead to the *iqta*' thus 'protected' becoming effectively the possession of the great emir who had sufficient resources to collect its revenue.[18]

But the main purpose of the *rawk* was to break up the old *iqta*' units, create new ones and redistribute the new *iqta*'s in such a way as to favour the sultan and weaken his enemies. The surveyors of the *rawk* (mainly Copts from the financial *diwan*s working under the supervision of emirs) divided the rural wealth of Egypt into 24 parts. The sources differ as to how those 24 parts were then distributed, but it seems that four parts were assigned to the sultan as his private estate (*khass*), certainly more than his predecessors had possessed. Even more important was the way that the redistribution was used to weaken the old guard of the *halqa* — from whom Kitbugha had formerly drawn so much of his support. Paradoxically, this was done by increasing the number of *iqta*'s which might be made available to the *halqa*. New *iqta*'s were created for new *halqa* troops, new recruits who would not necessarily feel any solidarity with the *Wafidiyya*, Kurds and others who had supported Kitbugha. Depending on which account one follows either ten or 14 twenty-fourths were assigned to the emirs and old *halqa*, and either one or two twenty-fourths were set aside for new *halqa* soldiers. The *iqta*'s available for new troops were created by an overall diminishment of the size and value of the *iqta*'s of emirs and *halqa* soldiers by between a half and a third.

Lajin's reform would not only have strengthened his position internally; it would in principle have increased the strength of Egypt's standing army. However, the redistribution of *iqta*'s was intensely unpopular. Lajin's *na'ib*, Mankutamur al-Husami, who was held to have masterminded the operation, seems to have profited vastly from the redistribution. More important, the old *halqa* troops complained that, as a result of the *rawk*, their *iqta*'s were now too small to pay for their military equipment, or even their subsistence. The *rawk* was completed in October 1298. Lajin and Mankutamur now began to talk of following up the *rawk* with an enquiry into military pay and pensions. The unpopularity of these schemes may have been among the factors which led to Lajin's murder in January 1299.

Lajin died before the newly available *iqta*'s could be reassigned to new *halqa* troops. In the years that followed, established emirs and court favourites were successful in getting their hands on most of them. As a result of this and of the fact that all *halqa iqta*'s had been reduced in value, the *halqa*'s fighting capacity and status declined drastically. Because the *halqa iqta*'s were so small, the *halqa* troops and lesser emirs were more than ever dependent on the *himaya* of powerful emirs. Thus the Husami *rawk* unintentionally initiated a decline in the *halqa* which was to be fraught with long-term consequences for the Mamluk Sultanate.

Presumably the men that Lajin, had he lived, would have recruited into the *halqa* would have been drawn from the native Egyptian townspeople and peasantry, particularly from the towns' unemployed or underemployed people who were looking for a new career. Certainly they were later to enter the *halqa* in large numbers.[19] In fact during his short reign Lajin had generally been able to count on the support of the urban poor. Here is another indication that the power struggle in Egypt and Syria in this period did not constitute a closed system in which the contending factions were recruited from mamluks alone. Just as Kitbugha had been able to draw on the support of *Wafidiyya* and Kurds, so Lajin made his appeal to the mobs of Cairo. Kitbugha had been so unpopular with the people of Cairo that he had had a new *maydan* for equestrian exercises constructed so that he would not have to ride through the most heavily populated areas of Cairo.[20] Some of Kitbugha's unpopularity was due to factors beyond his control. During his reign (1294–6) there was a prolonged famine in Egypt. In the summer of 1295 the Nile failed to flood and there were severe food shortages in Cairo. The following year the famine was even worse — in part, doubtless, because seed corn had been eaten and livestock slaughtered in the previous year. Sandstorms ruined most of Egypt's crops and now drought affected much of Syria and the Hejaz too. (In such circumstances the arrival of thousands of Oirat *Wafidiyya* in Syria could hardly have been welcome.) In Cairo people starved to death in their thousands and there were rumours of cannibalism. There were also rumours that Kitbugha's vizier, Fakhr al-Din al-Khalili, and some of Kitbugha's emirs were profiting from grain sales.[21] Sultan Lajin, on the other hand, was luckier in his weather and in the popular support he received. In particular he seems to have been popular with the *harafish* (singular, *harfush*) — that is, the organised gangs of beggars and urban poor. When Lajin recovered from a serious riding accident in 1297 the *harafish* gathered to cheer him as he rode through the streets of Cairo. In 1307, by contrast, the populace demonstrated in front of the citadel in favour of al-Nasir Muhammad and against Baybars and Salar, and in 1310 the *harafish* pelted Baybars II as he fled before al-Nasir Muhammad's advance on Cairo.[22]

The popularity or unpopularity of sultans and emirs in this period depended to a considerable extent on the stand they took on religious issues. The mamluks involved themselves in religious affairs, both from conviction and as a matter of expediency. None of the protagonists in the struggle for power at the turn of the century was indifferent to religion. All had been educated in the reign of Qalawun and had received religious instruction. Kitbugha was pious. As well as going on the *hajj*, he performed lesser pilgrimages to the tomb of Hud and to a shrine which guarded a footprint of the Prophet. He was also a patron of at least two Sufi orders. Lajin was by all accounts intensely if conventionally pious. He lived austerely and did the supererogatory fasts and his suppression of canonically irregular taxes seems to have been intended to be more than the customary, and temporary, gesture to mark the inauguration of a new reign. He too went on the *hajj*. Salar also went on the *hajj* and during the first reign of al-Nasir Muhammad worked to secure the release of the religious polemicist Ibn Taymiyya — whether from policy or from conviction is not clear. Baybars al-Jashnakir as emir and sultan was advised and deeply influenced by the Sufi shaykh al-Nasr al-Manbiji. He was a strong partisan for the Sufis and their lavish patron. Al-Nasir Muhammad ibn Qalawun also went on the *hajj* and initally at least seems to have sympathised with the teachings of Ibn Taymiyya. Other Mansuri emirs interested themselves in Islamic theology, law, traditions or Sufism.[23]

Just as the military interested themselves in religious issues, so the religious figures of the age, whether they liked it or not, were involved in politics. The caliph, the chief *qadis* in Cairo and Damascus and the leading *'ulama'* all had to consent to the accession of a new sultan. When al-Nasir Muhammad fled to Kerak and Baybars al-Jashnakir usurped the throne, the latter took particular pains to have the legitimacy of his accession attested to by the leading *'ulama'*. He hoped that the declared advocacy of the leading religious figures of the age would guarantee popular support. He could not, however, browbeat Ibn Taymiyya into accepting the legality of al-Nasir Muhammad's abdication and his own usurpation. Although Baybars II took pains to have himself invested sultan by the caliph not once, but twice, this proved of no avail when al-Nasir Muhammad returned from Kerak to retake the throne.[24]

Fatwas (formal legal opinions given by jurists of standing) were sought by mamluks on a wide variety of issues of great importance to them. More often than not the '*ulama*' co-operated with the mamluks. They preached and issued *fatwas* against the Mongols and the heretics of the Lebanese mountains, for instance. Then again senior members of the '*ulama*' caste could often be persuaded to abrogate the terms of a legacy or of a *waqf* settlement, if a sultan or an emir put pressure on them to do so. At times, however, the '*ulama*' could prove awkward. For example, Taqi al-Din ibn Daqiq al-'Id, the Shafi'ite chief *qadi* from 1295 until his death in 1302, clashed with Lajin's *na'ib*, Mankutamur, and refused to sanction the latter's appropriation of a deceased merchant's legacy. Later, in 1300, he successfully headed the opposition of the '*ulama*' to a general emergency tax at the time of a Mongol invasion of Syria. He asserted that there was no justification for such an uncanonical tax when it was so evident that the emirs and their wives continued to live in luxury. It was within the powers of the sultans to depose him, yet none dared to do so.[25]

The mamluks experienced even more problems with the curmudgeonly scholar and jurist Ibn Taymiyya (1263–1328).[26] Ibn Taymiyya's family had fled before the Mongols from the Harran into the Mamluk lands in the 1260s. Ibn Taymiyya himself became a leading spokesman for the Hanbali *madhhab* in Syria (on the whole, a more rigorous school of law than the Hanafi *madhhab* to which most of the mamluks belonged or the Shafi'i *madhhab* to which most of their Sunni Muslim subjects belonged). When not in prison or in exile in Egypt, Ibn Taymiyya taught at a Hanbali *madrasa* in Damascus. His personal influence, however, was much greater than his teaching post might suggest. Because of his reputation for scholarship and unbending probity, his opinion was sought on a great number of topics and he duly issued *fatwas* and polemics on those topics. On every issue he sought to assert the supremacy of *shari'a* law and to urge a return to the practice of the Prophet and the Prophet's Companions. There was nothing good about innovation.

This meant that he was opposed to a rather wide range of ideas, institutions and practices. He was against influence of the Christians and Jews in Mamluk politics and the economy, and the lax enforcement of discriminatory legislation aimed at them; against craft corporations; against suggestive female dress; against bedouin superstitions; against the monist and anti-nomian ideas of certain Sufis; against backgammon; against the Mamluk emirs' overriding of the *shari'a*; against the spread of Mongol customs among the mamluks; against firewalking; against the lesser pilgrimages (such as those performed by Kitbugha); against the cult of saints' tombs and the intercessory power of saints; against the practice of rolling eggs at the Coptic Easter festival; against Shi'ite heterodoxy; against hashish; against the chivalric cult of *futuwwa*; against the cult of Palestine as a second Holy Land; against state control of food prices. There were so many ways in which the Mamluk Sultanate fell short of being the ideal Islamic state.

Ibn Taymiyya's opinions were listened to with respect by those outside his own *madhhab*; in particular, many of the leading '*ulama*' in Damascus — al-Dhahabi and his circle, for example — supported his stand on some of these issues. A few of the mamluk emirs professed themselves his disciples. The paramount shaykh of the bedouin Arabs in Syria, 'Isa ibn Muhanna, was his friend. More than that, Ibn Taymiyya could count on a street following, particularly when he preached against the Christians. The occasions when he was arrested resulted in popular rioting. After his death in 1328, his funeral took on the nature of a mass demonstration. On the occasions when their aims converged, Ibn Taymiyya could be very useful to the mamluks. He preached the *jihad* against the heretics in the Lebanese mountains and against the Mongols. He headed the passive resistance to the occupation of Damascus by the Mongols and their ally, Sayf al-Din Qibjaq, in 1300. He issued a *fatwa* excusing the mamluk troops from observing the Ramadan fast before the Battle of Marj al-Suffar against the Mongols in 1303. He could prove unco-operative, however. He refused to testify to the validity of al-Nasir Muhammad's abdication in 1309, but on the other hand he later resisted al-Nasir Muhammad's pressure on him to denounce those who had so testified.

Swift to denounce what he detected as heresy or error, Ibn

Taymiyya was himself so denounced by his enemies. In particular, his anthropomorphic conception of God was alleged to be heretical and his teachings on divorce law held to be in error. Sufis, influential at court, who felt themselves threatened by Ibn Taymiyya's attacks on some (but not all) aspects of Sufism were prominent among Ibn Taymiyya's accusers. Sultans and emirs were obliged to take sides in these issues. Kitbugha and Baybars II, who favoured the Sufis, were on the whole hostile. Aqush al-Afram, the Na'ib of Damascus from 1300 until 1310, favoured Ibn Taymiyya and so for a time did the young sultan al-Nasir Muhammed. The Sufis, too, could command urban mobs, and the mamluks, whose prestige may have suffered because of their factional fighting and their failure to keep the Mongols out of Syria in 1299, bowed to pressure first from one side and then the other.

On one thing Sufis and Islamic fundamentalists were united. That was in their hostility to Christians.[27] The roots of this antagonism were various. Probably the most important cause of resentment was the overwhelming Coptic presence in the financial bureaus of the sultans and of the emirs and in related commercial ventures. There was perhaps a tendency on the part of the military in power to use Christians as cat's paws in planning and enforcing unpopular financial measures. Copts, for instance, had done most of the work on the Husami *rawk*. Though Copts no longer enjoyed the same pre-eminence in commerce that they had had under the Fatimids, the wealth of a few Copts still gave rise to jealousy, and there were a few Copts in the wealthy corporation of Karimi merchants. Then again the Christians were suspected of constituting a fifth column for the Mongols and the Crusaders, and a few Christians do indeed seem to have collaborated during the Mongol occupation of Damascus in 1300. Maghribis who had suffered from the Christian *reconquista* in Spain and Christian naval raids on the North African coast urged the sultans of Egypt to treat the Christians less kindly. Cairo's housing was very close packed and grain and fodder were stored in the centre of the city. This made Cairo and Damascus very vulnerable to fire. Such fires were blamed on the activities of Christian arsonists.

There was widespread rioting against the Christians in 1293 in the reign of al-Ashraf Khalil and again in 1301 when al-Nasir Muhammad nominally ruled, but Baybars al-Jashnakir was actually responsible for announcing the enforcement of discriminatory legislation against them. There would be further disturbances in the third reign of al-Nasir Muhammad. In 1301 the *harafish* beggars played a prominent part in the rioting, and Baybars al-Jashnakir, urged on by the Sufis, was not inclined to deal with the Christians kindly.

In the bad times, the *ahl al-dhimma* (people of the pact — that is, the Christians and the less numerous and less influential Jews) were forced to wear distinctive dress. The Christians wore blue turbans and belts and the Jews yellow. They were forbidden to ride horses or mules in the towns; churches were sacked or closed. Copts were dismissed from the financial bureaus and the chancery, unless they agreed to convert to Islam. A number acquiesced, despite the protests of some of the '*ulama*' that such forced conversions were against the law of Islam. The converts were known as *musalima* and they continued to be denounced by some Muslims on the grounds that their adoption of Islam had been merely tactical. It was alleged that the *musalima* continued to serve their former co-religionarists as protectors and apologists. Such allegations may not have been groundless.   227 566

In the years that followed intense bouts of anti-Christian activity, discriminatory measures such as those listed above were inevitably relaxed. Foreign Christian regimes interceded with the sultans on their behalf — Ethiopia, Georgia and European powers such as Venice, Genoa, Aragon and Castile which had trading relations with Egypt. In the long run also the rehabilitation of Coptic functionaries was made necessary by the fact that emirs could not afford to do without them.

Mamluk factional strife may have encouraged the '*ulama*' to take a more critical approach towards their masters. Much more damaging was the fact that Mamluk internal strife gave the Mongols renewed hope of conquering Syria in the late 1290s. In October 1298, the Na'ib of Damascus, Sayf al-Din Qibjaq, fearing that he was about to be deposed and perhaps killed at the urging of Lajin's *na'ib al-saltana*, Mankutamur, fled from Damascus with a number of other prominent emirs and crossed the Euphrates into Mongol lands. As has been mentioned above, Qibjaq's father had been a *silahdar* at the court of the Ilkhanate. It was natural that Qibjaq should seek Ilkhan Ghazan's help in restoring his position in Syria.[28] It was natural also that Ghazan, who received Qibjaq in April 1299, should be eager to profit from these troubles in the Mamluk camp, for Lajin, and then Baybars and Salar after him, had been trying to destabilise the Mongol position in Asia Minor. In

1297 Lajin sent an expedition to Cilicia which was successful in occupying most of the important Cilician towns and in forcing the Armenians to agree to pay half a million dirhams in tribute. The Mamluks also encouraged the Qaramanli Turkomans to harass the Mongols in Anatolia. Further, when Sulemish, an important Mongol general in Anatolia, rebelled in the winter of 1298–9, the Mamluks promised him support. After Sulemish's early reverses, he was received in Cairo and then sent back to Anatolia with additional assistance. Sulemish, however, was speedily apprehended and killed.[29] In the summer of 1299 the Mamluks had also taken the offensive against the Mongols in Upper Iraq and captured Mardin. In the winter of 1299 therefore Ghazan crossed the Euphrates with a mixed army of Mongols, Armenians and Georgians and with the Mamluk emirs Qibjaq and Baktimur among his commanders. By now Lajin and Mankutamur had been murdered and Qibjaq's life would no longer have been in danger from his enemies in Egypt. However, it was too late. Qibjaq was for the time being committed to the Mongol cause. Ghazan's army did not pause to invest Aleppo or Hama. The Mamluks seem to have been taken by surprise by Ghazan's winter offensive. The main army was hurried out of Egypt. While at Gaza on its way to encounter the Mongols, the army was thrown into turmoil by a plot by the Mongol Oirat *Wafidiyya* to murder the sultan and his officers and to put the Mongol mamluk Kitbugha back on the throne. After the plot had been foiled, hundreds of Oirats were killed.

The Mamluk army pressed on to intercept the Mongol army some way north of Homs at a place called Wadi al-Khazinder on 23 December 1299. By then, however, the army was exhausted by the forced marches that it had made and, though the battle was prolonged its final issue was disastrous for the Mamluks. They fled in disorder back to Egypt and Druze hillsmen from Kasrawan harassed and plundered the retreating troops. The Battle of Wadi al-Khazindar was the first and only major defeat ever experienced by the Mamluks at the hands of the Mongols. As a result of his victory, Ghazan was able to occupy Homs and seize the army's treasury which had been left there, and in January the town of Damascus surrendered without fighting (the citadel, however, held out). The following month Ghazan returned to Iran. He left Syria under a dual administration. In Damascus Qibjaq and a Mongol general Qutlugh-shah were jointly governors and in the north Baktimur and another Mongol similarly shared control. But the

Mongol occupation of Syria collapsed very rapidly. The Mongols had plundered and mulcted Damascus too thoroughly for their rule to be popular there. Their armies lacked the siege engines and perhaps also the will to take any of the Mamluk forts or citadels. Qibjaq and Baktimur corresponded with the junta in Egypt and they negotiated their redefection back to the Mamluk side that spring, while the Mongol army withdrew.[30]

Ghazan attempted to recoup his position in a second invasion in the winter of 1301, but, though he advanced down beyond Aleppo, the expedition had eventually to be abandoned because of heavy rains. Later that year and the following year, Ghazan and Sultan al-Nasir Muhammad exchanged embassies which mingled conciliatory promises with threats. Ghazan, like Teguder Ahmad before him, seems to have been aware of the advantages to be gained from an opening of the frontiers to peaceful commerce.[31] In 1302, however, two further groups of Mamluk emirs, losers in the incessant factional strife, defected to the Mongols and urged Ghazan to make yet another attempt to conquer Syria. Qutlughshah was sent into Syria in 1303, but his army was routed at the Battle of Marj al-Suffar, not far from Damascus, on 20 April.[32] Ghazan died in the spring of 1304. There was, however, a further skirmish next year when a Mamluk foray into Cilicia encouraged a few hundred Mongols, including some of Salar's relatives, to defect from Anatolia. These *Wafidiyya* eluded capture by a larger Mongol army.[33]

With the Mongol threat much diminished after the death of Ghazan, the Mamluks were free to turn their attention to a major area of disaffection in Syria, Kasrawan, a highland region to the north-east of Beirut. As has been noted above, the Druze and other tribesmen in that region had harried the mamluks fleeing from the field of Wadi al-Khazindar. Also the Lebanese coast was vulnerable to Frankish piracy and there was plainly a danger that the tribesmen of the hinterland could be roused to revolt by promises of Frankish money and arms. In 1300 Jamal al-Din Aqush al-Afram, Na'ib of Damascus, set out with a punitive expedition against Kasrawan. Ibn Taymiyya was recruited to preach against the heretics of the region. There was considerable confusion as to the nature of the heresy of Kasrawan. Druze chieftains, possibly assisted by Nusayri Shi'ites and Maronite Christians, headed resistance to the Mamluks, but Ibn Taymiyya's *fatwa* denounced a generalised amalgam of tenets held by various Shi'ite sects, including some of those of the Persian

Isma'ili Nasir al-Din al-Tusi. In any event, it is clear that while the Mamluks were successful in whipping up Sunni orthodox feelings against the Kasrawanis, their real aim was to establish military control of the Lebanon and its hillsmen, whatever denomination they belonged to. Aqush al-Afram's first expedition was successful in securing some of the plunder that the Kasrawanis had acquired in the previous winter and in exacting tribute from them, but he was not strong enough to impose a permanent Mamluk presence in the area. In 1305 the Kasrawanis broke out in open revolt, but this time they were well beaten. The area was split up into *iqta*'s and loyal Turkoman tribesmen settled there.[34]

Nineteen years had passed since Qalawun, the master of the Mansuris, had died. Internecine feuding and blood-letting at the top were the chief features of the period. That the Mamluks were generally able to defend Egypt and Syria against the attacks of the Mongols and the Franks was due more to the weakness of their enemies than to Mamluk strength. Yet when Qalawun's son al-Nasir Muhammad returned to the throne for the third time in 1310, the Mansuri emirs continued to hold a near monopoly of political power, and it did not seem likely that the young sultan would be able to assert effective control for himself and bring to an end the pattern of senior emirs using the sultan's rule to veil their manoeuvrings for real power.

Notes

1. The chief published sources covering the political events of this period are: Abu'l-Fida, *al-Mukhtasar fi Akhbar al-Bashar*, vol.4 (Istanbul, 1869–70) (translated for this period by P. M. Holt as *The Memoirs of a Syrian Prince* (Wiesbaden, 1983)); Ibn al-Suqa'i, *Tali Kitab Wafayat al-A'yan*, J. Sublet (trans. and ed.) (Damascus, 1974); Ibn al-Dawadari, *Kanz al-Durar*, vol.8, U. Haarmann (ed.) (Freiburg, 1979), vol.9, H. R. Roemer (ed.) (Cairo, 1960); al-Jazari, *La Chronique de Damas d'al-Jazari (années 689–698 H.)*, summary translation by J. Sauvaget (Paris 1949); Mufaddal Ibn Abi al-Fada'il, 'Histoire des sultans mamluks', E. Blochet (ed. and trans.) in *Patrologia Orientalis*, vol.14 (1920), vol.20 (1929); Anonymous, in *Beiträge zur Geschichte der Mamlukensultane*, K. V. Zettersteen (ed.) (Leiden, 1929); Ibn al-Furat, *Tarikh al-Duwal wa'l-Muluk*, vol.8, Q. Zurayq and N. Izz al-Din (eds) (Beirut, 1939); al-Maqrizi, *Kitab al-Suluk*, vol.1, pt.3, vol.2, pt. 1, M. M. Ziada (ed.) (Cairo, 1939–41); Ibn Taghribirdi, *al-Nujum al-Zahira*, vol.8 (Cairo, n.d).

See also S. M. Elham, *Kitbuga und Lagin. Studien zur Mamluken — Geschichte nach Baibars al-Mansuri und an-Nuwairi* (Freiburg, 1977); P. M. Holt, 'The Sultanate of Lajin (696–8/1296–9)', *BSOAS*, vol.36 (1973), pp.521–32; D. P. Little, *An Introduction to Mamluk Historiography* (Wiesbaden, 1970)); M. Chapoutot-Remadi, 'Une Grande Crise à la fin du XIIIe siècle en Egypte', *JESHO*, vol.26 (1983), pp.217–45.

2. On Mamluk executions, see Ibn al-Nafis, *The Theologus Autodidactus of Ibn al-Nafis*, M. Meyerhoff and J. Schacht (eds and trans.) (Oxford, 1968), 'Excursus F', pp.81–2; Ibn Sasra, *A Chronicle of Damascus*, W. M. Brinner (ed. and trans.) (Berkeley and Los Angeles, 1963), p.12n.

3. For the career of Sanjar al-Halabi, see Ibn Taghribirdi, *Nujum*, vol.8, p.39.

4. On Baysari, see in particular Ibn Taghribirdi, *Nujum*, vol.8, pp.185–6; L. A. Mayer, *Saracenic Heraldry* (Oxford, 1933), p.112.

5. On Baktash, see Ibn al-Suqa'i, *Tali*, pp.73–4; Ibn Taghribirdi, *Nujum*, vol.8, p.224.

6. D. Ayalon, 'Studies on the Structure of the Mamluk Army' (part 2), *BSOAS*, vol.15 (1953), p.462.

7. Maqrizi, *Suluk*, vol. 1, pt.3, p.942; B. Grekov and A. Yakubovsky, *La Horde d'Or* (Paris, 1939), p.88; D. Ayalon, 'The Great Yasa of Chingiz Khan. A re-examination (C1)' *SI*, vol.36 (1972), pp.117–18. On p.118, however, Ayalon understands 'al-Mansur' to refer to Qalawun. The context indicates that Baybars al-Mansuri was referring to al-Mansur Lajin.

8. D. Ayalon, *L'Esclavage du Mamelouk* (Jerusalem, 1951), pp.29–31, 34–7; D. P. Little, *Introduction*, pp.125–6.

9. M. Mahdi, *Ibn Khaldun's Philosophy of History* (Chicago, 1964), p.196 and n.

10. R. Syme, *The Roman Revolution* (Oxford, 1939), pp.12, 157.

11. K. B. McFarlane, *England in the Fifteenth Century* (London, 1981), p.19.

12. Maqrizi, *Suluk*, vol.1, pt.3, p.824.

13. Elham, *Kitbuga und Lagin*, pp.75–6; Holt, 'Sultanate of Lajin', p.524.

14. D. Ayalon, 'The Wafidiyya in the Mamluk Kingdom', *Islamic Culture*, vol.25 (1951), pp.91, 99–100; J. A. Boyle (ed.), *The Cambridge History of Iran*, vol. 5 (Cambridge, 1968), p.381; Elham, *Kitbug und Lagin*, pp.77–8; I. M. Lapidus, *Muslim Cities in the Later Middle Ages* (Cambridge, Mass., 1967), p.176; Little, *Introduction*, index *sv* 'Oirat'.

15. Little, *Introduction*, p.126.

16. D. P. Little, 'Notes on Aitamis, a Mongol Mamluk' in U. Haarmann and P. Bachmann (eds), *Die Islamische Welt zwischen Mittelalter und Neuzeit* (Wiesbaden, 1979), p.392; Little, *Introduction*, p.129.

17. This account of *rawk* is based mainly on the excellent introduction in H. Halm, '*Ägypten nach den mamlukischen Lehens-registern. I. Oberägypten und das Fayyum* (Wiesbaden, 1979), pp.17–23. See also Ayalon, 'Studies in the Structure' (part 2), pp.451–3; Holt, 'Sultanate of Lajin', pp.527–9; H. Rabie, *The Financial System of Egypt* (London, 1972), pp.52–3; Chapoutot-Remadi, 'Une Grande Crise', pp. 241–2.

18. On *himaya*, see Halm, *Ägypten*, p.17; C. Cahen, 'Notes pour l'histoire de la himaya' in *Mélanges Louis Massignon*, vol.1 (Damascus, 1956), pp.287–303.

19. Ayalon, 'Studies on the Structure' (part 2), p.453.

20. D. Ayalon, 'Notes on the Furusiyya Exercises and Games in the Mamluk Sultanate', *Scripta Hierosolymitana*, vol.9 (1969), p.39.

21. Maqrizi, 'Le Traité de famine', G. Wiet (ed. and trans.), *JESHO*, vol.5 (1962), pp.32–41; Elham, *Kitbuga und Lagin*, p.78; Chapoutot-Remadi, 'Une Grande Crise', pp.219–38.

22. Maqrizi, *Suluk*, vol.2, pt. 1, pp.35–6; Ibn Taghribirdi, *Nujum*, vol.8, pp.173–4; W. M. Brinner, 'The Significance of the Harafish and their "Sultan" ', *JESHO*, vol.6 (1963), pp.196–7; I. M. Lapidus, *Muslim Cities*, p.180.

23. On the religiosity of the period, see H. Laoust, *Essai sur les doctrines sociales et politiques de Taki-d-din Ahmad b. Taimiya (1262–1382)* (Cairo, 1939); Laoust, 'Le Hanbalisme sous les Mamlouks Bahrides (658–784/1260–1382)', *REI*, vol.28 (1960), pp.1–71; D. P. Little, 'Religion under the Mamluks', *Muslim World*, vol.73 (1983), pp.165–81.

24. On the role of the caliph in this period, see J.-C. Garcin, 'Histoire, opposition

politique et pietisme traditionaliste dans le Husn al-Muhadarat de Suyuti', *Annales Islamologiques,* vol.7 (1967), pp.49, 55–6.

25. J. H. Escovitz, 'The Office of Qadi al-qudat in Cairo under the Bahri Mamluks', unpublished PhD thesis (Institute of Islamic Studies, McGill University, 1978), pp.155–6, 161–2; J.-C. Garcin, *Un Centre Musulman de la haute Égypte medievale: Qus* (Cairo, 1976), pp.408–9; *Garcin,* 'Histoire, opposition', pp.69–70, 75; Laoust, 'Le Hanbalisme', pp.10–11, 17–18; E. Sivan, *L'Islam et la Croisade* (Paris, 1968), pp.178–80.

26. On Ibn Taymiyya, see D. P. Little, 'The Historical and Historigraphical Significance of the Detention of Ibn Taymiyya', *IJMES,* vol.4 (1973), pp.311–27; Laoust, *Essai;* G. Makdisi, 'Ibn Taymiyya: A Sufi of the Qadiriya Order', *American Journal of Arabic Studies,* vol.1 (1973), pp.118–29; M. U. Memon, *Ibn Taymiyya's Struggle against Popular Religion* (Hague, 1976); E. Sivan, 'Ibn Taymiyya: Father of the Islamic Revolution. Medieval Theology and Modern Politics', *Encounter* (May 1983), pp.41–50; 'Ibn Taimiya' in *EI(2).*

27. On the Copts and their persecution, see C. E. Bosworth, 'Christian and Jewish Religious Dignitaries in Mamluk Egypt and Syria', *IJMES,* vol.3 (1972), pp.59–74; D. P. Little, 'Coptic Conversion to Islam under the Bahri Mamluks 692–755/1293–1354', *BSOAS,* vol.39 (1976), pp.552–69; D. Richards, 'The Coptic Bureaucracy under the Mamluks' in *Colloque International sur l'Histoire du Caire* (Cairo, 1969), pp.373–81; E. Sivan, *L'Islam et la Croisade,* pp.181–3.

28. Boyle, *Iran,* vol.5, p.386; and see above p.91.

29. Boyle, *Iran,* vol.5, pp.386–7; C. Cahen, *Pre-Ottoman Turkey* (London, 1968), pp.300–1; 'Cilicia' in *EI(2).*

30. On the Mongol campaigns of 1299–1300, see Boyle, *Iran,* vol.5, pp.388–9; Little, *Introduction, passim;* J. Richard, 'Isol le Pisan: Un Aventurier franc governeur d'une province mongole?', *Central Asiatic Journal,* vol.14 (1970), pp.186–94; S. Schein, '*Gesta Dei per Mongolos 1300.* The Genesis of a Non-event', *English Historical Review,* vol.94 (1979), pp.805–19; J. de Somogyi, 'Adh-Dhahabi's Record of the Destruction of Damascus by the Mongols in 699–700/1299–1301' in S. Lowinger and J. de Somogy (eds), *Ignace Goldziher Memorial Volume,* vol.2 (Budapest, 1948), pp.353–86.

31. Boyle, *Iran,* vol.5, pp.389–90, 392; H. Horst, 'Eine Gesandschaft des Mamluken al-Malik al-Nasir am Ilhan-Hof in Persien' in W. Hoernbach (ed.), *Der Orient in der Forschung* (Wiesbaden, 1967), pp.348–70.

32. Boyle, *Iran,* vol.5, p.392–4.

33. Little, *Introduction,* pp.8, 16–17; 'Cilicia' in *EI(2).*

34. H. Laoust, 'Remarques sur les expeditions de Kasrawan sous les Mamlouks', *Bulletin du Musée de Beyrouth,* vol.4 (1940), pp.93–115; Little, *Introduction,* index sv 'Gabal al-Kasrawan'; K. S. Salibi, *Maronite Historians of Mediaeval Lebanon* (Beirut, 1959), pp.119–20, 140.

6 THE THIRD REIGN OF AL-NASIR MUHAMMAD IBN QALAWUN, 1310–41

The cult of Qalawun had not diminished during the 19 years of turbulence. Indeed, whereas formerly mamluks on emancipation had taken their oath of loyalty to the reigning sultan at the tomb of al-Salih Ayyub, the ceremony now took place at the tomb of Qalawun in the Mansuri complex of mosque, *madrasa* and hospital which dominated the Bayn al-Qasrayn area to the north of the citadel.[1] The structures of administration and military organisation were substantially unchanged from what they had been in Qalawun's time. The only major reforms had been attempted by Lajin and he had been killed before those reforms could bear fruit, for good or ill. During those years Qalawun's son, al-Nasir Muhammad, had served the emirs — first Kitbugha and Lajin, later Baybars and Salar — as a sort of mascot. By the time of his accession to the throne for the third time, in 1310, al-Nasir Muhammad was 24 and he had learnt a great deal from the years of humiliation on the throne and of exile away from it.[2]

To a considerable extent Kitbugha's tenure of the throne had been doomed by the Nile's failure to rise sufficiently. Baybars II faced the same problem in 1309. Food prices rose. The sultan whose ill fate had brought this upon Egypt was jeered at and pelted by the *harafish* as he attempted to flee before the triumphant al-Nasir Muhammad. Baybars had relied on quite a narrow group of Burji and Circassian emirs. Aqush al-Afram the *na'ib* in Damascus had previously wept tears of joy when he had heard of Baybars's accession in 1309. Aqush al-Afram was a fellow-Burji and a Circassian; his future had then seemed assured.[3] Sayf al-Din Salar, the *na'ib* in Cairo, on the other hand, was Baybars's disappointed rival rather than his committed supporter. The other *na'ib*s in Syria — most prominently Qurasunqur al-Mansuri at Aleppo, Qibjaq al-Mansuri at Hama, Baktimur al-Jawakandar al-Mansuri at Safed, and Asandamur al-Kurji at Tripoli — were either favourable to al-Nasir Muhammad's return or neutral. Doubtless they hoped to control the sultan's third reign, as others had controlled his previous reigns.

However, the return of al-Nasir Muhammad was not solely due to the support of disaffected Mansuris. The small army which carried him to success in Damascus and then in Cairo was comprised largely of bedouin from the Kerak region and of al-Nasir Muhammad's own Nasiri mamluks. During his periods of exile al-Nasir Muhammad had striven to win the support of the Arabs of Kerak, and it is probably to those early years in the wilderness of Kerak that one should trace the origins of the cult of the bedouin Arab that was to be such a prominent feature of the reigns of al-Nasir Muhammad and some of his children. Secondly, although the young al-Nasir Muhammad's political guardians had kept him on a tight financial leash, denying him all luxuries, the sultan had been able to accumulate a small corps of mamluks formerly in the service of his brother, al-Ashraf Khalil. Some had been inherited by al-Nasir Muhammad directly after Khalil's murder, while others had come to him only after the murder of Lajin. Among those who were destined to play a great part in future events were Tankiz al-Husami, Arghun al-Dawadar and Aytamish al-Muhammadi. Thirty-two of al-Nasir's mamluks were promoted to the rank of emir and given official duties immediately after al-Nasir Muhammad's reaccession.[4]

However, in order to advance his Nasiri mamluks further it would be necessary for the sultan to dispose of those Mansuri emirs who had also played a role in returning him to the throne. He would have to kick away the unreliable props. Initially, of course, these emirs had been rewarded by being promoted to more senior governorships or confirmed in the ones they held. Qarasunqur moved to Damascus, Qibjaq moved from Hama to replace Qarasunqur at Aleppo, and so on. Baktimur al-Jawkandar, who in 1307 and prior to his demotion to the governorship of Safed had been part of the ruling junta in Cairo with Baybars and Salar, was in 1307 chosen by the sultan for the top job of *na'ib al-saltana* in Egypt. Nevertheless, all these distinguished emirs were marked men. Sayf al-Din Qibjaq at Aleppo was lucky enough to die of natural causes in 1310 but Baktimur, the *na'ib* in Egypt, was arrested in 1311 on a conspiracy charge, accused of plotting to dethrone al-Nasir Muhammad and replace him with 'Alam al-Din Musa, a son of the sultan's deceased older brother, al-Salih 'Ali. So were a number of other Mansuris, including Qutlubak (the governor of Safed) and Asandamur (who had replaced Qibjaq at Aleppo). Many of the emirs arrested in 1311 were later strangled in 1316.[5] Qaransunqur, nervous of the sultan from the first, transferred himself from Damascus to Aleppo to put a greater distance between them, and then fled to the Mongols in 1312. Six hundred mamluks followed him into exile.[6]

The years of humiliation and exile had made the sultan suspicious to a fault and, as we shall see, surprise arrests of royal servants and the deaths of former favourites in dubious circumstances were to continue as a feature of this otherwise relatively peaceful reign. After the early purges the top governorships were confined to a very small bank of trusted emirs. Sayf al-Din Tankiz al-Husami was Na'ib of Damascus from 1312 until 1340. After Baktimur al-Jawkandar's arrest in 1311, Baybars al-Mansuri was briefly *na'ib* in Egypt. Then from 1312 until 1317 the post was held by Arghun al-Nasiri. After the latter's transfer to Aleppo the office of *na'ib* in Egypt was temporarily suppressed (until the end of al-Nasir's reign). After Qarasunqur's flight to the Mongols in 1312 the office of Na'ib of Aleppo was briefly held by a nonentity. Then 'Ala al-Din Altunbugha was Na'ib of Aleppo from 1314 until 1317, when he was honourably transferred to Egypt and replaced by Arghun. The former returned to govern Aleppo again after Arghun's death in 1331 and continued to hold this position until the end of the reign.

It would be a mistake to regard these emirs as simply or even mainly garrison commanders or political thugs. Despite their formal military training, they were men of high culture. Arghun al-Nasiri wrote Arabic with a good hand, worked in the chancery before he became governor of Egypt, collected books on a great scale, studied the traditions of Bukhari and Hanafi law and actually issued *fatwa*s on religious questions.[7] Baybars al-Mansuri had headed the chancery in the reign of Qalawun, was literate in Arabic and composed with the aid of one of his Christian scribes a chronicle which is one of the main sources for the history of the period.[8] Tankiz was a pious and charitable man. For most of al-Nasir Muhammad's third reign, Tankiz was the effective king of the most important part of Syria and his long tenure of the governorship of Damascus saw a massive programme of urban restoration undertaken in that city. Mosques, *madrasa*s, schools and markets were erected and, most importantly, a new aqueduct was built to assure the city's water supply. Similar works were undertaken in Beirut, Jerusalem, Safed and elsewhere. Abuses in the management of the *waqf*s of Damascus were stamped out, and the money thus saved was used for further works of restoration of religious buildings.[9]

In Egypt the sultan set about acquiring a younger group of mamluks as his intimates. He seems to have been partial to pretty faces and the fashionable physiognomy for a mamluk was Mongol.

Qawsun al-Nasiri was of Mongol origin and cost the sultan 80,000 dirhams. Bashtak al-Nasiri, who was purchased by the sultan on the basis of his alleged resemblance to Ilkhan Abu Sa'id, cost 6,000 dirhams.[10] Once he was securely established on the throne, al-Nasir Muhammad set about buying mamluks at a great rate. The high prices he was prepared to pay led to competition among the Mongols to sell to him. According to al-Maqrizi, traders were paying up to 40,000 dirhams for a single mamluk. Despite al-Nasir's readiness to pay great sums for his mamluks, it does not seem that the numbers in the service of the sultan ever equalled the corps assembled by Baybars, Qalawun and al-Ashraf Khalil, and it is also possible that high prices in the fourteenth century reflect a diminishing supply of white slaves.[11]

It may be that his need to buy mamluks was made more intense by the fact that, by the beginning of his third reign, the influx of *Wafidiyya* into the Mamluk lands had declined to a trickle. The most important *Wafidi* emir during this period, the Mongol Badr al-Din Jankali ibn Muhammad ibn al-Baba, had come over to the Mamluks somewhat earlier, in 1303. Badr al-Din Jankali proved to be an enthusiast for the ideas of Ibn Taymiyya and intervened repeatedly in religious affairs, particularly criticising the corruption of the *qadi*s. He was also granted an emirate of one hundred and sat in the *majli*s of emirs as one of the sultan's most senior and respected advisors. His daughter married the sultan's son. Badr al-Din Jankali, however, was one of the last great *Wafidis* and there were to be few such marriages subsequently.[12]

Whereas Baybars I and Qalawun seem to have favoured marriage with *Wafidis*, al-Nasir Muhammad pursued the new dynastic policy of binding his favoured Nasiri emirs yet more closely to him through a complicated series of marriage alliances. He had 14 sons and 11 daughters. His older sons married daughters of Baktimur al-Saqi and Tuquzdamur al-Hamawi. His daughters married Qawsun, Bashtak, Abu Bakr (the son of Arghun) and various other less powerful Nasiri emirs.[13] That the Mongols still retained their social prestige is indicated by the series of missions sent by the sultan to the lands of the Golden Horde to secure a Mongol princess. In the end al-Nasir Muhammad did briefly marry Tulubiyya, a great-great-grand-daughter of Chingiz Khan.[14] The royal harem swelled to an unprecedented size. Besides wives and concubines, al-Nasir Muhammad maintained an establishment of 1,200 slave girls. There is some evidence to suggest that the women of the harem and their attendant eunuchs did occasionally exercise influence on political decisions.[15] Nevertheless, it is clear that there were strict limits to that influence when it is compared first to the power wielded by emirs and, second, to that wielded by functionaries of the scribal class.

It was necessary to find ways of vastly increasing royal income in order to finance the purchase of mamluks and to maintain an unprecedentedly large court establishment. Not only that, but after the mamluks had been purchased, trained and emancipated, they would have to be assigned *iqta*‘s. We must now turn to consider the background of the Nasiri *rawk* of 1315 in Egypt and the related Syrian *rawk*s. Of course it was not long since Lajin had ordered the Husami *rawk* (1298). However, the Husami *rawk* had applied to Egypt only. Moreover, Lajin had been killed before his proposed redistribution could be made fully effective. Also al-Nasir Muhammad had acquired so much new *iqta*‘ land from the defeated Mansuri emirs — in particular, the estates of Baybars al-Jashnakir and Salar — that a systematic survey and redistribution would be desirable. Finally, important irrigation work had been undertaken in 1310 and this must have altered the value of some *iqta*‘ lands.

As far as Egypt is concerned, the *rawk* survey itself was preceded by a survey of irrigation works made by a team of ten emirs in 1314–15. The *rawk* itself was completed a little later, in 1315. As a result of the new distribution of land that followed, where before the sultan had held four-twenty-fourths of Egypt as his *khass*, his share now went up to ten-twenty-fourths and the rest of the emirs and *halqa* were left holding the remainder between them. Al-Nasir Muhammad, unlike Lajin, did not set aside any new *iqta*‘ land for the maintenance of new *halqa* troops. Indeed, while the new *iqta*‘s that were now assigned to the *halqa* appeared to retain their approximate former value in the form of tax income received by the *muqta*‘, they were in fact worth less. This was because whereas previously the income of the *muqta*‘ was based solely or mainly on the *kharaj* tax (generally a fixed proportion of the agricultural produce within the *iqta*‘), now the *jizya* or *jawali* tax was assigned to the *muqta*‘ and included in the estimate of the value of the *iqta*‘. The *jizya* tax was the annual poll tax levied on all non-Muslims resident within the Sultanate and in principle the *jizya* paid by the Coptic peasantry should have provided its recipient with a major source of income. However, though the sultan relinquished his right to collect this tax outside his *khass* lands (and was thus saved the expense of collecting it), the emirs who now received it did not benefit as much as they should in principle have done. The reason for this was that under the new system it was easy for Copts to evade the tax by slipping from village to village and pretending to the *muqta*'s that they had paid the poll tax elsewhere. The relatively small and inefficient financial *diwan*s of the emirs were ill-equipped to check on such evasion.

The result of all this was that the value of all *iqta*'s, outside the royal *khass* lands, was diminished. The incomes of the great emirs were reduced and their dependence on the sultan correspondingly increased. The smaller *iqta*'s of the *halqa* were so much reduced that from henceforth it became more or less impossible to maintain and equip proper soldiers from their income. The status and income of the *halqa* had declined as an unintentional result of the Husami *rawk*. Now it declined still further as a deliberate result of the Nasiri *rawk*. All sorts of riff-raff, such as pedlars and artisans, acquired *halqa iqta*'s. They did so not in the hope of serving in the army, but of using the *halqa* income as a sort of pension to supplement what they earned elsewhere. Henceforth the Mamluk sultans in their campaigns relied more and more on relatively large numbers of mamluk soldiers and much less on the free-born troops of the *halqa*. The mamluks were of course much better soldiers, but they were expensive and politically turbulent.

The Nasiri *rawk* was not popular. Some of the mamluks attempted to refuse their new *iqta*'s in a protest before the sultan which took place as the diplomas for the *iqta*'s were being handed out in 1316. The new way of collecting the *jizya* tax was particularly criticised by the Muslims and the Nasiri *rawk* came to be regarded in some circles as a Coptic conspiracy to ruin Egypt. This was a view which was encouraged by the fact that Copts played a large part in the surveying and calculating done for the survey. More than that, the idea of the *rawk* was alleged to have been proposed to the sultan by a Coptic convert to Islam, Taqi al-Din ibn Amin al-Mulk, the controller of the sultan's finances (*nazir al-dawawin*). The other figure most closely associated with the unpopular redistribution of *iqta*'s was also a Coptic convert to Islam, Fakhr al-Din ibn al-Qibti, the financial supervisor of the army (*nazir al-juyush*), and of course it was the Copts who were supposed to have benefited from the handing over of the *jizya* tax to the emirs.

Though the Nasiri *rawk* was primarily concerned with the redistribution of cultivable land as *iqta*', associated with this reform were a large number of subsidiary reforms and peripheral effects arising from the *rawk*. Some should be noted here. As a result of the sultan handing over most of the *jizya* tax to the emirs, he was saved the expense of collecting it. On the other hand, as financial officials travelled less through the provinces, he was less well informed about them and had less control over them. He had less *locus* to intervene in the internal affairs of an *iqta'*. Secondly, though he now had more *khass* land than before, some of these royal estates were for the first time given out as *iqta's* to royal mamluks. These mamluks, those who had not yet received emirates and who lodged in the royal barracks in the Cairo Citadel, had hitherto received only pay and rations. From now on inadequate pay was to be supplemented by income from *iqta's*. Thirdly, *iqta's* based on taxes other than those levied on land and agriculture were abolished (e.g. the *iqta'* on the customs revenue of Alexandria). Generally, the collection of all sorts of minor taxes was abolished or simplified or redistributed among the various *diwans*. The vizier's *diwan*, for instance, responsible for the provisions of the royal kitchen, got a larger allocation than before. *Iqta's* were more carefully divided and scattered throughout Egypt, so as to weaken the regional power of the *muqta's*. Overall — in the short run, at least — the effect of the Nasiri *rawk* was enormously to increase the power and income of the sultan.[16]

The above remarks apply to Egypt only. It is much less clear what happened in the Syrian provinces. A *rawk* was carried out in the Damascus province in 1313, in the Tripoli province in 1317 and in the Aleppo province in 1325.[17] As far as Egypt was concerned, not only did the chroniclers record in some detail how the *rawk* was carried out, but registers of *iqta's* from the late fourteenth and from the fifteenth centuries survive which shed a great deal of light on the aims and consequences of that *rawk*. Such information is not available for Syria. However, a royal edict issued in 1317 concerning taxation and administration in the province of Tripoli may well embody some of the conclusions of the survey conducted there earlier in the year. The edict ordered the abolition of miscellaneous taxes — such as those on coastal shipping, local festivities, salt and slaves. As in Egypt, *iqta's* based on fiscal sources other than landed taxes were abolished. The private prisons of emirs were abolished. Tighter control of the local Nusayri heretics was instituted. However, the edict gives no indication as to how *iqta's* were allocated after the survey, and we know even less about the other

Syrian *rawks*. All that can be said is that the *halqa* always held a relatively larger number of *iqta*'s in Syria than in Egypt, and that there is no evidence that the Nasiri *rawks* did anything to diminish the predominance of *halqa iqta*'s in Syria. As far as the Mamluk emirs were concerned, *iqta*'s in Syria were less esteemed and generally less valuable than those in Egypt. Transfer from, say, an emirate of the *tablakhana* (i.e. of forty) in Syria to an emirate of the *tablakhana* in Egypt was reckoned to be a promotion. Finally, the Aleppan *rawk* seems to have been made to coincide with an inspection of frontier defences and fortification.

The splendours of al-Nasir Muhammad ibn Qalawun's Sultanate were based on tight control of his subjects' affairs by the financial *diwan*s of the sultan. Under earlier sultans, financial administration had been dominated by the *na'ib al-saltana*, the *ustadar* and the vizier. This does not seem to have been the case in this period. Indeed, the post of *na'ib al-saltana* was left vacant from 1326 onwards.[18] Similarly, the post of vizier was suspended between 1314 and 1323 and again between 1331 and 1339.[19] Most of the financial responsibilities of these officials were transferred to the *nazir al-khass* (overseer of crown property). The *nazir al-khass* thus became the most powerful official under the sultan.[20] To some extent the enormous increase in power of the *nazir al-khass* may be attributed to the increase in the size of the sultan's *khass* estates as a result of the Nasiri *rawk*. However, the institution of this office and the appointment of Karim al-Din al-Kabir to the post in 1310 antedated the *rawk* and, moreover, the *nazir al-khass*'s responsibilities were not restricted solely or even mainly to estate management. Karim al-Din, a former Copt with a scribal background, was appointed to the office after he had advised the sultan to make the *matjar* (the state commercial office which dealt with commodities and operated monopolies on a large scale) royal property (*khass*), and its revenues were accordingly transferred from the state treasury to the sultan's private purse. Thanks to the labours of Karim al-Din and successors, the sultan became the greatest entrepreneur in his lands, engaging in import and export both in the Mediterranean and in the Red Sea, as well as grain sales, and sugar and textile production. Karim al-Din himself established offices in every town in Egypt and Syria for buying and selling and had merchants working for him in the Red Sea. In this manner he accumulated a private fortune (a thin line or no line at all divided state enterprise from the private enterprises of its officials).[21] State

intervention in private commerce became an even more pronounced feature of royal policy later under al-Nashu (another
former Copt) who was *nazir al-khass* from 1333 until 1338.
Al-Nashu instituted a form of *gabelle* in Egypt, known as *tarh*, by
which private merchants were forced to buy certain designated
commodities at artificially high prices from the sultan. Among those
commodities were cloth, wood, furs and iron.[22] *Pari passu* with the
ruthless promotion of royal enterprises went the harrying and closer
supervision of the sultan's rivals among the wealthy emirs. The
sugar presses of prosperous emirs were taxed and the rates at which
emirs could sell their grain were uncompetitively fixed. Additional
revenue was raised by closer scrutiny and heavier taxation of individuals to whom state enterprises (such as emerald mines or molasses
factories) had been farmed out, by taxing the inheritance of orphans,
by forcing merchants to accept debased coinage from the royal mints
at unrealistic rates and by other expedient innovations.

The Copts staffed most of the financial *diwan*s, and the heads of
those *diwan*s were normally recent converts from the Coptic faith.
For instance, Karim al-Din al-Kabir's nephew, Karim al-Din
al-Saghir, was *nazir al-dawla* (superintendent of the state treasury)
during the period when his uncle ran the royal treasury.
Additionally, he was overseer of the Karimi spice merchants and
the royal sugar factories.[23] Because of the nature of their jobs, such
men were not likely to be popular. When anti-Christian riots broke
out in Cairo and Alexandria in 1321 and there were rumours of
Christian arsonists, Karim al-Din al-Kabir interceded for his former
co-religionarists with the sultan.[24] On the other hand, perhaps the
unpopularity of such officials had contributed to the unpopularity of
the Coptic community. Karim al-Din, along with other functionaries and emirs engaged in making money, sought to insure his future
in various ways — he was, for instance, generous with presents to
emirs and their wives. Karim al-Din was also alleged to have money
deposited with European merchants in Egypt ready for a quick
getaway. Money could be protected from confiscation by making it
over as a *waqf* for the maintenance of a pious endowment while
stipulating that the stipendiaries of the pious establishment should
be one's relatives. However, such bequests could be and sometimes
were successfully challenged in the *qadi*s' courts. Money could
simply be hidden and indeed thesaurisation on a large scale may
well have been a factor in Egypt's and Syria's recurrent currency
crises.

Nevertheless, it was more or less inevitable that successful officials would be disgraced and that their visible wealth would be confiscated. These proceedings provided an important additional source of royal revenue, and were so much a matter of course that the confiscations may have been regarded as the sultan reappropriating wealth which had been made available to his servants for use. Such downfalls could be spectacular. In 1323 Karim al-Din al-Kabir was suddenly arrested and forced to sign a statement to the effect that all his wealth was the sultan's. A great deal of money was taken from him that year before he was sent into exile. The following year more money was squeezed out of him before he died. It was given out that he had hanged himself with his turban cloth, but many thought that he had been murdered by the state that he had served.[25] Taqi al-Din ibn Amin al-Mulk, the man who had instituted the Nasiri *rawk*, was suddenly disgraced in 1316. After the sultan had threatened him, Taqi al-Din took to his bed and died of fear.[26] His estate yielded disappointingly little. Al-Nashu, who had taken pains to live in apparent austerity, was seized in 1339 and died under torture, but not before immense sums had been produced from their places of concealment.[27] Perhaps such men were expendable, the sultan's dispensable agents. The *shadd al-dawawin*, a mamluk officer with financial responsibilities, generally conducted the investigation of disgraced officials, and torture was the favoured mode of investigation. However, members of the scribal class were not the only victims. Former favourites among the emirs were no less vulnerable. Almas the *hajib*, who had always taken pains to live austerely from fear of the sultan, was suddenly arrested in 1333. He was starved to death and after his demise found to have been a wealthy man.[28] After the death of Baktimur al-Saqi in suspicious circumstances in 1332 (poison from the hand of the sultan?), his immense wealth became royal property.[29] So did 360,000 gold dinars, 1,500,000 silver dirhams, cloth worth 640,000 dinars as well as livestock, houses, shops and land.[30] In such a way was wealth concentrated in the hands of a few favoured individuals and from there transferred into the hands of one individual.

Commerce and industry were generally left to the officials of the *diwan*, but al-Nasir Muhammad took a more direct interest in another area of state enterprise — the rearing of livestock. Horses were the sultan's great love. By the time of his death the sultan had 7,800 horses in the royal stables and pastures in and around Cairo.

He was prepared to pay as much for a good mare as he was for a beautiful mamluk in top condition (30,000 dinars). The sultan's amazing memory embraced the names of his horses and their pedigrees. He had the Maydan al-Mahari built for the rearing of colts and fillies. He and his court summered at Siryaqus, some way to the north-east of Cairo, where there was full scope for equestrian activities — *furusiyya* exercises, horse races, polo and hunting. The *amir akhur* (emir of the stables), previously an officer of little intrinsic significance, now became an important channel of access to the sultan, and the scope of his responsibilities was expanded to cover relations with the bedouin chiefs.[31] (In other regions bedouin affairs were normally dealt with by a mamluk officer known as the *mihmandar*.)[32]

Horses came from levies on the Arab tribes of Barqa (Western Libya) and Upper Egypt, but the best horses were hand-reared by the bedouin of the Fadl tribe in Syria. In the early years of his third reign the sultan's relations with the Banu Muhanna, the paramount clan within the Fadl, had been fraught. Their shaykh was accused of being an accomplice in the flight of Qarasunqur al-Mansuri to the Mongols and of having other dealings with the Mongols. Even so, the sultan's desire for their horses led to the channelling of large sums of money to the Banu Muhanna. On the other hand, the increased wealth of the Banu Mahanna and their confederates created political problems for al-Nasir Muhammad's successors. With the cult of the horse came the cult of the bedouin at the Mamluk court. The sultan's older sons – Anuk, Ibrahim and Ahmad – were sent to be educated in the bedouin environment of Kerak. Kerak became the Balmoral (or even the Gordonstoun) of the fourteenth-century Sultanate.[33]

It would be a serious mistake to consider the sultan's hippomania as pure extravagance and self-indulgence. Horses were a necessity for the army. Emirs of a hundred and emirs of forty received horses from the sultan twice a year, royal mamluks received horses from the sultan when they were emancipated and other emirs occasionally received them. Furthermore, though it is hard to think of the sultan's favourite brood mares ending up in the kitchens, horseflesh was eaten by the mamluks and – as on the Kipchak steppes — eaten on great occasions. At the wedding feast of Emir Qawsun to a daughter of the sultan, 50 horses were consumed. Horseflesh was similarly served at the wedding feast of Prince

Anuk. The wealthy Emir Bashtak al-Nasiri had 50 horses and sheep served at his table every day.[34] Mutton, however, was more normal fare for less wealthy mamluks.

Related to the sultan's passion for horses was his intense interest in sheep farming. He wished to improve the breed. Turkomans were encouraged to bring their herds from Syria to Egypt and there are indications that a great deal of *khass* land in Upper Egypt which had formerly been cultivated was now turned over to pasturage for sheep. A select flock was kept near Cairo for the sultan's inspection. This was something more than playing at being a gentleman farmer. At the time of his death the sultan's sheep numbered 30,000. Besides the profits from sales of wool, mutton was crucial for the provisioning of the mamluk army. The royal mamluks received a daily ration of meat. Additionally, it was the custom for the sultan to provide emirs, mamluks and civilian dignitaries with whole sheep to be sacrificed at the annual festival of the *'Id al-Adha*.[35] Shortfalls in the provision of sheep for both these purposes were to cause serious political disturbances later on in the Mamluk period. As it was, the sultan's concern to sponsor sheep farming paralleled the similar concerns of the Christian kings of Spain and Southern Italy in the same period.[36] Naturally the sultan also took an interest in the acquisition and cross-breeding of camels. The camels were important for the army, being used for the baggage train, and at the start of a major campaign every mamluk received a camel from the royal stables.

In every aspect of economic life the state's interests were apparent and indeed some enterprises required the initiative or at least the protection of the state for them to be feasible at all. The most obvious example of this was in the maintenance of the great canals and the improvement of major irrigation works. Work on the canals had implications not only for rural crop yield, but for the watering of orchards in and near the towns, for urban reclamation and for commercial transport. The Nile was Egypt's highway, especially for bulk commodities. Many European travellers in the Mamluk period comment on the crucial role of river boats in commercial transport. Alexandria, Egypt's most important port was in this period situated to the west of the westernmost of the arms of the Nile Delta. A canal was necessary to connect the port to the Nile and Alexandria's commercial prosperity was very vulnerable to the silting up. In 1311 major work was undertaken to maintain and improve this canal. In 1313 improvements to irrigation in the Giza area were made. In 1323 a new canal was dug to the west of old Cairo and some of the new land thus reclaimed, the Bulaq area, swiftly became Cairo's commercial port and a flourishing suburb in its own right.[37]

Motives of public good and private glory mingled in the architectural work undertaken in Cairo and elsewhere in this period. Al-Nasir Muhammad's reputation as an architectural patron would be even greater than it is today, if it were not for the fact that two of his greatest works — the Qasr al-Ablaq, or 'Striped Palace', within the citadel, and the 'New Mosque' — have since perished. Even so, it is apparent that his third reign was one of the most important architectural periods in Cairo's history, from the point of view of both aesthetics and of urban renewal. A large building programme was necessary, if only because of the great earthquake that had devastated much of Cairo in 1303. Beyond that, the Luq, Maqs and Bulaq areas on the edge of Cairo were settled with the encouragement of the sultan. The architecturally splendid City of the Dead grew up to the east of old Cairo. New souks were built. So were some 30 new mosques. A new aqueduct was constructed to provide Fustat with water. (Water that did not come from aqueducts came from the Nile on the backs of camels, a great source of street congestion.) Besides being a great builder in his own right, the sultan and the emir responsible for architecture (the *shadd al-'ama'ir*) took a hand in providing materials and designs for the mosques of favoured emirs — particularly of the sultan's sons-in-law.[38] The markets, shops and industries, constructed to provide incomes for the maintenance of pious *waqf* foundations, were of course generators of wealth in al-Nasir Muhammad's Cairo and Tankiz's Damascus.

It is far from certain whether Egypt's and Syria's prosperity in this period depended to any great extent on the profits of the transit trade from the Indies to Europe. The lives, property and commercial privileges of the Venetians trading in the Sultanate may have been protected by a commercial treaty negotiated earlier, in 1302. The Genoese do not seem to have been protected by any treaty at all. During al-Nasir Muhammad's third reign a series of embassies passed between the sultan and the kings of Aragon. However, their negotiations seem to have been at least as much concerned with the status of Christian shrines and pilgrims as they were with securing commercial privileges for Catalan merchants.[39] Moreover, commerce with Europe in this period was hampered on the Christian side by the attempts of the Papacy and Crusading powers to impose trade sanctions against the Sultanate. On the Muslim side it seems that the Karimi spice merchants may have regarded the Genoese and Venetian traders more as rivals than as customers. Such feelings seem to have lain behind the fierce outbreak of anti-Christian and anti-foreigner rioting that broke out in 1327. The Wali of Alexandria had to request reinforcements from Cairo to protect the foreign community.[40]

In order to circumvent the embargoes which were occasionally enforced by the republics of Genoa and Pisa, it was sometimes necessary to trade indirectly with Italy via Cyprus, and Cyprus's role in this covert trade may have been the reason for Karim al-Din al-Kabir's plan to expand and improve the harbour of Lattakia, shortly before his downfall.[41] Regular Venetian convoys to Alexandria and Beirut did not begin until some years after al-Nasir Muhammad's death.

Trade with the East, however, certainly was important and dictated al-Nasir Muhammad's diplomatic relations with Muhammad ibn Tughluq, the Sultan of Delhi, and with Rasulid Yemen.[42] There were 200 Karimi merchants, mostly specialising in trade through the Red Sea, in this period. The sultan relied on them for huge (and forced?) loans and in the reigns of his children the political influence of the Karimi merchants would increase.[43] Just as the state intervened in commerce, so merchants were active in politics and diplomacy. During the Alexandria disturbances a wealthy merchant who claimed to have an armed retinue of between 100 and 200 men offered to keep order there for the sultan. (His offer was rejected and he was eliminated.) A Genoese merchant in the service of al-Nasir was used in negotiations with the Mongols of the Crimea.[44] Majd al-Din al-Sallami, one of the Karimi merchant princes who traded on behalf of the sultan's *khass*, played a large part in the negotiations which led to the Treaty of Aleppo between the Sultanate and the Mongol Ilkhanate in 1322.[45]

From 1304 until 1316 Mongol Iran was ruled by Oljeitu Khudabanda, who resembled Donovan's 'Universal Soldier' in being by turns a Sunni Muslim, a Buddhist, a Christian and a Shamanist before settling for Shi'i Islam. In 1312, encouraged by the renegade Emir Qarasunqur, he attempted an invasion of Syria. The siege of Rahaba on the Euphrates proved bloody and difficult and Oljeitu was forced to withdraw after having failed to take it. It was to be the last attempt of the Mongols on Mamluk Syria.[46] Peace and security on the northern and eastern frontiers of the Sultanate go a long way to explaining the prosperity within it. There was no full-scale mobilisation of the Egyptian *halqa* between 1310 and 1340. In 1317 Abu Sa'id, who had declared himself a Sunni Muslim, succeeded Ilkhan Oljeitu. In 1321 Timurtash, the Mongol governor in Anatolia, rebelled against Abu Sa'id. It may have been this revolt which led the Ilkhan to send the Karimi merchant and slave trader Majd al-Din al-Sallami to propose peace to the Mamluk sultan in 1320. Al-Sallami went back to Iran in 1322 with Aytamish al-Muhammadi, one of the favoured Mongol mamluks, and a formal peace was negotiated. (It is not clear why modern historians refer to it as the Treaty of Aleppo.) Aytamish went on a second mission in 1326. However, relations in fact remained tense. Al-Nasir Muhammad toyed with the idea of helping the rebel Timurtash in Anatolia. Then in 1327 the defeated Timurtash took refuge in Cairo. It was not until the exchange of embassies in 1328 that peace could truly be seen to have been made. The land frontiers were opened to trade and the renegades Timurtash and Qarasunqur were executed by their respective hosts. Abu Sa'id's reign was turbulent and marked by other revolts.

Having ceased to be a military threat, Mongol Iran became a cultural influence upon the Sultanate. There were many channels of influence — *Wafidiyya,* mamluks of Mongol origin, immigrant Sufi groups from Iran and Iraq (such as the Qalandariyya and the Rifa'i), diplomatic missions and commerce. A few examples at random must suffice. Al-Nasir's mosque within the citadel is decorated with faience tiles in the Iranian manner. The spiral minarets of Qawsun's mosque were closely modelled on minarets seen in Tabriz during Aytamish's mission in 1322. A splendidly illuminated Koran executed for the Ilkhan Oljeitu and furnished with a Shi'ite litany ended up in a Sufi *khanqah* founded in Cairo by Baktimur al-Saqi. Ibn Taymiyya blamed the Mongols for introducing the vile practice of eating hashish to Syria. Ibn al-Dawadari, chronicler and grandson of a mamluk emir, interested himself in the mythological origins of the Mongols. Aytamish al-Muhammadi, one of the sultan's favourite emirs, was esteemed for his knowledge of Mongol genealogy and history and was alleged to have enforced the *yasa* (Mongol code of behaviour and discipline) upon the sultan's *khassaki* mamluks.

The fifteenth-century chroniclers al-Maqrizi and Ibn Taghribirdi were to claim that the Mongol *yasa* formed the basis of the code of justice enforced by the Mamluks, but as we have seen their evidence is not convincing and is not confirmed by earlier sources.[47] What does seem to be true, though, is that from this period onwards there was a steady encroachment upon *shari'a* justice by mamluk emirs empowered by the sultan to exercise *siyasa* justice (that is, justice based upon the independent discretion of the sultan). A milestone in this process was the temporary abolition of the office of *na'ib al-saltana* in 1327. The *na'ib* was replaced in some of his functions — in particular, the administration of *siyasa* justice — by the chief *hajib*. Sayf al-Din Almas, the first emir to hold the newly upgraded post, seems to have been ill-fitted to exercise justice over the sultan's Muslim subjects. He knew no Arabic and was later accused of homosexual rape as well as other crimes.[48] Later on in the fourteenth century the power to exercise independent justice would be further devolved to the tribunals of other emirs to the discontent of the *'ulama'*.

Al-Nasir Muhammad's third reign was relatively peaceful on other fronts besides the Mongol one. The Mamluks retained a formal suzerainty over the Hejaz, ruling through the Sharifs in Mecca and Medina. The pretensions of Ilkhan Oljeitu and the Rasulid sultans of the Yemen to some sort of symbolic presence in the Hejaz were successfully resisted. Aytamish al-Muhammadi was sent with an army to bring to an end feuding between members of the Sharifian families. Minor expeditions were sent to intervene in the turbulent affairs of the Yemen in 1315, 1322 and in 1331. The Mamluk sultans claimed ultimate overlordship of the Yemen, a claim which the Rasulids were prepared to accept only sometimes.[49]

The Christian kingdom of Cilician Armenia had agreed to pay the Mamluks an annual tribute of half a million dirhems in 1297 during the reign of Lajin. In 1315 al-Nasir Muhammad was successful in getting this payment doubled. However, there were repeated defaults and these led to Mamluk punitive expeditions in 1320, 1322, 1335 and 1337. The 1332 expedition briefly occupied the major commercial port, Ayas, and added 50 per cent of its customs revenues to the tribute. The 1337 expedition occupied and then devastated the Armenian capital of Sis, but Cilician Armenia was not to be finally conquered until 1375.[50] Mamluk expeditionary forces entered Nubia in 1315–16 and 1323, but here again there seems to have been no intention of permanently occupying territory. Indeed, the turbulence of the Arabs in the south of Upper Egypt would have made any permanent Mamluk presence in Nubia difficult to supply and reinforce. Only the Red Sea port of Aydhab had a *wali* and a garrison to protect it from the bedouin.[51]

In 1340 the sultan fell ill and his condition slowly deteriorated. It is probable that the downfall of those overmighty subjects Tankiz and Nashu should be seen in the context of the sultan's concern to secure the succession for his son, Sayf al-Din Abu Bakr. Baktimur al-Saqi, the man who might have been expected to dominate the reign of the next sultan, conveniently (too conveniently?) died in 1332. Still Tankiz was more powerful in Syria than Baktimur had ever been in Egypt. There had been a number of issues over which the sultan and Tankiz had clashed in the last years of the reign — Tankiz's fierce treatment of Christians accused of arson, his interception of correspondence from Cilician Armenia, his reluctance to allow his sons to be betrothed to the sultan's daughters. The real fear must have been, though, that when the sultan died Tankiz would lead Syria in revolt. So Tankiz was arrested, tortured and killed in July 1340. Al-Nashu, the *nazir al-khass*, had always had enemies, but Tankiz had been one of the most powerful spokesmen on his behalf. Al-Nashu's downfall followed swiftly upon that of Tankiz and his end was similarly painful.

Al-Nasir Muhammad died in 1341. He emerges from contemporary accounts as a man possessed of an amazing memory. It embraced not only the genealogies of his stud horses but the names of his mamluks and scribes and the details of pay slips. He was always ready to immerse himself in the details of administration. He was pious and austere in observing the prescriptions of Islam, flamboyant and extravagant where no such constraints applied. He exercised intelligence in choosing the men who served him, but was capricious and a little paranoid in his treatment of those he had chosen. He was certainly one of the greatest Mamluk sultans; he was perhaps one of the nastiest.

Notes

1. Al-Maqrizi, *al-Mawa'iz wa'l-i'tibar fi dhikr al-Khitat-wa'l-athar* (Cairo, Bulaq ed., 1853), vol.2, pp.380–81.

2. The chief published sources for the third reign of al-Nasir Muhammad are Abu'l-Fida, *al-Mukhtasar fi Akhbar al-Bashar*, vol.4 (Istanbul, 1869–70) (translated for this period by P. M. Holt as *The Memoirs of a Syrian Prince* (Wiesbaden, 1983); Ibn al-Suqa'i, *Tali Kitab Wafayat al A'yan*, J. Sublet (trans. and ed.) (Damascus, 1974); Ibn al-Dawadari, *Kanz al-Durar*, vol.9, H. R. Roemer (ed.) (Cairo, 1960); Mufaddal Ibn Abi Fada'il, 'Histoire des sultans mamlouks', E. Blochet (ed. and

trans.) in *Patrologia Orientalis*, vol.20 (1929), continued by S. Kortantamer (trans. and ed.) as *Ägypten und Syrien zwischen 1317 und 1341 in der Chronik des Mufaddal b. Abi l-Fada'il* (Feiburg im Breisgau, 1973); Baktash al-Fakhri in *Beitrage zur Geschichte der Mamlukensultane*, K. V. Zettersteen (ed.) (Leiden, 1919), pp.145–249; al-Shuja'i, *Die Chronik as-Suga'is*, vol.1, B. Schäfer (ed.) (Wiesbaden, 1977); al-Maqrizi, *Kitab al-Suluk*, vol.2, pts 1 and 2, M. M. Ziada (ed.) (Cairo, 1941–2); Ibn Taghribirdi, *al-Nujum al-Zahira*, vol.9 (Cairo, n.d.). See also D. P. Little, 'An Analysis of the Relation between Four Mamluk Chronicles', *Journal of Semitic Studies*, vol.19 (1974), pp.252–68; Little, 'The Recovery of a Lost Source for Bahri Mamluk History: al-Yusufi's Nuzhat al-Nasir fi Sirat al-Malik al-Nasir', *JAOS*, vol.94 (1974), pp.42–54; H. N. al-Hajji, *The Internal Affairs in Egypt during the Third Reign of Sultan al-Nasir Muhammad* (Kuwait, 1978), should only be used with caution.

3. Ibn Taghribirdi, *al-Nujum al-Zahira*, vol.8 (Cairo, 1939), p.236.

4. Maqrizi, *Suluk*, vol.2, pt.1, p.77.

5. Ibn al-Dawadari, *Kanz*, vol.9, pp.208–13; Baktash al-Fakhri in *Beitrage*, pp.153–6; Maqrizi, *Suluk*, vol.2, pt. 1, pp.89–94. See also al-Hajji, *Internal Affairs*, pp.74–9 for further references.

6. D. P. Little, *An Introduction to Mamluk Historiography* (Wiesbaden, 1970) p. 101–21.

7. Al-Safadi, *al-Wafi bi al-Wafayat*, vol.8 (Istanbul and Wiesbaden, 1931–), pp.358–60; Ibn Hajar al-Asqalani, *al-Durar al-Kamina*, vol.1 (Hyderabad, 1929–32), pp.351–2; Ibn Taghribirdi, *Nujum*, vol.9, pp.288–9; H. Laoust, 'Le Hanbalisme sous les Mamlouks Bahrides (658-784/1260–1382)', *REI*, vol.28 (1960), p.27.

8. E. Ashtor, 'Études sur quelques chroniques mamloukes', *Israel Oriental Studies* (1971), pp.273–6; Little, *Introduction*, pp.4–10.

9. I. M. Lapidus, *Muslim Cities in the Later Middle Ages* (Cambridge, Mass. 1967), pp.22, 70, 75, 262–3n.

10. Ibn Hajar, *Durar*, vol.1, p.477, vol.3, p.357.

11. Maqrizi, *al-Khitat*, vol.1, p.95, vol.2, p.218; Maqrizi, *Suluk*, vol.2, pt.2, pp.524–5; Ibn Taghribirdi, *Nujum*, vol.9, p.166.

12. Ibn Taghribirdi, *Nujum*, vol.10, pp.43–4; D. Ayalon, 'The Wafidiyya in the Mamluk Kingdom', *Islamic Culture*, vol.25 (1951), p.93; H. Laoust, *Essai sur les doctrines sociales et politiques de Taki-d-din Ahmad b. Taimiya (1262–1328)* (Cairo, 1939), pp.478–9 and n.

13. Maqrizi, *Suluk*, vol.2, pt.2, p.536; A. 'Abd al-Raziq, *La Femme au temps des Mamelouks en Égypte* (Cairo, 1973), pp.269–302 (*passim*).

14. 'Abd al-Raziq, *La Femme*, pp.298–9.

15. D. Ayalon, 'The Eunuchs in the Mamluk Sultanate' in M. Rosen-Ayalon (ed.), *Studies in Memory of Gaston Wiet* (Jerusalem, 1977), pp.283, 288–9.

16. This account of the *rawk* is chiefly based on H. Halm, *Ägypten nach den mamlukischen Lehensregistern*, vol.1 (Wiesbaden, 1979), pp.24–9. See also D. Ayalon, 'Studies on the Structure of the Mamluk Army' (part 2), *BSOAS*, vol.15 (1953), pp.452–3; H. Rabie, *The Financial System of Egypt A. H. 564–74/A.D. 1169–1341* (London, 1972), pp.53–6.

17. On the Syrian *rawks*, see Maqrizi, *Suluk*, vol.2, pt.1, pp.127, 264; H. Rabie, *Financial System*, p.53n.; A. N. Poliak, *Feudalism in Egypt, Syria, Palestine and the Lebanon 1250–1900* (London, 1939), pp.24–5; U. Vermeulen, 'Some Remarks on a Rescript of al-Nasir Muhammad B. Qala'un on the Abolition of Taxes and the Nusayris (Mamlaka of Tripoli) 717/1317', *Orientalia Lovaniensa Periodica*, vol.1, (1970), pp.195–201.

18. Ibn Taghribirdi, *Nujum*, vol.9, p.174.

19. A. 'Abd al-Raziq, 'Le Vizirat et les vizirs d'Egypte au temps des Mamluks',

Annales Islamologiques, vol.16 (1980), pp.198–9; Rabie, *Financial System,* p.142.

20. Rabie, *Financial System,* pp.143–4.

21. S. Y. Labib, *Handelsgeschichte Ägyptens im Spätmittelalter* (Wiesbaden, 1964), p.67n.; Rabie, *Financial System,* p.94; E. Ashtor, *Levant Trade in the Later Middle Ages* (Princeton, 1983), p.274; *EI(2) sv* 'Ibn Sadid'.

22. Labib, *Handelsgeschichte,* pp.186–92; Lapidus, *Muslim Cities,* p.56; Rabie, *Financial System,* p.82.

23. *EI(2) sv* 'Ibn Sadid'.

24. On the riots in Alexandria, see Ibn Battuta, *The Travels of Ibn Battuta,* vol.1 (Cambridge, 1958), pp.27–8; Labib, *Handelsgeschichte,* pp.229–33.

25. Kortantamer, *Ägypten und Syrien,* pp.98–9.

26. Maqrizi, *Suluk,* vol.2, pt.1, p.169.

27. Ibn Hajar, *Durar,* vol.2, pp.429–30.

28. Al-Safadi, *al-Wafi,* vol.9, pp.370–1.

29. Ibn Battuta, *Travels,* vol.1, p.53, vol.2, pp.53–4; Maqrizi, *Suluk,* vol.2, pt.2, pp.364–5; Little, 'The Recovery of a Lost Source', pp.49–50, 53–4.

30. Lapidus, *Muslim Cities,* p.50.

31. Maqrizi, *Khitat,* vol.2, pp.199–201; Ibn Taghribirdi, *Nujum,* vol.7, pp.167–70; D. Ayalon, 'The System of Payment in Mamluk Military Society' (part 2), *JESHO,* vol.1 (1957–8), pp.264–6.

32. M. A. Hiyari, 'The Origins and Development of the Amirate of the Arabs during the Seventh/Thirteenth and Eighth/Fourteenth Centuries', *BSOAS,* vol.38 (1975), p.521–2.

33. Ayalon, 'The Eunuchs', pp.292–3.

34. On Mamluk consumption of horseflesh, see Maqrizi, *Suluk,* vol.2, p.288; Ibn Taghribirdi, *Nujum,* vol.10, p.74.

35. Ayalon, 'The System of Payment' (part 2), pp.258–61; J.-C. Garcin, *Un Centre Musulman de la haute Egypte medievale: Qus* (Cairo, 1976), p.236.

36. See, for instance, N. J. G. Pounds, *An Economic History of Medieval Europe* (London, 1974), pp.206–7.

37. H. Rabie, 'Some Technical Aspects of Agriculture in Medieval Egypt' in A. L. Udovitch (ed.), *The Islamic Middle East, 700–1900: Studies in Economic and Social History* (Princeton, 1981), pp.60–2; T. Sato, 'Irrigation in Rural Egypt from the 12th to the 14th Centuries', *Orient,* vol.8 (1972), pp.81–92.

38. V. Meinecke-Berg, 'Quellen zu Topographie und Baugeschichte in Kairo unter Sultan an-Nasir b. Qala'un', *Zeitschrift fur Deutsches Morgenlandisches Gesellschaft,* supp.3 (XIX Deutscher Orientalistentag, 1975), 1977, pp.538–50.

39. On trade with Europe in the early fourteenth century, see F. Gabrieli, 'Venezia e i Mamelucchi' in A. Pertusi (ed.), *Venezia e l'Oriente fra tardo Medioevo e Rinascimento* (Venice, 1966), pp.421–2; S. Y. Labib, *Handelsgeschichte,* pp.75–80; Ashtor, *Levant Trade,* pp.17–63.

40. Ibn Battuta, *Travels,* vol.1, pp.27–8; Labib, *Handelsgeschichte,* pp.229–33; A. Salim, *Tarikh al-Iskandariyya wa hadarataha* (Alexandria, 1982), pp.229–31; Ashtor, *Levant Trade,* pp.52–4.

41. Labib, *Handelsgeschichte,* p.67n.

42. S. Digby, 'The Maritime Trade of India, in T. Raychaudhuri and I. Habib (eds), *The Cambridge Economic History of India,* vol.1 (Cambridge, 1982), pp.146, 156; Labib, *Handelsgeschichte,* pp.82–4, 89–94.

43. E. Ashtor, 'The Karimi Merchants', *JRAS* (1956), pp.45–56; Ashtor, *A Social and Economic History of the Near East in the Middle Ages* (London, 1976), pp.300–1; Labib, *Handelsgeschichte,* pp.112–18; Lapidus, *Muslim Cities,* pp.121–2, 125–6.

44. Labib, *Handelsgeschichte,* p.76.

45. Kortantamer, *Ägypten und Syrien,* p.74 and n., p.81; D. Ayalon, *L'Esclavage du Mamelouk* (Jerusalem, 1951), p.3; Labib, *Handelsgeschichte,* pp.71–2; J. M.

Rogers, 'Evidence for Mamluk-Mongol Relations 1260–1360' in *Colloque International sur l'Histoire du Caire* (Cairo, 1974), p.399.

46. J. A. Boyle, 'Dynastic and Political History of the Ilkhans' in J. A. Boyle (ed.), *The Cambridge History of Iran*, vol.5 (Cambridge, 1968), pp.397–413; Labib, *Handelsgeschichte*, pp.71–2; D. P. Little, 'Notes on Aitamis, A Mongol Mamluk' in U. Haarmann and P. Bachmann (eds), *Die islamische Welt zwischen Mittelalter und Neuzeit: Festschrift fur Hans Robert Roemer zum 65 Geburstag* (Beirut, 1979), pp.390, 395–7; Rogers, 'Evidence for Mamluk-Mongol Relations', pp.385–6, 388, 399.

47. On the cultural influence of the Mongols on the Mamluks, see D. Ayalon, 'The Great Yasa of Chingiz Khan: A Re-examination', *SI*, vol.33 (1971), pp.97–140, vol.34 (1971), pp.151–80, vol.36 (1972), pp.113–58, vol.38 (1973), pp.107–56; Little, 'Notes on Aitamis', pp.387–401; Little, 'The Founding of Sultaniyya: A Mamluk Version', *Iran*, vol.16 (1978), pp.170–5; Rogers, 'Evidence for Mongol-Mamluk Relations', pp.385–404.

48. On Almas, see Safadi, *Wafi*, vol.9 (1974), pp.370–1; Ibn Taghribirdi, *Nujum*, vol.9, pp.108–9, 301–2.

49. J. Jomier, *Le Mahmal et la caravane des pèlerins de la Mecque XIII-XX siècles* (Cairo, 1953), pp.44–5; Labib, *Handelsgeschichte*, pp.87–90; D. P. Little, 'The History of Arabia during the Bahri Mamluk Period According to Three Mamluk Historians' in *Studies in the History of Arabia*, vol.1, *Sources for the History of Arabia*, pt.2 (Riyad, 1979), pp.17–23; *EI(1) sv* 'Mecca'.

50. *EI(2) sv* 'Cilicia'.

51. Y. F. Hasan, *The Arabs and the Sudan* (Khartoum, 1973), pp.76–9, 118, 120.

7 THE QALAWUNID EPIGONES, 1341–82

The death of al-Nasir Muhammad ibn Qalawun ushered in a renewed period of turbulence. This time the turbulence was more prolonged and this time the struggle to control the throne coincided with severe social and economic problems in Egypt and Syria. Whether the social and economic problems should be blamed on the political instability is of course another matter. Study of this confused epoch is complicated by the difficulty in determining who really exercised the powers of the Sultanate. Not all of al-Nasir Muhammad's descendants were degenerates or minors – putty in the hands of powerful emirs — but plainly in cases where that was so, it would be necessary to identify the background and intentions of the emirs and, since abrupt switches in policy resulted from the frequent coups and murders at the top, it is difficult to find a narrative thread that will make sense of it all.[1]

For over 40 years after the death of al-Nasir Muhammad, the Sultanate was to be ruled by his children and grandchildren and governed by his Nasiri emirs. When earlier, in 1326, Ibn Battuta, the North African globe-trotter, had visited Cairo, he listed those favourite emirs of the sultan whom he understood to be most important in Egypt: Baktimur al-Saqi, Arghun al-Dawadar, Mughultay al-Jamali, Tashtimur al-Badri, Badr al-Din Jankali ibn al-Baba, Jamal al-Din Aqush al-Ashrafi, Tuquzdamur al-Nasiri, Bahadur al-Hijazi, Qawsun and Bashtak.[2] Of the ten emirs listed, the first three died during al-Nasir Muhammad's reign. The remaining seven had a dominant role in the politicking and civil strife of the years immediately after the sultan's death. But by 1345 (when Tuquzdamur died in disgrace) all of the remaining seven were dead and most of them had died violently. In other words, the events of the first four or five years after al-Nasir Muhammad's death were dominated by the feuds of small groups of senior Nasiri emirs who had grown wealthy in peacetime. Thereafter, another group of Nasiri emirs — on the whole, younger than the first — took over. The feuding in the years 1341–5 was something of a family affair. Emir Tuquzdamur's daughters married Sultans al-Mansur Abu Bakr, al-Salih Ismail and al-Kamil Sha'ban. Bashtak and Qawsun both married daughters of al-Nasir Muhammad, as did

Maliktimur al-Hijazi, a younger emir who was to become an intimate drinking companion of al-Mansur Abu Bakr.[3]

By now Egypt and Syria had experienced some 30 years of freedom from civil strife and no one questioned the rights of the descendants of Qalawun to the throne. Therefore the succession to the throne in 1341 should not have been contentious, but it was. Al-Nasir Muhammad's favourite son, Anuk, had been groomed to succeed to the throne; he, however, had died in 1339. Al-Nasir Muhammad had passed over the next oldest of his sons, Ahmad, as too capricious and frivolous to become sultan and chosen instead Abu Bakr as his successor. Though there was hardly a rule of primogeniture for succession to the Mamluk throne, the exclusion of Ahmad from inheritance gave ambitious emirs opportunities for intrigue. Secondly, although after the convenient death of Baktimur al-Saqi in 1332, that overmighty emir's enormous wealth had been confiscated by the sultan, most of it had been subsequently redistributed. The royal favourites Bashtak and Qawsun were the chief beneficiaries and together they were as dangerously overmighty as Baktimur had ever been. Bashtak had, with the sultan's complaisance, acquired most of Baktimur's *iqta*'s and his right to exercise *himaya* in Sharqiyya (the Eastern Delta province) as well as Baktimur's palace, stable, widow and favourite slave girl. Bashtak's *iqta*'s were estimated to be worth 100,000 dinars a year. Qawsun was similarly wealthy and was able to purchase the palace of Baysari (the richest emir at the end of the thirteenth and beginning of the fourteenth centuries). Qawsun was one of the great sugar industrialists of the age; indeed, following his death and the plundering of his palace by the mob, the exchange value of gold in relation to silver fell on the Cairo markets. Both Bashtak and Qawsun had manipulated the grain market in the 1330s.[4]

After the death of al-Nasir Muhammad these two men manoeuvred for ascendancy over the new sultan, al-Mansur Abu Bakr (1341). Bashtak was handsome and flamboyant, but also notorious as a rake; neither was he liked for his pomposity and arrogance (although he could speak Arabic perfectly well, he insisted on addressing his servants in Turkish, making use of an interpreter). Bashtak was also known to have previously favoured the succession of the older son, Ahmad. This weakened his position against Qawsun and he was swiftly imprisoned and killed. In the meantime the sultan — who was 20 years old and competent and popular enough — intrigued to free himself from the tutelage of

Qawsun, who had been appointed his *atabak*. However, Qawsun was in a strong position after the removal of Bashtak. Though his rank was formally that of emir of one hundred (mamluks), his wealth allowed him to keep 700 mamluks in his employ. Two months after the accession of al-Mansur Abu Bakr, Qawsun went up to the citadel and arrested the sultan. Abu Bakr's *na'ib al-saltana* and father-in-law, the gentle and pious Emir Tuquzdamur, was powerless to protect him. The other emirs were astounded by Qawsun's effrontery. In time they would all get used to this kind of thing. Abu Bakr was formally deposed and sent to Upper Egypt where he was murdered soon after.

Qawsun then produced another brother, Kuchuk, from the harem. Kuchuk means 'little' in Turkish, and this prince was in fact only seven years old. Al-Ashraf Kuchuk's accession was of course required to rubber stamp Qawsun's war of elimination against his rivals among the powerful emirs. Yet, though he was largely successful in securing the key positions in Egypt, he was unable to secure the assent of all the Syrian *na'ibs* to his *de facto* rule. From the 1340s onwards the governors of Syria played an increasingly large part in determining who should rule in Cairo. This was especially true of the *na'ibs* of Aleppo. Damascus was still probably the largest city in Syria and seat of the senior Syrian governor, but Aleppo was growing rapidly in importance. In part, this was due to the growth in the overland trade which resulted from the opening of the frontiers between the Ilkhanate and the Mamluk Sultanate in the 1320s. In part, the growing power of the Na'ib of Aleppo was due to the increased strategic role of Aleppo in meeting the growing threat from the Turkoman principalities in Anatolia and Iraq.[5]

In any event it was Tashtimur al-Badri, the Na'ib of Aleppo, who was first to proclaim his opposition to Qawsun and his puppet. Having done so, he withdrew from Aleppo and, taking a large part of the Aleppan army with him, found refuge with Eretna (a former lieutenant of the Mongols who had established himself in an independent principality in the region of Sivas in Eastern Turkey). Tashtimur's nickname, Himmis Akhdar, referred to his fondness for the lower-class dish of green chickpeas. Tashtimur had been a popular emir in Cairo. According to Ibn Battuta, he used to distribute alms lavishly to the *harafish* beggars of Cairo, so that, although he was twice imprisoned by al-Nasir Muhammad, the *harafish* successfully rioted to secure his release.[6]

The other threat to Qawsun's regime was the continued liberty and independence of Ahmad, the oldest of al-Nasir Muhammad's surviving sons. Ahmad's residence in the fortified palace of Kerak and his command of the loyalty of the local bedouin population allowed him to defy Qawsun's authority. Qawsun sent an army out of Egypt to besiege Kerak. Unwisely he chose Emir Qutlubugha al-Fakhri to command that army. Qutlubugha was extremely fond of green chickpeas: not only that, but he and Tashtimur al-Badri were old friends and comrades-in-arms. (Tashtimur was reputed to be the brains of the pair, while Qutlubugha's wildness and outspokenness gained him the reputation of being *majnun* — mad.) No sooner had Qutlubugha led his army out of Egypt than he proclaimed his allegiance to Ahmad at Kerak. Tashtimur began to make his way back from the Eretnid lands and the other Syrian governors, headed by Altunbugha al-Hajib, the man who had replaced Tankiz as Na'ib of Damascus, joined their cause. In Cairo Yalbugha al-Yahyawi, another of al-Nasir Muhammad's favourites, also declared his support for the revolt. A conspiracy of emirs culminated in the arrest of Qawsun and the deposing of his puppet. Qawsun was strangled in prison, while Kuchuk was sent back to the harem. Al-Ashraf Kuchuk's reign had lasted five months.

Ahmad was now acclaimed sultan and took the regnal name al-Nasir. His reign began and ended in the year 1342. It began with widespread support among the elite of the emirs and indeed Ahmad was linked by marriage to two of them: he had married a daughter of Emir Tayarbugha, while his mother, Bayad, a former singing girl in the harem of his father, was now married to Emir Maliktimur al-Sirjawi. However, it seems that al-Nasir Ahmad did not wish to feel beholden to those who had restored him to his birthright, nor did he wish to govern the Mamluk empire from Cairo. In fact Tashtimur and his allies demanded a great deal as a reward for placing al-Nasir Ahmad on the throne, and it seems that Tashtimur wished to use Ahmad as his puppet, just as Qawsun had used Abu Bakr. Though Ahmad came to Cairo to be installed as the new Sultan al-Nasir, he stayed there less than two months. Conflicts rapidly developed between the sultan and his kingmaker, in particular over the resources of the defeated Emir Qawsun. Tashtimur appropriated much of Qawsun's former wealth, including some sugar and molasses factories. Al-Nasir Ahmad, as a counter-measure, took over Qawsun's mamluks and brought them into the citadel, making them royal mamluks and rewarding them with *halqa iqta*'s. Tashtimur tried to deny other emirs access to the citadel. Al-Nasir Ahmad, with the backing of the eunuch commander of the royal mamluks and some of the Nasiri emirs, was successful in arresting Tashtimur and his chief ally, Qutlubugha al-Fakhri.

Soon afterwards al-Nasir Ahmad set out for Kerak, taking with him not only his prisoners, but also the royal treasury, the royal insignia and the vast flocks of sheep that had belonged to his father and to Qawsun, as well as cattle, horses and camels. He proposed to govern the Mamluk empire from Kerak, where he could be free from the pressure of mamluk factions. Though he set off from Cairo with a huge escort of emirs and royal mamluks, he discharged most of them en route. The only officials he took with him into Kerak were the chief financial official Jamal al-Kufat, *nazir al-khass* and *nazir al-jaysh*, and 'Ala al-Din 'Ali ibn Fadlallah, *katib al-sirr* (head of the chancery). Egypt was entrusted to a *na'ib al-ghayba*, the caliph was sent to Jerusalem and a large section of the royal mamluks was sent to Hebron and then to Gaza. In Kerak al-Nasir Ahmad was served and defended by the locals, who seem to have been mostly Christian Arabs. Ahmad's father had frequently sojourned at Kerak. The place was strongly fortified and strategically located between Egypt, Syria and the Hejaz. Ahmad's attempt to relocate the centre of government had a certain amount to be said for it, but of course he could never expect to get the assent of the Egyptian emirs to the move. There was some fruitless correspondence between Cairo and Kerak in which, among other things, Ahmad asked for supplies to be sent from Upper Egypt, apparently unaware that a bedouin revolt had broken out there. Unpleasant rumours reached Egypt about Ahmad's dissipations and his passion for all things Arab — including Arab boys. When the Egyptian emirs learnt of the execution of Tashtimur and Qutlubugha at Kerak they declared Ahmad deposed. During a reign which had lasted little over three months, al-Nasir Ahmad had succeeded in doing a great deal of damage to the Sultanate. In the summer of 1342 a half-brother, Isma'il, was installed as sultan and took the regnal name al-Salih. At 17 he was some seven years younger than his brother Ahmad, but still mature enough to govern.

The emirs took an oath to al-Salih Isma'il and al-Salih Isma'il took an oath to them. They promised to be loyal and he promised not to arrest or injure them. (This sort of reciprocal oath had also been sworn on the accessions of Baybars I and Lajin.) Inevitably, this was an oath which was to be repeatedly broken — most notably a year later when the *na'ib al-saltana*, Aqsunqur al-Sallari, was deposed. Allegedly this was because the viceregent had been exercising his functions too indulgently, but probably it was to make way for the sultan's stepfather, Arghun al-Ala'i. However, al-Salih Isma'il does seem to have paid greater attention to the consensus of his emirs than had his predecessors. Emirs did not die under torture and the shortness of al-Salih Isma'il's reign (1342–5) was due to death from natural causes, not political unpopularity. Like his father Isma'il combined intense piety and austerity with extravagance and an inordinate fondness for women. Al-Salih Isma'il was accustomed to ride out with an escort of 200 concubines dressed in precious silks. One of his great pleasures was to pick teams from his concubines to play polo against one another.

The wives, concubines and eunuchs of the harem were alleged to exercise influence on political decisions in the 1340s and 1350s. Arab chroniclers are somewhat reticent on the topic, but one woman in particular, Ittifaq, seems to have been the Lola Montez of her age. Ittifaq had begun her career as one of the black concubines and singers in the harem of al-Nasir Muhammad. Subsequently, she married three Mamluk sultans — al-Salih Isma'il, al-Kamil Sha'ban and al-Muzaffar Hajji — then a Mamluk vizier and finally a Merinid sultan.[7] The chief eunuch also became more influential than ever in al-Salih Isma'il's reign. 'Anbar al-Sahrati had been tutor to the young Isma'il. Now he used his influence to advance the interests of the court eunuchs in general and his own interests in particular. He acquired eunuchs, mamluks and trading offices.

Al-Salih Isma'il seems to have been able to indulge the harem despite the fact that he was very short of funds at the beginning of the reign. It had been necessary to consolidate his accession by a generous distribution of offices and largesse. More important, al-Nasir Ahmad had taken most of his father's treasury with him to Kerak. It took no less than eight expeditions before Kerak was captured and Ahmad executed in 1344. Al-Salih Isma'il had had to depend on funds exacted from Persian merchants to finance the final successful expedition. It may have been the sultan's financial straits which led him to look favourably on a Venetian embassy which arrived in the same year. New commercial privileges, more favourable than those which had been granted in the last commercial treaty of 1302, were granted by al-Salih Isma'il to the Venetians in 1345. From 1345 onwards annual convoys, eventually

numbering as many as ten galleys, started arriving in Alexandria.
(The numbers of galleys may not sound very great, but of course the
Venetians came mainly to purchase low-bulk, high-value spices.)[8]
The Venetians for their part were now very keen to trade with Egypt
and Syria, since political changes in the Black Sea region had made
it difficult for them to trade there. Since the fall of Acre in 1291
there had been relatively little trade between the Western
commercial powers and the Sultanate. In part this had been due to
papal embargoes against trade with the Mamluks and in part due to
the rival attractions of markets in Cilician Armenia, Turkey,
Byzantium and the Black Sea region. Venice's overtures now
signalled a relaxation in papal attitudes and a shift in Mediterranean
trading patterns. One by one Venice's commercial rivals followed
its example. In time the concessions granted to Christian traders
would become more generous and the immunities offered to
communities of European merchants resident in the Sultanate
would become more all-inclusive, and the extension of such
concessions and immunities would prove in the long term to be
fraught with unwelcome consequences for the Islamic regimes in the
Eastern Mediterranean.[9]

During the 1340s there was a rapid turnover of sultans and emirs
in power. The damaging effects of this on the government were to
some extent mitigated by the relatively longer tenures of civilian
officials in the administration. For example, Jamal al-Kufat had
been appointed *nazir al-khass* to succeed his relative, al-Nashu,
after the latter's downfall in the reign of al-Nashir Muhammad. He
continued to hold this office under the next four sultans and added
to it the offices of *nazir al-jaysh* (superintendent of army finances)
and *nazir al-dawla* (superintendent of state finances). He thus
enjoyed unprecedented control over the finances of the Sultanate
and was only divested of office and tortured to death in 1344.[10]

A similar observation applies to the chancery. In the late
thirteenth century the chancery, and especially its senior post, that
of *katib al-sirr*, had been dominated by the Banu 'Abd al-Zahir and
their relatives and allies. In the early fourteenth century the Banu
Fadlallah acquired a similarly commanding position over the
chancery. Like the Banu 'Abd al-Zahir, the Banu Fadlallah were a
cultured clan of Muslim Arabs. Though there were Copts and
musalima in the chancery they never acquired the ascendance over it
which they had over the financial *diwan*s. They may have been
excluded from the top chancery posts because these involved

negotiating with and spying on Christian powers, as well as the taking of oaths on treaties. 'Ala al-Din 'Ali ibn Fadlallah succeeded his father as *katib al-sirr* in the reign of al-Nasir Muhammad and after the latter's death he continued in office under the next ten sultans, dying in office in 1368.[11]

To take a third and final example, the young royal mamluks in the barracks of the Cairo Citadel were by convention instructed and officered by eunuchs. The *muqaddam al-sultaniyya* was almost invariably a eunuch. 'Anbar al-Sahrati held this office for much of al-Nasir Muhammad's reign, and he served the next four sultans in the same post, reaching the apogee of his power under al-Salih Isma'il (whose tutor he had been). 'Anbar dealt in property and commerce and his wealth was such that he built a polo *maydan* for his private use.[12] The power of such eunuchs was based as much on their influence over the royal mamluks as it was on their access to the royal harem.

However, the power of the eunuchs and the harem should not be exaggerated. They were obvious targets for *'ulama'* looking for signs of the decay of the age. Their influence was for the most part confined to palace and family affairs. 'Anbar al-Sahrati's power was exceptional and was based on his command of the royal mamluks. In this decade as in others ultimate power was based on alliances among the princes, emirs and royal mamluks.

A distinctive feature of this period is the huge number of unemancipated Nasiri mamluks in Cairo, to which each of al-Nasir Muhammad's successors added his own quota. For some time after the break-up of the retinues of Bashtak and Qawsun, no emir had a retinue anywhere near the size of the corps of royal mamluks. Additionally, many of the mamluks of defeated and disgraced emirs, such as Qawsun, were taken into the ranks of the royal mamluks. Such mamluks were known as *sayfi*s. The influx of *sayfi*s increased the number of royal mamluks, but diminished their discipline, for the cohesive blocs of new entrants formed factions in the barracks which aimed at controlling rather than serving their royal masters. It is also true that while the Nasiri mamluks were loyal to the House of Qalawun, they were not loyal to any particular one of his descendants. We find young sultans and their 'protectors' among the powerful emirs paying for the loyalty of sections of the Nasiri mamluks by promoting them to emirates or by giving them *halqa iqta*'s even before they had been emancipated. The younger sons of al-Nasir Muhammad had been educated for pleasure, not responsibility. Their attention to the drudgery of government was in most cases fitful. Sport and dalliance took up much of their time. The great beauties of the age, most notably the daughters of Tankiz and Baktimur al-Saqi, were passed from sultan to sultan. (Ittifaq, who enjoyed a similar career, was esteemed not for her beauty, but for her intelligence and her vocal skill.)[13]

Al-Salih Isma'il fell ill in the summer of 1345. He was not yet 20 when he died in August of that year. Before dying he had nominated his full brother Sha'ban to succeed him. Al-Kamil Sha'ban was perhaps 17 years old at the time of accession. He was to reign for a little over a year. Arghun al-'Ala'i, a relatively low-ranking mamluk in the *jamdariyya* guards corps, was a leading figure in Egypt during this brief reign. Arghun was not even an emir, but his influence derived partly from his reputation for efficient administration and the personal fortune which he had carefully siphoned off from the administration. Even more important, he had married the mother of Isma'il and Sha'ban after her divorce from al-Nasir Muhammad and subsequently acted as *lala* (nurse or guardian) to the two young princes.[14]

Although Arghun's authority was extensive, he did not have everything his own way. The sultan had a personality of his own — which appears to have been unpleasant. He used to say, 'My name is Thu'ban ['The Snake'] not Sha'ban.' He was later accused by his enemies of drunkenness, cruelty and indolence. The court eunuchs remained as influential under Sha'ban as they had under Isma'il. Above all, Arghun was opposed by Ghurlu, an emir who specialised in financial administration and who now held the post of *shadd al-dawawin* (inspector of bureaus). Since the financial problems evident in the reign of al-Salih Isma'il continued under al-Kamil Sha'ban, Ghurlu decided to sell off *halqa iqta*'s to the highest bidders, whether those purchasers had military backgrounds or not. An office was established, the *diwan al-badal* (office of exchange), to handle these transactions and it also sold middle- and low-rank administrative posts. To some extent the establishment of this office can only have made what was already common practice more formal and more systematic.[15]

In 1346 Yalbugha al-Yahyawi, the Na'ib of Damascus, raised the standard of revolt. Yalbugha had already been bold enough to protest at the excessive power of the eunuchs and against the arbitrary arrest and execution of emirs in Egypt. In rebelling, Yalbugha was encouraged by rumours of Prince Hajji's opposition to his half-brother, the sultan, and spurred on by fears that he, Yalbugha, was to be the sultan's next victim. News of Yalbugha's revolt in turn inspired Maliktimur al-Hijazi and other Egyptian emirs to move against Sha'ban and depose him. Sha'ban was swiftly disposed of in prison and Arghun was also to die in captivity a few years later.

Hajji was proclaimed sultan in September 1346 and took the regnal name al-Muzaffar. He was 14 years old and fond of polo, torture and playing with pigeons. He preferred the company of low-caste wrestlers and pigeon racers to that of his senior emirs. According to one story, when a delegation of emirs came to reproach him for his misrule, he slaughtered some pigeons before their eyes and told them that he would deal similarly with those of his subjects who gave him trouble (a vivid gesture which reminds one of Turanshah and his candles). Ghurlu's ascendancy increased in this reign and it seems to have been on his advice that al-Muzaffar Hajji spent lavishly in buying the loyalty of the royal mamluks and their eunuch commander, al-Sahrati. Ghurlu also urged the sultan to increase their numbers by buying Circassian slaves (Ghurlu himself was a Circassian). Ghurlu's determination to concentrate all power in his hands and the concomitant purges of promising rivals drove the leading emirs headed by the *na'ib al-saltana*, Ariqtay al-Nasiri, against Ghurlu. Ghurlu was deposed from office and murdered at prayer.[16] Hajji did not long survive his creature. Rumours of a further purge contemplated by the sultan brought about a revolt by the senior emirs and his death in July 1347.[17]

Another son of al-Nasir Muhammad was installed as the new Sultan al-Nasir Hasan. The new ruler was a minor (he was probably eleven). By convention he would have to be declared of age no later than his fifteenth Islamic lunar year. In the meantime a junta of Nasiri emirs — including the *na'ib* Baybugha, the vizier Manjak and Emir Taz — took over the administration and the royal treasury. They forced the resale of many of the recently acquired Circassian mamluks and, as part of a general programme of reductions in expenditure, cut down on royal ceremonial.[18] The reserves accumulated by al-Nasir Hasan's father had by now vanished — and the financial problems of the regime were within months to be enormously increased by the arrival of the Black Death in Egypt.

This bubonic plague originated in Central Asia. From there it spread to the Black Sea region. Janibeg, Khan of the Golden Horde, loaded his mangonels with plague-stricken corpses during his siege of the Italian commercial colony of Caffa on the Sea of Azov. It seems likely that the plague was carried on merchant ships from the Black Sea to Alexandria. People began dying of the plague in Alexandria in the autumn of 1347. The resistance of the Egyptians to the virus was weakened by a famine that was already widespread in Egypt that year due to a shortfall in the flooding of the Nile. People's responses to the plague were confused by their misconception as to what it was. It was commonly thought to have been decreed by God as a punishment for the vicious and a test for the virtuous. It was commonly thought that the plague was not contagious but travelled from land to land as a dark cloud or an invisible vapour. It was allegedly commonly observed that animals and fishes also died of its effects. By the spring of 1348 it had spread through the Delta and in the autumn and winter of that year it extended its sway over Upper Egypt and Syria. By February 1349 it was observed to be subsiding in Egypt and a month or two later in Syria also.[19]

There is no reliable evidence at all on which to base an estimate of the numbers of those who died in the Sultanate as a result of the Black Death. The guesses of modern experts, for what they are worth, tend to calculate that about a third of the population of Egypt and Syria died of the plague in these years. This is an estimate that agrees well with those that have been made for some areas of Europe that were affected by the Black Death. However, it is unlikely that mortality within the Sultanate was evenly spread. In particular, remarkably few emirs of a hundred seem to have died in the relevant years. An examination of Ibn Taghribirdi's biographical dictionary and his chronicle suggests that only three died of any causes in the period concerned (and there should have been approximately 24 emirs of one hundred at any one time). What this suggests is, perhaps, that wealth and good eating were the best defence against the infection. The governing elite survived the plague remarkably well, the sultan spending the time when contagion was at its worst at his summer residence of Siryaqus.

Whereas the demographic toll from the Black Death seems to have been no less high in Western Europe than in Egypt and Syria, in the West — most obviously in England and Italy — population, commerce, agriculture, and the crafts recovered in the course of the next century. In Egypt and Syria this does not seem to have happened. The population never regained its pre-Black Death level. The reason for this is thought to be that Egypt and Syria, unlike Western Europe, were subsequently and recurrently visited by epidemics of pneumonic plague. Pneumonic plague, unlike bubonic plague, is a winter plague, is infectious rather than contagious and has a higher mortality rate. The Mamluk lands were especially likely to suffer high fatalities from pneumonic plague, because the resistance of their inhabitants was regularly weakened by famine and drought. It has been estimated that there were, in the period 1347–1517, 55 outbreaks of plague in Egypt of which 20 were major epidemics. Whereas the mamluk elite seems to have suffered relatively lightly from the first great epidemic, this was certainly not the case later. Chroniclers rarely forbear to comment that those who suffered most from the subsequent plagues were children, foreigners and imported mamluks (that is, those who had acquired no resistance to the virus). In the long run the ravages of plagues made an important contribution to the depletion of the ranks of the mamluks and the resultant ill discipline in the barracks.[20]

The cyclical return of plague may not have been the only factor in holding the population down. It has been suggested that pessimism about the bad times led to an increased leniency in jurists' attitudes to birth control and to its increased practice among the people.[21] However, it is by no means certain that there is any clear correlation between hard times and the decision not to have children: some work suggests the reverse. On the other hand, amenorrhoea — female infertility due to malnutrition — must have affected the populations of Egypt and Syria adversely in the late fourteenth and fifteenth centuries.

One particular feature of medieval Egypt's population history has drawn comment from modern historians — namely the alleged failure of the mamluk elite to reproduce themselves genetically. It has been noted that it is difficult to trace a mamluk family for more than three generations.[22] On the other hand, it is also difficult to trace an '*ulama*' or a Karimi family for more than three generations in this period.[23] The difficulty seems to reflect the fragility of tenure on status and wealth, rather than some specific mamluk genetic failing. Incidentally, such modern speculations are interestingly anticipated by medieval Western observers who attempted to explain from a distance the mamluk phenomenon. According to William of Adam, writing in the early fourteenth century, Egypt ate up its inhabitants, and abortion ravaged its population. Therefore merchants imported specially fattened-up boys for the homosexual pleasure of the mamluk elite. James of Verona (*c*.1335) had made similar remarks about unnatural vice among the Mamluks.[24]

The short-term effects of the Black Death in the 1340s and 1350s are not easy to assess. In the towns high mortality may have led to accelerated and undeserved promotion among the young mamluks. Unlike emirs of one hundred, young royal mamluks were not necessarily very well nourished. During the vizierate of Emir Manjak al-Yusufi the quality of meat rations deteriorated drastically.[25] The mamluk retinues of dead emirs would generally have reverted to the sultan, contributing to an increased concentration of power around the citadel. Among the civilian population high mortality would have led to the concentration of fortunes in fewer hands. There is evidence to indicate that after the Black Death the shortage of skilled labour in the towns allowed artisans to charge more for their work. According to the fifteenth-century chronicler and essayist al-Maqrizi, the mortality was such that some crafts were wiped out altogether. But here, as elsewhere, al-Maqrizi's testimony should be treated with caution. He always was a terrible Jeremiah about everything.

In the countryside high mortality among the peasants may have altered the balance of population in favour of the bedouin — certainly this and other effects of the Black Death should be borne in mind when considering the great bedouin revolts in Upper Egypt in the 1350s. Peasant mortality led to long-term labour shortage in the countryside. Landlords and *muqta's* resorted to harsh methods to keep the peasants on their estates. The price of grain does not seem to have risen in the same way that the price of manufactured products did. A smaller labour force produced absolutely less food (but more *per capita* as they abandoned marginal lands) and this food was sold at relatively cheap prices to the diminished urban markets. It was not only the settled peasants who were adversely affected by this phenomenon, but also the bedouin and Turkoman meat producers, for they depended no less than the peasants on urban demand. The drift of peasants from the land was encouraged by the fact that in these years of famine, bedouin revolt or mamluk lawlessness in the countryside, the centres of distribution of food for the starving were in the towns where the granaries of the sultan and the emirs were.

The fall in agricultural revenues hit the mamluk *muqta's* very hard, for their revenues were largely based on levies in kind on cereal crops. In the late Mamluk period the increased frequency and intensity of reports of mamluk oppression, disorder and protection rackets in the countryside should be taken as evidence of the increased need of the mamluks and other officials, rather than as indicating that the mamluks of the late fourteenth and the fifteenth centuries were somehow intrinsically less virtuous and more greedy than their predecessors. The sultan — as, in a sense, the greatest *muqta'* in his lands — was similarly affected by a decline in fiscal revenue. Perhaps the worst affected of all were those *'ulama'* whose income came from fixed *waqf* stipends based on allocations of agricultural produce revenue. The *'ulama'* were poorly placed to compensate themselves.

Finally, turning to the matter of *iqta'* land, the Black Death and subsequent epidemics led to the rapid transmission of *iqta'*s from one tenant to another. Baybugha al-Arus, the *na'ib al-saltana*, allowed the sons of *iqta'* holders to inherit *iqta'*s, but, even so, this still left many *iqta'*s potentially without tenants.[26] From 1349 onwards Baybugha's bloodbrother and ally, the vizier Manjak al-Yusufi, finding himself short of money, handed over *halqa iqta'*s to royal mamluks and officials in lieu of cash.[27] Additionally, many civilians — artisans, rope makers, tailors, and so forth — bought their way into the *halqa* so as to assure for themselves what was effectively a pension from the *iqta'*. (However, this was hardly a new development. As early as the reign of al-Salih Ayyub there had been complaints about this sort of thing.)

Al-Nasir Hasan's first reign brought his subjects no fortune. Both Egypt and Syria suffered from plague, famine and bedouin disturbances. In 1348 the regime was rocked by scandal in Damascus when the Na'ib of Tripoli turned up with what may or may not have been a forged royal warrant and used it to arrest and kill Arghunshah, the Na'ib of Damascus. The murderer was pursued and eventually killed and the sultan disclaimed all responsibility, but the vizier Manjak confiscated Arghunshah's property. In Egypt, Circassian mamluks attempted a coup in 1347 in a bid to regain the favourable position that they had enjoyed under al-Muzaffar Hajji. The leading Turkish emirs combined to scotch this plot. On other issues, however, the ruling junta of nine emirs was split. Taz al-Nasiri was leader of the majority faction, but much of the administration was in the hands of Baybugha al-Arus and Manjak al-Yusufi. Baybugha's upright management of affairs as *na'ib al-saltana* won him popularity among the citizens of Cairo.

He left the necessary dirty work of government to his close ally, Vizier Manjak al-Yusufi. Manjak was an expert in the related fields of fiscal policy and torture. He had first come to prominence as the officer who executed Sultan al-Nasir Ahmad. Subsequently, he had acquired a reputation for toughness as *hajib* in Damascus. As vizier in Egypt he took the lead in enforcing necessary economies. He cut down on the pay and meat rations of the royal mamluks and dismissed droves of palace entertainers and servants; he also reorganised the *diwans*.[28] Al-Nasir Hasan was made to pay for the extravagance of his brother Al-Muzaffar Hajji. Al-Nasir Hasan for his part formed an alliance with the *amir akhur* Mughultay and together they sought to use the rift between Taz al-Nasiri and Baybugha to secure some freedom for manoeuvre for themselves. But in 1351 Taz took advantage of Baybugha's absence on the *hajj* to stage a coup against him and Manjak. Baybugha was arrested in the Hejaz and at the same time Manjak was seized in Cairo. A little later Taz's ally Sarghitmish went to the citadel to enforce Al-Nasir Hasan's abdication. Hasan was imprisoned in the harem where he was to spend the next four years devoting himself to study.

This readjustment of the balance of power among the emirs was marked by the installation as sultan of another of the sons of Al-Nasir Muhammad, Al-Salih Salih, in August 1351. Al-Salih Salih was not yet 14 when he came to the throne. He was a popular choice among the Syrians for he was, through his mother, the grandson of Tankiz, the uncrowned king of Damascus between 1310 and 1340. Soon after Salih's elevation Mughultay went to prison in Alexandria. However, the governing junta did seek to broaden the basis of its support by releasing Manjak and Baybugha from confinement and Baybugha was made *na'ib* in Aleppo.

The trust of the ruling junta (Taz, Shaykhun and Sarghitmish in Baybugha was not justified. In the summer of 1352 Baybugha raised the standard of revolt. In his advance on Damascus that summer Baybugha was accompanied not only by mamluk troops from Aleppo and Tripoli and bedouin from the Fadl confederacy, but also by Dulghadirid Turkoman tribesmen. Qaraja ibn Dulghadir, a Turkoman tribal chief, had in the 1330s established himself in Eastern Anatolia, in the Malatya region, under mamluk patronage — specifically with the assistance of Tankiz, Na'ib of Damascus. Qaraja's decision to intervene in Mamluk factional politics was a harbinger of future problems that the Mamluks were to experience in Syria with Turkoman princes. In 1352 Baybugha's descent through Syria with a large Turkoman army had something of the character of a foreign invasion and their looting of the suburbs of Damascus was compared by the citizens to that of Ghazan's Mongols more than half a century earlier. However, the advance out of Egypt of an army nominally commanded by the sultan, forced Baybugha and Qaraja to withdraw. Their army disintegrated. Qaraja betrayed Baybugha to his rivals and then fled to take refuge with Mahmud ibn 'Ala al-Din Eretna. Mahmud's father, Eretna had been another of the soldiers of fortune who had taken advantage of the break-up of the Mongol overlordship in Anatolia to carve out a principality for himself, though Eretna had started out not as a tribal leader, but as a general in the service of the Mongols. The elastic frontiers of Eretna's realm at times included Sivas, Kayseri, Ankara and Aksaray. Mahmud ibn Eretna swiftly betrayed Qaraja to the Mamluks. Both Baybugha and Qaraja were executed in 1354.[29]

Problems created in Syria by rebel emirs and Turkomans were taken advantage of by Arabs in Upper Egypt. From the early 1340s onwards the Mamluks had found it increasingly difficult to control the bedouin tribes there. There were mamluk garrisons at Qus and in other key towns in the region, but in normal years there was not a large military presence there and Mamluk control relied rather on playing one group of tribes off against another. (The two factional groupings were labelled according to traditional practice, but rather notionally, Qays and Yaman. This will be discussed in Volume 2 of this work.) However, in times of political weakness the Mamluks were unable to intervene in order to prevent one of the factions from gaining the ascendancy.

From about 1351 onwards much of Upper Egypt was effectively under the control of al-Ahdab. Al-Ahdab (his name means 'The Hump-backed') was leader of the Yamani faction of bedouins. However, he seems also to have been supported by many of the peasants of the region. It was in any case becoming increasingly difficult to distinguish sedentarised bedouin from peasants who may have taken up the raising of livestock. One of the aims of al-Ahdab's revolt was to seize grain destined for Cairo and the Delta towns. In the winter of 1353–4 Emir Shaykhun led an expedition into Upper Egypt. Despite some exemplary massacres, he was unable to inflict a convincing defeat on al-Ahdab. Therefore the Mamluks were obliged to come to terms with al-Ahdab and govern Upper Egypt in co-operation with the Yamani bedouin tribes. The rival Qaysi moiety then switched from being the loyal collaborators of the Mamluks to brigandage and revolt. It is impossible to know how much damage was done to the Mamluk economy generally by the deteriorating security situation in Upper Egypt, the interception of grain supplies, the peasants' flight from the land, and the growing power of the Arab tribal chiefs in determining affairs in the villages and *iqta*'s of the region, but the damage was certainly significant. It may even have been the single greatest factor behind the decline of Mamluk prosperity and power.[30]

In Cairo itself the most spectacular event to occur during the reign of al-Salih Salih was the rise and fall of 'Alam al-Din ibn Zunbur. Ibn Zunbur had been appointed vizier at the end of al-Nasir Hasan's first reign, in 1351. Very likely bribes had eased his way into this appointment. Under al-Salih Salih he combined the post of vizier with those of *nazir al-khass* and *nazir al-jaysh* — an unprecedented concentration of fiscal and administrative power. Under Ibn Zunbur's management the distinction between the funds of the state and his private purse became somewhat unclear. Ibn Zunbur kept a portion of his wealth concealed in a marble column in his palace and other hoards were secretly deposited with friendly emirs as insurance for the future. But there could be no concealing the scale of his wealth — his 25 sugar factories, his herds of sheep numbering 50,000- or 70,000-head and his 700 ships which plied the Nile carrying molasses, olive oil, honey, lead, copper, sulphur and many other commodities to his shops and warehouses.

Ibn Zunbur was one of the *musalima,* a convert from the Coptic faith. His chief enemy in the regime, Emir Sarghitmish, was noted both for his fanatical piety and his own entrepreneurial skills. For whatever motive, it was Sarghitmish who moved against Ibn Zunbur in 1352. Shaykhun, Sarghitmish's rival, was unable to protect Ibn Zunbur. The vizier was deposed, the visible portions of his wealth were sequestrated and he and his family were tortured to reveal the whereabouts of the hidden caches. He was found to be worth more than a million dinars. Sarghitmish and his friends among the '*ulama*' accused Ibn Zunbur not only of misappropriating state funds, but also of being an insincere convert to Islam. (However, an attempt to dissolve the *waqf*s of Ibn Zunbur was overruled.) Ibn Zunbur was exiled to Qus, where he died in 1353.[31]

The scale of Ibn Zunbur's wealth and propaganda put about by Sarghitmish's party about crypto-Christians in the administration may have been behind the renewed wave of anti-Christian rioting which broke out all over Egypt in 1354. Under popular pressure the sultan and his emirs were obliged to decree the strict enforcement of discriminatory legislation against the Christians, and, for a while, not only Copts but also *musalima* were dismissed from the *diwans*.[32]

By the beginning of 1354 it was evident that the triumvirate of Taz, Shaykhun and Sarghitmish could not hold together any longer. Taz and Sarghitmish were increasingly at odds. Taz tried and failed to win over Shaykhun. Shaykhun aligned himself and his 700 mamluks with Sarghitmish. In the autumn of 1354 while Taz was away in Upper Egypt, Sarghitmish staged a *putsch* and seized the citadel from Taz's partisans. Though there was street-fighting later when Taz returned, Taz was unable to reverse the coup and had to accept the governorship of Aleppo as compensation. Shaykhun and Sarghitmish marked their triumph by sending al-Salih Salih back to his mother and bringing al-Nasir Hasan out of the harem for a second reign (1354–61). Although Sarghitmish seems to have instigated the *putsch*, Shaykhun was its prime benefactor, and during the early years of Hasan's reign the *atabak* was the effective controller of the realm. Shaykhun and Sarghitmish were perhaps the last of a great generation of mamluks who had been thoroughly educated by al-Nasir Muhammad as a preparation for public service. Shaykhun interfered repeatedly in religious affairs and had been commended for his piety in washing the dead during the Black Death.[33] Sarghitmish also intervened in religious affairs. He was noted for his partisanship for Turkish '*ulama*' and adherents of the Hanafi *madhhab*. His attempts to secure precedence for the Hanafi chief *qadi* over the Shafi'i chief *qadi* made him widely unpopular. Both emirs were wealthy patrons of civilian scholars and religious architecture. Sarghitmish was eloquent, an expert both in the intricacies of Arabic and of *fiqh* (religious law). He loved the company of '*ulama*', we are told.[34] However, Sarghitmish and Shaykhun did not love one another.

Shaykhun's pre-eminence lasted until his murder at court in 1357. He was cut down in front of the sultan. Though a royal mamluk confessed to having murdered Shaykhun to settle a private grudge and was speedily executed, al-Nasir Hasan's disclaimers of any responsibility were widely disbelieved. In the short term the removal of Shaykhun only led to the ascendancy of Sarghitmish, who now became *atabak*. However, in August 1358, al-Nasir Hasan's mamluks seized, imprisoned (and later executed) Sarghitmish and al-Nasir Hasan's reign truly began at last.

The long years of humiliating tutelage had taught Hasan to distrust his father's emirs. To some extent Hasan's own corps of

Nasiri mamluks was used to ease the old guard out of key positions. Yalbugha al-Khassaki in particular was advanced to the rank of emir of one hundred, but the rank and file of al-Nasir Hasan's purchased mamluks seemed to have considered that they had a greater claim on his purse than he had on their loyalty. Therefore, to counterbalance the influence of the emirs, as well as to break the mould of Mamluk politics and to broaden the sexually narrow basis of power in Cairo, al-Nasir Hasan relied on the advice of the women and eunuchs of the palace. This, as we have seen, had its precedents in the reigns of some of his brothers. More interestingly, he promoted the interests of the *awlad al-nas*, his own sons and the sons of deceased Nasiri emirs. By the end of the reign nearly half the emirs who advised and supported the sultan in his *majlis* were *awlad al-nas* and most of the key governorships in Syria were similarly held by *awlad al-nas*.[35] (The pool of capable *awlad al-nas* which al-Nasir Hasan was able to draw on was of course a product of the long years of peace between 1310 and 1340, during which emirs had married, produced children and been able to secure the prosperity of those children.) Had al-Nasir Hasan's experiment succeeded, a truly feudal hereditary system might have been established in Egypt and Syria.

Yet within a year or two of the removal of Sarghitmish it became apparent that al-Nasir Hasan's coup had in fact inaugurated the eight-year-long, albeit uncrowned, reign of Yalbugha al-Khassaki, a reign which was to outlast several sultans and which only ended with Yalbugha's murder in 1366.[36] In the last years of his reign Hasan became increasingly unpopular. It was acknowledged that he was clever, but he was also greedy. The sultan economised on the *iqta*'s, pay and pensions of his officers and further siphoned money off from the state treasury (*bayt al-mal*) and into the crown estates (*khass*). Much of this money went into the sultan's massive building programme, particularly into the building of the Sultan Hasan mosque. This magnificent religious complex faced the citadel and its minarets overtopped the citadel's walls.[37] Construction was commenced in 1356, but work was still proceeding on it in 1361, when one of its minarets collapsed and killed hundreds of people. Its downfall was regarded as presaging the sultan's downfall. By 1361 al-Nasir Hasan's over-favoured emir, Yalbugha al-Khassaki, had been recognised by the sultan to be an overmighty subject and Yalbugha was not allowed to approach his lord without first being strip-searched. It was plain to everyone that the sultan would soon make a move against this former favourite, but Yalbugha struck first. Yalbugha rebelled, there was fighting outside Cairo and Hasan, when he discovered the extent of his unpopularity and the fact that Yalbugha had been suborning his mamluks, tried to make a run for Kerak. He was captured and imprisoned. It is not known how he died.

Since the supply of sons of al-Nasir Muhammad had run out, Yalbugha produced a grandson, one of the sons of al-Muzaffar Hajji, and proclaimed him as the new Sultan al-Mansur Muhammad in 1361. Within months of Yalbugha's coup the Syrian governors headed by Baydamur, Na'ib of Damascus, rebelled against the murderer of al-Nasir Hasan. However, faced by Yalbugha's rapid advance into Syria, their coalition fell apart. Yalbugha allowed Baydamur to retire to Jerusalem — in this period particularly the haven of disgraced but harmless political figures. Yalbugha was to have more problems with his protégé al-Mansur Muhammad. Despite his youth — he was perhaps only 14 at the time of his accession — Muhammad was showing signs of becoming an accomplished debauchee, and there were, moreover, hints of derangement in his sadistic treatment of his concubines. Still more serious for Yalbugha, the prince was insufficiently pliable. In May 1363 Muhammad was removed from the throne and sent back to the harem.

Al-Ashraf Sha'ban, who was now acclaimed as sultan, was the ten-year-old son of al-Nasir Hasan. Thus Yalbugha made use of the fiction of rule by the son of the man he had had murdered to continue undisturbed in the exercise of power until the disasters of 1365–6.

Yalbugha's power rested on the number of mamluks he owned. He was said to have between 1,500 and 3,000 in his service, a force which certainly exceeded the number of royal mamluks in the nominal service of the sultans. Yalbugha was a man of a different stamp from Shaykhun and Sarghitmish. He was not cultured and he reared his mamluks in his own image — as fighters rather than public servants. The discipline they endured was strict but capricious. A mamluk who answered his master back was liable to have his tongue cut out. The way Yalbugha brought up his mamluks is of some importance, for not only did they constitute the dominant faction during his lifetime, but after his death emirs who had risen from the ranks of the Yalbughawi mamluks continued to dominate the governorships and military commands in Egypt and Syria until the early years of the Circassian regime. Indeed, many of the Circassians — including Barquq himself — seem to have been initially recruited by Yalbugha.

From 1361 to 1366 Yalbugha held the office of *atabak al-'asakir*. The prestige of his position as, effectively, protector of the realm must have been severely damaged by his failure to counter Cypriot and Crusading attacks on the Mamluk lands; it is noteworthy that his downfall occurred only a year after the Alexandria Crusade. The expedition led against Alexandria by King Peter I of Cyprus was only the culmination of a struggle that had been going on since the 1340s between Christians and Muslims, a struggle for control over the ports and commerce of the Eastern Mediterranean. In particular, Cyprus and Egypt struggled for control over the ports on the south coast of Asia Minor. The ending of hostilities between Mamluks and Mongols had not led to a cessation of Mamluk attacks on Cilician Armenia. An attack in 1322 had led to the Mamluks' acquiring rights to annual tribute from the Armenian port of Ayas. An expedition in 1337 succeeded in temporarily occupying the Armenian capital, Sis. In 1355 the Mamluks occupied the ports of Tarsus, Adana and Massisa.[38] Mamluk penetration into Cilicia allowed them to establish closer contacts with the Turkoman beylicates that were forming in Anatolia and the lands to the east after the break-up of Mongol power, in particular the Qaraman principality to the north-west of Cilicia and the Dulghadirid principality to the north-east. Also, as we have seen, the ports on the south-east coast of Asia Minor were staging-posts for the transmission of strategically crucial supplies of wood, iron and white slaves, and in this period much of the overland spice and silk trade seems to have debouched at these ports. At the same time as the Mamluks were seeking to extend their hegemony over South-east Asia Minor, Venice was strengthening its commercial ties with the Mamluk empire. New commercial agreements and treaties were negotiated in 1355 and 1361, Venetian convoys began to visit Beirut as well as Alexandria, and the Venetians purchased 'graces' from Papal agents which allowed them to trade with the infidel despite the sporadically applied Crusading embargo against such trade.

The increase of Venice's direct trade with Mamluk ports seems to have weakened Cyprus's commercial position and led to a decline in the number of Venetian ships calling at Cypriot ports. There had always been a considerable amount of commerce between the Christian kingdoms of Cyprus and Armenia. From 1359 onwards, with the accession of Peter I to the Cypriot throne, contacts with Cilician Armenia became yet closer, the Cypriots offering support against the neighbouring Turkoman principalities. In 1360 Cypriots occupied and garrisoned the Cilician port of Gorighos at the invitation of the Armenian king and in 1361 a mixed force of Cypriots and Crusaders seized the port of Adalya from Tekke, a Turkoman principality on the coast to the west of Cilicia. Turkoman pirates harried Christian shipping in the region. Christian pirates based on Cyprus and Rhodes attacked Muslim ships and raided the coastline of Mamluk Syria. Peter I had also inherited the title to the throne of the defunct Crusader principality of Jerusalem.

These factors, then — commercial and piratical rivalry, support for Cilician Armenia against the Mamluk-backed Turkoman principalities, and Peter's Crusading pretensions — seem to have been the key factors in Peter's decision to lead a Crusader fleet against Alexandria in 1365.[39] Whether it was Peter's initial intention simply to sack the port, or whether he intended to use the captured port as a base for conquest of the rest of Egypt, or as a bargaining counter to secure the surrender by the Mamluks of the former kingdom of Jerusalem, is not clear.

The picture we glean of Alexandria in the 1360s is a mixed one. Commercially it was doing well, but this commercial prosperity may have benefited relatively few people. Its population seems to have declined drastically since the 1340s. After the Black Death in 1347, the *Dar al-Tiraz*, the state-run factory for the manufacture of precious fabrics, had to close temporarily for lack of workers. On the other hand, al-Ashraf Sha'ban took a personal interest in the industry's revival and there were still said to be 1,400 looms in Alexandria in the 1390s.[40] Politically, Alexandria had little importance despite its role as a source of revenue and also its use as a place of imprisonment or exile for the disgraced. The governor of Alexandria was an emir of middling rank, and at the time of the Cypriot landing he was actually away on the *hajj*. The Crusaders took the town on 10 October, having faced very little resistance, and once within its walls set to plundering and massacring. Yalbugha in Cairo was slow to react, for he believed that the report of the Crusader landing was a trick to get him out of Cairo and to stage a coup in his absence. However, a relief force was slowly assembled and slowly it advanced up the Delta (the Nile waters were still high at this time of the year). In the meantime the Crusaders had been unable to take the bridge over the canal that linked Alexandria with the Nile. Moreover, now that they had secured their plunder, many of Peter's motley band of 'Crusaders' were eager to withdraw. So after only a week at Alexandria the Crusaders sailed away.

Though the Venetians had participated with reluctance in the expedition and were only too eager to negotiate a peace on Cyprus's behalf, the war dragged on for several years. Neither Peter nor Yalbugha had a temperament that disposed them to compromise and peace. Cypriot and other vessels raided Tripoli, Sidon, Lattakia, Tortosa and Beirut, as well as the Cilician ports of Ayas and Bodrum which were under Mamluk control, and Alexandria was attacked again. Peace was only successfully negotiated in 1370 after the death of the two protagonists. In 1369 Armenia had already accepted new and humiliating terms from the Mamluks. It is possible that the Cypriot naval expeditions had delayed for a while the final downfall of Cilician Armenia, but in 1375 the Mamluks overran Armenia and this time they were finally successful in occupying it. Thenceforth, authority in Cilicia was shared between Mamluk governors and Turkomans of the vassal principality of Ramadan.[41]

Venetian commerce with the Mamluks was only briefly interrupted; indeed, its trade with the Mamluk lands continued to grow throughout the remainder of the fourteenth century. Alexandria itself, however, must have experienced some problems arising from the silting-up of its canal to the Nile from the 1370s onwards. After the Alexandria Crusade the governorship of the city was upgraded from an emirate of forty to an emirate of one hundred and the port's defences were reconstructed. Another predictable response to the Crusade was a renewed wave of persecution of Copts in Egypt and of harassment of the Maronites in the Lebanon. Immediately after the Crusade the property of the Christian Church in Egypt was declared confiscate. This decree was reversed later under Western diplomatic pressure. The Alexandria débâcle also encouraged an upsurge of military enthusiasm in Egypt. The decree went out that emirs must set aside adequate portions of their *iqta*'s for the maintenance of troopers. Yalbugha presided over the building of a revenge fleet. *Furusiyya* exercises were revived and manuscripts on *furusiyya* were commissioned. It would be naive to credit the revival of *furusiyya* in the late 1360s and the 1370s to the personality of Sultan al-Ashraf Sha'ban.[42] The direction of affairs was in the hands of Yalbugha and, after his death, his Yalbughawi successors.

Yalbugha was killed in 1366 by some of his own mamluks who had been unable to endure their master's harsh discipline any longer. Though the sultan approved their action, he was not fully master of the changed situation. In 1366 he probably still had less than a couple of hundred mamluks in his service. Power passed into the hands of such Yalbughawi emirs as Tashtimur, Yalbugha al-Yalbughawi, Qaratay, Barka and Barquq.

Despite the manoeuvrings and occasional outbreaks of street-fighting between rival groupings of these emirs, the rest of al-Ashraf Sha'ban's reign after the death of Yalbugha was not entirely without achievement. As has been noted, commerce with the Venetians grew and Cilicia was conquered in this period. In 1376 a new survey of *iqta*'s and other forms of tenure in Egypt was carried out and the data of the Nasiri *rawk* of 1315 thus brought up to date,[43] but the results of the survey suggest that Egypt's commercial and military capacity had been severely damaged by the events of 1374–5. In 1374 the Nile did not rise sufficiently. The famine that ensued continued into the following year and swift on the heels of the famine came the first great outbreak of pneumonic plague since the Black Death. This time it is clear that the mamluks themselves suffered particularly heavily from the plague's ravages. This plague and subsequent epidemics particularly threatened those who had not been in Egypt and survived previous outbreaks — that is, foreigners, children and mamluks.[44] New and hitherto unknown mamluks came to the fore in military politics. Other problems were faced by the *na'ib*s of Aleppo who had to deal with a growing nomad problem. In 1368 bedouins of the Syrian Fadl and Kilab tribes killed Aleppo's *na'ib* and ravaged Aleppan territory.[45] Also from the 1370s onwards the Turkomans of the Dulghadirid principality menaced the northern frontiers of the province of Aleppo. Punitive expeditions mounted against the Turkomans were not effective.

In the course of the 1370s Sha'ban's power grew. In part this was due to his acquisition of most of Yalbugha's mamluks. He became an effective ruler and actually a popular ruler, for he was sane, competent and pious. In 1377 he made preparations to go on the *hajj*. He made careful dispositions to safeguard his realm in his absence, but his care was insufficient. In March 1377 the Yalbughawi mamluks staged a coup and took the Cairo citadel. Al-Ashraf Sha'ban was captured a little later and strangled. The emir Barquq was prominent among the Yalbughawi plotters.

Barquq, a Circassian mamluk, had originally been acquired by

Yalbugha al-Khassaki. After the latter's murder in 1366 he had spent some time in prison before entering the service of al-Ashraf Sha'ban. As a mamluk he served that sultan as a *silahdar*.[46]

Al-Ashraf Sha'ban's infant son, al-Mansur 'Ali, was placed on the throne by his father's murderers. In Egypt the dominant group was formed mainly by Yalbughawi emirs. These were years of small-scale scuffles fought between disorderly emirs with small retinues and uncertain futures. In Syria Tashtimur al-'Ala'i, Na'ib of Damascus, was the dominant figure (he had previously been al-Ashraf Sha'ban's *dawadar* until becoming implicated in a premature plot against that sultan). Barquq advanced his status by marrying Tashtimur's daughter. The following year he intrigued with Tashtimur's mamluks and had Tashtimur arrested. By 1376 he had become *atabak* of the armies and had seized and killed the chief of his former allies among the Yalbughawi mamluks, Emir Barka. It is conventional to date the beginning of the Circassian Mamluk Sultanate to 1382, but, from the 1360s onwards, Yalbugha's mainly Circassian mamluks had played a dominant part in affairs, and the Circassian mamluk Barquq was already sultan in all but name in 1376. When al-Mansur 'Ali died of a sickness in 1382, Barquq replaced him with another infant from the Qalawunid line, al-Salih Hajji II. Then Barquq hastily decided that he was in a strong enough position to take the throne for himself. Disorders in Syria demanded that there be a strong man at the helm. Hajji II was deposed by al-Zahir Barquq, the first in the sequence of Circassian Mamluk sultans. But, as events were to prove, Barquq's open usurpation of the throne was premature, and ushered in a new and prolonged period of political turbulence and civil war.

Notes

1. The chief sources in print on this period are: Ibn al-Wardi, *Tatimmat al-Mukhtasar* in Abu'l-Fida, *al-Mukhtasar fi akhbar al-bashar*, vol. 4 (Istanbul, 1870), pp. 100–55; al-Shuja'i, *Tarikh al-Malik al-Nasir Muhammad b.Qalawun al-Salihi wa awladihi*, B. Schäfer (ed) (Wiesbaden, 1977); Ibn Kathir, *al-Bidaya wa al-Nihaya*, vol.14 (Cairo, 1939); al-Maqrizi, *Kitab al-Suluk*, vol.2, pt.3, M. M. Ziada (ed.) (Cairo, 1958), vol.3, pt.1, S. Ashour (ed.) (Cairo, 1970); Ibn Taghribirdi, *al-Nujum al-Zahira*, vols10–11 (Cairo, n.d.). See also, B. Schäfer, *Beiträge zur Mamlukischen Historiographie nach dem Tod al-Malik an-Nasirs* (Freiburg im Breisgau, 1971).

2. Ibn Battuta, *The Travels of Ibn Battuta*, H. A. R. Gibb (ed.) vol. 1 (Cambridge, 1958), pp.53–4.

3. A. 'Abd al-Raziq, *La Femme au temps des Mamelouks en Egypte* (Cairo, 1973), pp.280–1, 283–4.

4. On Bashtak, see Ibn Hajar al-Asqalani, *al-Durar al-Kamina*, vol.1 (Hyderabad, 1929–32), pp.477–9; Khalil b. Aybak al-Safadi, *al-Wafi bi al-Wafayat* (17 vols, Wiesbaden, 1931–32), vol.10, pp.142–4; Ibn Taghribirdi, *Nujum*, vol.10, pp.18–20, 74–5; Ibn Hajar, *Durar*, vol.1, pp.477–8; S. Kortantamer, *Ägypten und Syrien zwischen 1317 und 1341 in der Chronik des Mufaddal b. Abi al-Fada'il* (Freiburg im Breisgau, 1973), p.166 n.4; al-Maqrizi, *Khitat*, vol.2, pp.34–5. On Qawsun, see Ibn Hajar, *Durar*, vol.3, pp.257–8; Ibn Taghribirdi, *Nujum*, vol.10, pp.44–7; L.A. Ibrahim, 'The Great Hanqah of the Amir Qawsun in Cairo', *Mitteilungen des Deutschen Archäologischen Instituts*, vol.30 (1974), pp.37–64, especially p.38n.

5. On the growth of Aleppo in the fourteenth century, see I.M. Lapidus, *Muslim Cities in the Later Middle Ages* (Cambridge, Mass., 1967), pp.20–1.

6. Ibn Battuta, *Travels*, vol.1, p.54.

7. Ibn Hajar, *Durar*, vol.1, p.80, vol.2, pp.261–2; 'Abd-al-Raziq, *La Femme*, p.285; D. Ayalon, 'The Eunuchs in the Mamluk Sultanate' in M. Rosen-Ayalon (ed.), *Studies in Memory of Gaston Wiet* (Jerusalem, 1977), p.289n.

8. On trade with Venice, see F. Gabrieli, 'Venezia e i Mamelucchi' in A. Pertusi (ed.), *Venezia e l'Oriente fra tardo Medioevo e Rinascimento* (Venice, 1966), p.422; S. Y. Labib, *Handelsgeschichte Agyptens im Spätmittelalter* (Wiesbaden, 1964), p.75; E. Ashtor, *Levant Trade in the Later Middle Ages* (Princeton, 1983), pp.67–70.

9. Ashtor, *Levant Trade, passim.*

10. Ibn Hajar, *Durar*, vol.1, p.79; Ibn Taghribirdi, *Nujum*, vol.10, p.111; D. P. Little, 'The Recovery of a Lost Source for Bahri Mamluk History: al-Yusufi's Nuzhat al-Nazir fi Sirat al-Malik al-Nasir', *JAOS*, vol.94 (1974), p.49.

11. Ibn Taghribirdi, *Nujum*, vol.7, pp.339–40, vol.11, p.102; *EI(2)* sv 'Ibn Fadlallah'.

12. Ibn Hajar, *Durar*, vol.3, pp.199–200; Ayalon 'The Eunuchs', pp.271, 285, 293–4.

13. 'Abd al-Raziq, *La Femme*, pp.279, 283, 285; Ayalon, 'The Eunuchs', p.289n.

14. On Arghun al-'Ala'i, see Safadi, *Wafi*, vol.8, p.355; Ibn Taghribirdi, *Nujum*, vol.10, pp.185–6.

15. On the *diwan al-badal*, see D. Ayalon, 'Studies on the structure of the Mamluk Army' (part 2), *BSOAS*, vol.15 (1953), p.475.

16. Ibn Hajar, *Durar*, vol.1, p.390; Ibn Taghribirdi, *Nujum*, vol.10, pp.166–8, 188.

17. On Muzaffar Hajji's character and tastes, see Ibn Hajar, *Durar*, vol.2, p.4; Maqrizi, *Suluk*, vol.2, pt.2. pp.729, 740; Ibn Taghribirdi, *Nujum*, vol.10, p.188.

18. Maqrizi, *Suluk*, vol.2, pt.3, pp. 745–7; Ibn Taghribirdi, *Nujum*, vol.10, p.188.

19. D. Ayalon, 'The Plague and its Effects upon the Mamluk Army', *JRAS* (1946), pp.67–73; M. W. Dols, *The Black Death in the Middle East* (Princeton, 1977); A. Udovitch, 'England to Egypt, 1350–1500: Long-term Trends and Long-distance Trade' in M. A. Cook (ed.), *Studies in the Economic History of the Middle East* (London, 1970), pp.115–28.

20. D. Ayalon, 'The Plague', pp.67–73; M. W. Dols, 'The Second Plague Pandemic and its Recurrences in the Middle East', *JESHO*, vol.22 (1979), pp.162–89.

21. B. F. Musallam, *Sex and Society in Islam* (Cambridge, 1983), pp.116–19.

22. Lapidus, *Muslim Cities*, p.117.

23. E. Ashtor, 'The Karimi Merchants', *JRAS* (1956), pp.50–1; Lapidus, *Muslim Cities*, p.110.

24. N. Daniel, *The Arabs and Mediaeval Europe*, (2nd edn, London, 1979), pp.224–5; Daniel, *Islam and the West: The Making of an Image* (Edinburgh, 1960), pp.144, 357n.

25. D. Ayalon, 'The System of Payment in Mamluk Military Society' (part 2), *JESHO*, vol.1 (1957–8), p.259.

26. Safadi, *Wafi*, vol.10, p.356.

27. Ayalon, 'Studies on the Structure' (part 2), pp.453–4.

28. Ibn Hajar, *Durar*, vol.4, pp.360–1; Ayalon, 'The System of Payment' (part 2), p.276.

29. Ibn Hajar, *Durar*, vol.1, pp.511–12; Ibn Kathir, *Bidaya*, vol.14, pp.243–7; Maqrizi, *Suluk*, vol.2, pt.3, pp.867–74, 891, 905; Ibn Taghribirdi, *Nujum*, vol.10, pp.270–7, 284, 293; *EI(2) sv* 'Dhu'l-Kadr'.

30. J.-C. Garcin, *Un Centre Musulman de la haute Égypte médiévale: Qus* (Cairo, 1976), pp.382–4, 404; Y.F. Hasan, *The Arabs and the Sudan* (Edinburgh, 1967), pp.103–5; A. H. Saleh, 'Les Relations entre les Mamluks et les Bedouins d'Égypte' *Annali Instituto orientale di Napoli* (new series), vol.30 (1980), pp.377–9.

31. Ibn Taghribirdi, *Nujum*, vol.10, pp.281–2, 299.

32. D. P. Little, 'Coptic Conversion to Islam under the Bahri Mamluks 692–755/1293–1354', *BSOAS*, vol.39 (1976), pp.566–9; U. Vermeulen, 'The Rescript of al-Malik as-Salih Salih against the dhimmis (755 A.H./1345 A.D.)', *Orientalia Lovanensia Periodica*, vol.9 (1978), pp.175–84.

33. Ibn Hajar, *Durar*, vol.2, pp.293–4; Safadi, *Wafi*, vol.16, pp.211–12; Ibn Taghribirdi, *Nujum*, vol.10, pp.324–5.

34. Ibn Hajar, *Durar*, vol.2, pp.305–6; Ibn Taghribirdi, *Nujum*, vol.10, p.328.

35. D. Ayalon, 'Studies on the Structure' (part 2), p.457.

36. On the career and character of Yalbugha, see Ibn Hajar, *Durar*, vol.4, pp.438–40; Ayalon 'Studies on the Structure' (part 2), pp.460–2.

37. M. Rogers, *The Spread of Islam* (Oxford, 1976), pp.101–6.

38. *EI(2) sv* 'Cilicia'.

39. On the Alexandria Crusade, see A. S. Atiya, *The Crusade in the Later Middle Ages* (London, 1938), pp.330–71; P. W. Edbury, 'The Crusading Policy of King Peter I of Cyprus' in P. M. Holt (ed.), *The Eastern Mediterranean Lands in the Period of the Crusades* (Warminster, 1977), pp.90–105; B. Flemming, *Landschaftsgeschichte von Pamphylien, Pisidien, und Lykien im Spätmittelalter* (Wiesbaden, 1964), pp.83–4, 86–9; G. Hill, *A History of Cyprus*, vol.2 (Cambridge, 1948), pp.317–60; Ashtor, *Levant Trade*, pp.88–92; S. A. Salim, *Tarikh al-Iskandariyya wa Hadaratahafi al-Asr al-Islami* (Alexandria, 1982), pp.310–49.

40. On Alexandria's economic condition, see Salim, *Tarikh*, pp.515–39; *EI(2) sv* 'Iskandariyya'.

41. *EI(2) sv* 'Cilicia'.

42. D. James, 'Mamluke Painting at the Time of the "Lusignan Crusade", 1365–70: A Study of the Chester Beatty Nihayat al-Su'l wa'l-umniya . . . Manuscript of 1366', *Humaniora Islamica*, vol.2 (1974), pp.73–87.

43. H. Halm, *Ägypten nach den mamlukischen Lehensregistern*, vol.1 (Wiesbaden, 1979), pp.29–35.

44. On these later plagues, see D. Ayalon, 'The Plague and its Effects upon the Mamluk Army', pp.67–73; M. W. Dols, 'The Second Plague Pandemic', pp.162–89.

45. Ibn Khaldun, *Kitab al-'Ibar wa Diwan al-Mubtada' wa-l-Khabar*, vol.5 (Cairo, 1867), pp.439–40; Maqrizi, *Suluk*, vol.3, pt.1, p.175.

46. On the career of Barquq, see *EI(2) sv* 'Barkuk'.

8 POSTSCRIPT

During the years 1260–1382 the Mamluk Sultanate neither advanced nor declined. Nor yet were its institutions static — they changed. The difficulty is to find a pattern to those changes. Though the mould of Mamluk politics was firmly set, there were repeated attempts to break that mould — in, for example, attempts to find support outside the mamluk military elite (as strictly defined) among the children of sultans and emirs, or among the *Wafidiyya* and the *halqa* free-born troops, or to seek to use the palace establishment or the urban mob or the tribesmen of Syria as alternative power bases. All these attempts failed. Still, it must be clear that the caste of white military slaves did not hold an absolute monopoly of political power.

By 1382 the union of Egypt and Syria and the continuation of that union could be taken for granted. But there was nothing God-given about that union (save perhaps in the minds of certain Cairo-based *'ulama'*). It had to be fought for, and it was the Mamluks who fought for it. Obviously they defended the lands they ruled against external enemies. Paradoxically and less obviously, their fights among themselves had cohesive results. As provincial governors and garrison commanders sought to take power at the centre, so they organised the resources of their provinces correspondingly. Education, patronage and, above all, the organisation of factions, all conduced to lead the thoughts of the ambitious and the able towards the centre. Though it was always possible for a rebellious emir to increase his following by recruiting Balabakki archers or bedouin and Turkoman tribesmen, in the end he was dependent on the size of his mamluk retinue to enforce his demands. For the mamluks so overwhelmingly excelled their subjects in the arts of war, and mamluks were, in the main, purchased, trained and garrisoned in Cairo.

The Mamluks give the impression of having exercised political thought at the points of their swords. The long-lived Mamluk Sultanate survived not in despite of violent factions. Rather, it actually thrived upon them. These factions were hardly more than coalitions formed by the greedy and the ambitious; they were in the main innocent of 'any common fund of party principle'. Yet this very absence of ideology or party principle militated against the

152

development of regional power bases and separatist interests. Factional strife, however accidentally it had originated, operated in the interests of the central authority. Those who appeared to challenge the central authority did not wish to destroy it, but rather to invest themselves with it. There are parallels here with certain faction-ridden political systems in sub-Saharan Africa.[1] Additionally, the Syrian towns and civil elite became dependent on patronage from Egypt to a degree which had not been the case in the Fatimid or Ayyubid periods. The brightest prospect many a Syrian *'alim* ever saw was the high road to Cairo.

At times the *'ulama'* grumbled about the hegemony of the Mamluks and the manner in which the military elite cut corners in the administration of justice and the prosecution of warfare. The Mamluk regime was hardly an ideal Islamic regime. Yet at other times the *'ulama'* went on record to express their gratitude to the Mamluks. And in fact it is the case that for long stretches in the thirteenth to sixteenth centuries the civilians of Egypt and Syria were adminstered by an elite which had actually been trained in the principles of administration. Moreover, this same elite actually had a stronger commitment to Islam and better knowledge of its tenets than the majority of their subjects. It is a little misleading to judge their Islamisation according to the unrealistically high standards of an Ibn Taymiyya or a Maqrizi. But there were, of course, many exceptions and I should not overstate the case. (If one studies any subject for a great length of time, one is likely to become unreasonably fond of the subject-matter.) Almas the *hajib* or Yalbugha al-Nasiri were hardly ideal Muslim governors, nor does Islam seem to have gone very deep with the governor of Alexandria in the 1320s: Ibn Battuta mentions how the latter worshipped the sun. But these men were, I think, exceptions. On the whole the mamluks are best understood as being public servants, so long as one also understands that they were the servants of God, not of their subjects.

Why does the Mamluk system look so unstable and yet prove so curiously durable? Or, to put it another way, why do faction leaders and their factions perish while the faction-driven system survives? The mutability of factional systems is well explained by Fredrik Barth in his study of Pathan factional organisation.[2] Barth treats factional conflict among the Pathans of the north-west frontier of India as a zero-sum game — that is, that the winner's gain must be the opponent's loss. The struggle for power in the Mamluk

Sultanate was not a zero-sum game in the strictest sense (various external factors and fudges enter the equation); nevertheless, it approaches it. In Barth's zero-sum game the participants in the quest for power and wealth make strategic choices about which faction to join in order to advance themselves. The strongest faction will win (tautologously, of course), but it is not in the interest of the leader of that winning faction that his support be too strong. If he comes to power with the support of too many of the most powerful men and too large a retinue, then the *per capita* rewards of success will be diminished. Ideally, a good political mover seeks to create a faction which is numerous enough to take power, but narrow enough to profit substantially from the seizure of power. In fact the ideal rarely happens: what usually occurs in reality is that someone who is bucking for the Sultanate rises to the top on the backs of a very broad coalition. Then, once he is in power, either he starts to purge the dispensable fringes of his coalition, or the less well-rewarded sections of that coalition take the initiative by seeking a *rapprochement* with the defeated party. For instance: the leader has come to power with the support of factions B and C against faction A. Having triumphed over faction A, the leader then decides to reward himself and faction B rather well and faction C hardly at all. Disgruntled faction C then goes over to join the defeated faction A. The new realignment A-C now stands a very good chance of winning against B. And so the turbulence goes on.

Again and again we see this happening in Mamluk politics. Party politics, ideology and 'irrational solidarity bonds' did not enter into it: each member of a faction simply calculated his own best selfish interest. The rapid turnover in sultans and in coalitions of emirs was a product of a multiplicity of entirely rational decisions. For the sultan, butter spread evenly over too many slices of bread was pretty much the same as no butter at all. So he moved against some of the men who put him in power. And in time the power-brokers of the Mamluk Sultanate became pretty canny about this and learned to anticipate it. So turbulence was built in to the system. As Ibn Taghribirdi remarked, 'When a thing is complete, it begins to fail.'

Mamluk politics looks chaotic, but it was in the main determined by rational choices — and not by some sort of tribal atavism or by irrational solidarity bonds. Certainly loyalty to the *ustadh* or the fellow-feeling of a mamluk towards his *khushdash* played a significant role in relation to factions — though probably a greater role in retrospectively describing them, than in actually determining their formation. There were clear limits to the force of such bonds. The mamluk barracks were not brainwashing centres and the mamluks were not oriental zombies. Even if a fanatical loyalty was inculcated in the barracks (and no source tells us how this was done), an awful lot of mamluks spent only a short time in the royal barracks, having been acquired from another emir or having arrived in Egypt at a relatively mature age (Baybars al-Bunduqdari and Qalawun al-Salihi are only two examples among many others). Professions of loyalty to the master or to fellow-slaves were more honoured in the breach than in the observance.

Why was Mamluk politics so violent? Or at least why does it look so violent? Well, to some extent the inbuilt turbulence of the Mamluks' zero-sum game allowed plenty of opportunities for violence. Then again it is tempting to plunder psychoanalysis or theories of group psychopathology for some sort of explanation. The Mamluks after all, had a very odd upbringing. (An interesting comparison might be made with the kibbutz-reared Sabras of contemporary Israel and what some have observed to be their bluntness, lack of sentimentality and drive to high achievement.)[3] Then again, more soberly, it should be pointed out that many of these mamluks were awfully young when they were given positions of immense responsibility. (Baybars's golden boy Bilik al-Khazindar is an obvious early example; he may not even have been 18 when he became *na'ib al-saltana* in Egypt.) They were young, naturally energetic, released from the constraints of barrack-room life and, for a while at least, unlikely to have been married. These young hoodlums did not behave so very differently from the youth of France or Italy in the same period.[4] But such speculations, though tempting, are probably best resisted, and these are not satisfactory answers.

In fact there is something rather theatrical about Mamluk violence (Turanshah with his candlesticks, Baktimur ripping out Baydara al-Mansuri's liver, Yalbugha cutting out the tongues of disorderly mamluks). Sometimes it reminds me of a gladiatorial conquest, sometimes of a Punch and Judy show ('That's the way to do it!'). The mamluk, the sword of Islam, needed to demonstrate his ability as a swordsman and his ruthlessness as a politician. In Western feudal society courage and the right to rule are things that could be inherited; they might be transmitted through the blood-line. In Egypt and Syria the ability to handle a sword and a horse had to be demonstrated.

The mamluk's theatrical demonstration was his ticket to the top. *Shuja'* (boldness) and *hazm* (decisiveness) are key words in the Arabic obituaries of Mamluk emirs. Those were the qualities they were judged by. The qualification for rule was ability to snatch the sceptre. Joe Fletcher has written about something rather similar in a brief study of Turkish and Mongolian succession practice. However, Fletcher rather misleadingly called it 'tanistry' although the parallels with tanistry as practised in Celtic societies are not exact.[5] The medieval Scots, for example, favoured succession by a member of the collateral branch of the royal house; the Mamluk emirs preferred to acclaim achievement.

On the other hand, failure was hard to cater for in the Mamluk system. Unless one was old or going blind or stroke-ridden, it was not easy to retire peacefully. Imprisonment or, occasionally, a spectacularly painful execution tended to follow dismissal from power. This is not surprising, given the highly urbanised form of Mamluk society and the fact that rural resources in the form of *iqta'*s could not normally be inherited. Because society was so centralised, fiscalised and urban, exile to the country seat was not on. Nor for that matter was it normally possible to sit out factional warfare in the provinces (as some English gentry did in the fifteenth century and again in the seventeenth century). There were no prizes for non-participation in the zero-sum game of the Mamluks, and the fighting was on one's doorstep. Even so, much of the 'factional strife' which terrorised the timorous shopkeepers of Cairo seems to have been more in the nature of demonstrations of strength than actual fighting. The two factions might ride out to face one another beneath the citadel and gradually men from one faction might drift over to join the faction which they judged to be the stronger.

How can one explain the Mamluk system? Self-interest took a man into a faction; demonstration of ability took him to the top of the faction and of the political system. It all makes sense — it is perhaps Western systems with their sentimental ideologies of rights, duties and inheritance which need examining. Qalawun's son al-Nasir Muhammad was succeeded on the throne by eleven of his descendants. Nevertheless, it must be admitted that only some of those descendants exercised real authority, and that the Qalawunid dynasty reigned in an ideological vacuum, without developing any explicit theory of hereditary succession, still less of one of primogeniture. It is the more general prevalence of a non-hereditary succession to the Mamluk Sultanate between 1260 and

1517 that has struck European historians as curious. But the rules governing succession to the throne in medieval Christendom were not always straightforward either. Cyril Mango has observed of the Byzantine emperor that

> More often than not, he owed his position to an unformulated, but generally respected, principle of heredity; alternatively, he may have been co-opted by his predecessor, chosen by an influential group or he may have owed his throne to a successful rebellion . . . To outside observers this system looked curiously unstable and ill-defined: some Arab authors believed that the Roman emperor owed his position to victory and was dismissed if he was unsuccessful.[6]

Similarly, Joshua Prawer on the Latin kingdom of Jerusalem has noted that 'As in almost every twelfth century kingdom, succession to the crown wavered between election and heredity.'[7] John Gillingham has argued the advantages of 'a ritual form of contest for control of the power and prestige which went with the crown' in the case of the Western (German) empire.[8]

And yet . . . and yet a sense of the oddity of the Mamluk regime persists. For it is not only succession to the Mamluk throne which is problematic. Almost as curious, surely, is the absence of any attempt by the Mamluk sultans to establish appanages for their younger sons. In this they differed from their Ayyubid predecessors and their Mongol contemporaries. Nor is it just a matter of monarchs and princes. Superficially at least, the non-hereditary aristocracy of emirs appears as a bizarre anticipation of modern meritocratic ideas. It may be that these features of Mamluk society willl appear less bizarre to those who come to them with a previous knowledge of Japanese samurai society or of the status of slaves among the pre-modern Matabele or Zulus; but certainly the peculiar characteristics of Mamluk society deserve further examination.

It is conventional to divide the history of the Mamluk Sultanate into two halves — that of the Bahri Turkish Sultanate from 1260 to 1382, and that of the Circassian Sultanate from 1382 to 1517, as if the change in racial origin of the sultans marked changes of greater significance. This is a little arbitrary. As we have seen, Circassians had already played a politically prominent role in the last decade of the thirteenth century and the first decade of the fourteenth century, and they were a prominent faction — often the predominant one — from the 1360s onwards; indeed, Barquq's real reign began long before he took the title al-Ashraf. After 1382 there were to be several at least temporarily successful Turkish counter-coups against the Circassians. By no means all the sultans and leading emirs in the 'Circassian era' were Circassians. The racial origin of those sultans and emirs who have been deemed to have been Circassians is often in fact doubtful. Above all, members of the Circassian elite in the later Mamluk period certainly owed more to their education in a Turco-Arab culture than to anything in their Caucasian infancy.

Nevertheless, there must be a dividing-point here and it is for better reasons. First, it is certainly true that in 1382 the grip of the house of Qalawun, which had lasted somewhat intermittently for over a century, was decisively broken. (Hajji II was to return to the throne for a second time in 1389 with the new regnal name al-Mansur, but it was for a few months only — and as the puppet of Circassian emirs.) From now on the Mamluk practice of 'tanistry' or succession to the throne by demonstrating ability in intrigue and warfare was to become even more overt than it had been hitherto.

Second, there is perhaps a change in the nature of the literary source materials and the way in which events were reported in the Circassian era. An important factor was the decline of Damascus as a centre of religious and literary culture. The teachers, lawyers and pious literary figures who had gathered around al-Dhahabi and al-Jazari in the late thirteenth and early fourteenth centuries found few descendants in fifteenth-century Damascus. Al-'Umari (died 1349) and Ibn Qayyim al-Jawziyya (died 1350) were perhaps the last great representatives of their intellectual world. In the Circassian era events were increasingly reported from an Egyptian perspective. This has actually led some modern historians to underestimate the importance of the Syrian military in Mamluk politics and the importance of Syrian agriculture and commerce in the Mamluk economy.

Third, although with the ending of any real military threat from the Mongols (c. 1312), Egypt and Syria had enjoyed some 60 years of relative peace, from the reign of Barquq onwards the Mamluks were confronted with new and more vigorous external enemies — first Timur and his successors, later the Aqqoyonlu, the Ottomans and the Portuguese.

Last, and most important, the great epidemics of 1347 and 1375 brought about massive social and economic changes, changes which were further confirmed by subsequent visitations of pneumonic plague. These changes cannot be overestimated. Most obviously they posed severe problems to the sultans who sought to maintain the level of recruitment of mamluks and the degree of discipline of those recruits. In the Circassian period — another paradox — the royal mamluks were less well treated by the sultans but they had more power. Underpaid and undernourished royal mamluks unionised themselves, as it were, and they went on strike or they rioted to secure their material needs. They were more obviously a sort of Praetorian guard in the Circassian period than in the Bahri. Generalising rather broadly, in the Circassian period the royal mamluks posed a greater threat to the authority of the sultan than the emirs and their mamluks did. And the disorderliness of royal mamluks and their interventions in politics in turn had many implications in internal and external affairs.

While the contribution of the Circassian mamluks to Bahri Mamluk politics has not been ignored in this volume it has been given relatively short shrift. In the volume which follows, this deficiency will in some part be remedied and events in the 1360s and 1370s will be examined to shed more light on the rise of Barquq and his Circassian successors. The second volume will bring the history of the Mamluk Sultanate down to the years 1516–17, when its armies were defeated by those of the Ottoman sultan and its lands absorbed into those of the Ottoman Sultanate.

Notes

1. M. Gluckman, *Custom and Conflict in Africa* (Oxford, 1955); Gluckman, *Politics, Law and Ritual in Tribal Society* (Oxford, 1965).

2. F. Barth, 'Segmentary Opposition and the Theory of Games: A Study of Pathan Organization', *Journal of the Royal Anthropological Institute*, vol.89 (1959), pp.5–22.

3. On education in the kibbutz, see B. Bettelheim, *Children of the Dream* (London, 1969).

4. G. Duby, 'Les "Jeunes" dans la société aristocratique dans la France du Nord-Ouest au XIIe siècle', *Annales: Économies, Sociétés, Civilisations*, vol.19 (1964), pp.835–46; L. Martines (ed.), *Violence and Civil Disorder in Italian Cities, 1200–1500*, (Berkeley, 1962).

5. J. Fletcher, 'Turco-Mongolian Monarchic Tradition in the Ottoman Empire' in *Essays Presented to Omeljian Pritsak, Harvard Ukrainian Studies*, vols 3–4 (1979–80), pp.236–51.

CHRONOLOGICAL LIST OF BAHRI MAMLUK SULTANS

	AH	AD
Shajar al-Durr	648	1250
al-Mu'izz Aybak	648–55	1250–7
al-Mansur 'Ali	655–7	1257–9
al-Muzaffar Qutuz	657–8	1259–60
al-Zahir Baybars	658–76	1260–77
al-Sa'id Berke Khan	676–8	1277–9
al-'Adil Salamish	678	1279
al-Mansur Qalawun	678–89	1279–90
al-Ashraf Khalil	689–93	1290–3
al-Nasir Muhammad	693–4	1293–4
al-'Adil Kitbugha	694–6	1294–6
al-Mansur Lajin	696–8	1296–8
al-Nasir Muhammad (2nd reign)	698–708	1298–1308
al-Muzaffar Baybars II	708–9	1308–10
al-Nasir Muhammad (3rd reign)	709–41	1310–41
al-Mansur Abu Bakr	741–2	1341
al-Ashraf Kuchuk	742	1341–2
al-Nasir Ahmad	742–3	1342
al-Salih Isma'il	743–6	1342–5
al-Kamil Sha'ban	746–7	1345–6
al-Muzaffar Hajji	747–8	1346–7
al-Nasir Hasan	748–52	1347–51
al-Salih Salih	752–5	1351–4
al-Nasir Hasan (2nd reign)	755–62	1354–61
al-Mansur Muhammad	762–4	1361–3
al-Ashraf Sha'ban	764–78	1363–77
al-Mansur 'Ali	778–83	1377–81
al-Salih Hajji	783–4	1381–2

BIBLIOGRAPHY OF PRIMARY ARABIC SOURCES

Abu al-Fida, Isma'il b. 'Ali, *al-Mukhtasar fi Akhbar al-Bashar*, 4 vols (Istanbul, 1869–70). Partly translated by P. M. Holt as *The Memoirs of a Syrian Prince: (672–732/1273–1331)*, (Wiesbaden, 1983)

Abu Shama, 'Abd al-Rahman b. Isma'il, *Kitab al-Rawdatayn fi Akhbar al-Dawlatayn*, 2 vols (Cairo, 1870)

Anonymous, *Beiträge zur Geschichte der Mamlukensultane in den Jahren 690–741 der Higra nach arabischen Handschriften*, K.V. Zettersteen (ed.) (Leiden, 1919)

Baktash al-Fakhri, in *Beiträge zur Geschichte der Mamlukensultane*, K.V. Zettersteen (ed.) (Leiden, 1919), pp.145–249

Baybars al-Mansuri, 'Zubdat al-fikra fi Tarikh al-Hijra', B. M. MS Or Add. 23325

Ibn 'Abd al-Zahir, Muhyi al-Din, *al-Altaf al-Khafiyya min al-Sira al-Sharifa al-Sultaniyya al-Malakiyya al-Ashrafiyya*, A. Moberg (ed.) (Lund, 1902)

—— *al-Rawd al-Zahir fi Sirat al-Malik al-Zahir*, A. Khowaiter (ed.) (Riyad, 1976). Translated in part as *Baybars I of Egypt*, F. Sadeque (trans. and ed.) (Dacca, 1956)

—— *Tashrif al-Ayyam wa'l 'Usur fi Sirat al-Malik al-Mansur*, M. Kamil (ed.) (Cairo, 1961)

Ibn al-Amid, al-Makin Jirjis, *Akhbar al-Ayyubiyyun*, selected, edited and translated by C. Cahen as 'La Chronique des Ayyoubides', *BEO*, vol.15 (1955–7), pp.109–84

Ibn Battuta, *The Travels of Ibn Battuta*, H.A.R. Gibb (trans.), 3 vols (Cambridge, Hakluyt Series, 1958–)

Ibn al-Dawadari, Abu Bakr, *Kanz al-Durar wa Jami' al-Ghurar*, vol.7, U. Haarmann (ed.) (Cairo, 1971); vol.8, H. R. Roemer (ed.) (Cairo, 1960)

Ibn al-Furat, Muhammad ibn Abd al-Rahim, *Tarikh al-Duwal wa'l-Muluk*, vol.7, Q. Zurayq (ed.) (Beirut, 1942); vol.8, Q. Zurayq and N. 'Izz al-Din (eds) (Beirut, 1939). Selected extracts for the years 1244–1277 edited and translated by U. and M. C. Lyons and J. Riley-Smith as *Ayyubids, Mamlukes and Crusaders*, 2 vols (Cambridge, 1971).

Ibn Hajar al-Asqalani, Ahmad ibn 'Ali, *al-Durar al-Kamina*, 4 vols (Hyderabad, 1929–32)

Ibn Kathir, 'Abdallah, *al-Bidaya wa'l-Nihaya*, 14 vols (Cairo, 1932–9)

Ibn Khaldun, 'Abd al-Rahman, *Kitab al 'Ibar wa Diwan al-Mubtada' wa'l-Khabar*, 7 vols (Bulaq, Cairo, 1867)

Ibn al-Nafis, 'Ala al-Din 'Ali b. Abi'l-Haram, *Kitab Fadil ibn Natiq*, edited and translated by M. Meyerhoff and J. Schacht as *The Theologus Autodidactus of Ibn al-Nafis* (Oxford, 1968)

Ibn Sasra, Muhammad b. Muhammad, *A Chronicle of Damascus*, W. M. Brinner (ed.) (Berkeley and Los Angeles, 1963)

Ibn Shaddad, 'Izz al-Din Muhammad b. Ibrahim, *Tarikh al-Malik al-Zahir/Die Geschichte des Sultans Baibars*, A. Hutait (ed.) (Wiesbaden, 1983)

Ibn al-Suqa'i, Fadlallah b. Abi Fakhr, *Tali Kitab Wafayat al-A'yan*, J. Sublet (ed. and trans.) (Damascus, 1974)

Ibn Taghribirdi, Abu'l-Mahasin, *al-Nujum al-Zahira*, 12 vols (Cairo, n.d.)

Ibn al-Wardi, Zayn al-Din 'Umar, *Tatimat al-Mukhtasar fi Akhbar al-Bashar*, in Abu al-Fida, *Mukhtasar*, vol.4, pp.134–55

Ibn Wasil, Jamal al-Din, 'Mufarrij al-Kurub fi Akhbar Bani Ayyub', MS Paris, Ar. 1702 and 1703

al-Jazari, Shams al-Din Muhammad, *Hawadith al-Zaman*, extracts selected and

162

translated by J. Sauvaget as *La Chronique de Damas d'al-Jazari (Années 689–698)* (Paris, 1949)

al-Maqrizi, Ahmad b. 'Ali, *Kitab al-Suluk li-Ma'rifat Duwal al-Muluk*, 6 vols, M. M. Ziada (ed.) (Cairo, 1956–8). Partly edited and translated by E. Quatremere as *Histoire des Sultans Mamlouks de l'Égypte*, 2 vols (Paris, 1845)

—— *Kitab al-Mawa'iz wa'l-I'tibar fi dhikr al-Khitat wa'l-Athar*, 2 vols (Bulaq, Cairo, 1853–4)

—— *Ighathat al-Umma bi Kashf al-Ghumma*, edited and translated by G. Wiet as 'Le Traité de famine de Maqrizi', *JESHO*, vol.5 (1960), pp.1–90

Mufaddal b. Abi'l-Fada'il, *al-Nahj al-Sadid wa'l-Dur al-Farid fi ma ba'd Tarikh Ibn al-'Amid*, edited and translated for the years 1259–1317 by E. Blochet as 'Moufazzal ibn Abil-Fazail. "Histoire des Sultans Mamlouks" ', *Patrologia Orentalis*, vol.12 (1919), pp.345–550; vol.14 (1920), pp.375–672; vol.20 (1929), pp.1–270. Edited and translated for the years 1317–41 by S. Kortantamer as *Ägypten und Syrien zwischen 1317 und 1341 in der Chronik des Mufaddal b. Abi l-Fada'il*, (Freiburg, 1973)

al-Qalqashandi, Ahmad b. 'Ali, *Subh al-A'sha*, 14 vols (Cairo, 1919–22)

al-Safadi, Khalil b. Aybak, *al-Wafi bi'l-Wafayat*, 17 vols (Damascus, Istanbul and Wiesbaden, 1931–)

Shafi b. 'Ali, Nasir al-Din, 'Al-Fadl al-Ma'thur min Sirat al-Malik al-Mansur', MS Bodleian, Oxford, no. Marsh 424

—— *Husn al-Manaqib*, A. Khowaiter (ed.) (Riyad, 1976)

al-Shuja'i, Shams al-Din, *Die Chronik as-Suga'is*, vol.1 (Arabic text) B. Schafer (ed.) (Wiesbaden, 1977)

al-Yunini, Qutb al-Din Musa, *Dhayl Mir'at al-Zaman*, 4 vols (Hyderabad, 1954–61)

BIBLIOGRAPHY OF NON-ARABIC PRIMARY SOURCES

Barbaro, Giosafat, *Travels to Tana and Persia,* W. Thomas (ed.) (London, 1873)
Bar Hebraeus, *The Chronography of Gregory Abu'l-Faraj,* E. A. Wallis Budge (ed. and trans.) (London, 1932)
Codex Cumanicus, G. Kuun (ed.) (Budapest, 1880)
Dawson, C., *The Mongol Mission* (London, 1955). (For John of Piano Carpini's *History of the Mongols* and Williams of Rubruck's *Journey.*)
Desimoni, C., 'Actes passés en 1271, 1274 et 1279 à l'Aias (Petit Armenie) et à Beyrouth par devant des notaires genois', *Archives de l'Orient Latin,* vol.1 (1881), pp.434–534
Jean de Joinville, *Histoire de Saint Louis,* N. de Wailly (ed.) (Paris, 1868)
Robert de Clari, *La Conquête de Constantinople,* P. Lauer (ed.), (Paris, 1974)
Skelton, R. A., Marston, T., and Painter, G., *The Vinland Map and the Tatar Relation* (New Haven and London, 1965), (For John of Piano Carpini.)

BIBLIOGRAPHY OF SECONDARY SOURCES

'Abd al-Raziq, A., *La Femme au temps des Mamelouks en Égypte* (Cairo, 1973)
———— 'Les Muhtasibs de Fustat au temps des Mamluks', *Annales Islamologiques*, vol.14 (1978), pp.127–46
———— 'Le Vizirat et les vizirs d'Égypte au temps des Mamluks', *Annales Islamologiques*, vol.16 (1980), pp.183–240
Allen, W. E. D., *A History of the Georgian People* (London, 1932)
Ankawi, A., 'Pilgrimage to Mecca in Mamluk Times', *Arabian Studies*, vol.1 (1974), pp.146–70
Ashtor, E., 'Étude sur quelques chroniques mamloukes', *Israel Oriental Studies*, vol.1 (1971), pp.272–97
———— 'Sheich Hidr, ein Beiträg zur Geschichte der Juden in Damascus', *Wiener Zeitschrift für die Kunde des Morgenlandes*, vol.44 (1937), pp.237–40
———— 'The Karimi Merchants', *Journal of the Royal Asiatic Society* (1956), pp.45–56
———— 'Some Unpublished Sources for the Bahri Period', *Scripta Hierosolymitana*, vol.9 (1961), pp.11–30
———— *A Social and Economic History of the Near East in the MiddleAges* (London, 1976)
———— *Levantine Trade in the Later Middle Ages* (Princeton, 1983)
Atiya. A. S., *The Crusade in the Later Middle Ages* (London, 1938)
Aubin, J., 'Comment Tamerlane prenait les villes', *SI,* vol. 19 (1969), pp. 83–122
Ayalon, D. 'The Plague and its Effects upon the Mamluk Army', *JRAS* (1946), pp.67–73
———— 'The Circassians in the Mamluk Kingdom', *JAOS*, vol.69 (1949), pp.135–47
———— *L'Esclavage du Mamelouk* (Jerusalem, 1951)
———— 'The Wafidiyya in the Mamluk Kingdom', *Islamic Culture,* vol.25 (1951), pp.81–104
———— 'Le Regiment Bahriyya dans l'armée Mamelouk', *Revue des Études Islamiques* (1952) pp.133–41
———— 'Studies on the Structure of the Mamluk Army', *BSOAS*, vol.15 (1953), pp.203–28 (part 1); pp.448–76 (part 2); vol.16 (1954), pp.57–90 (part 3)
———— 'The System of Payment in Mamluk Military Society', *JESHO,* vol.1 (1957–8), pp.37–65, 257–96
———— 'Notes on the Furusiyya Exercises and Games in the Mamluk Sultanate', *Scripta Hierosolymitana,* vol.9 (1969), pp.31–62
———— 'The Great Yasa of Chingiz Khan. A Reexamination', *Studia Islamica*, vol.33 (1971), pp.97–140 (part A); vol.34 (1971), pp.151–80 (part B); vol.36 (1972), pp.113–58 (part C1); vol.38 (1973), pp.107–56 (part C2)
———— 'Discharges from Service, Banishments and Imprisonments in Mamluk Society', *Israel Oriental Studies,* vol.3 (1972), pp.25–50
———— 'Aspects of the Mamluk Phenomenon', *Der Islam*, vol.53 (1976), pp.196–225 (part 1); vol.54 (1977), pp.1–32 (part 2)
———— 'The Eunuchs in the Mamluk Sultanate', in M. Rosen-Ayalon (ed.), *Studies in Memory of Gaston Wiet* (Jerusalem, 1977), pp. 267–96
Balog, P., *The Coinage of the Mamluk Sultans of Egypt and Syria,* (New York, 1964)
———— 'A Dirhem of al-Kamil Shams al-Din Sunquor, Rebel Sultan of Syria', *Revue Numismatique*, vol.11 (1969), pp.296–9
Barrie, J. M., *Peter Pan* (London, 1904)
Barthold, W., *Turkestan Down to the Mongol Invasion* (London, 3rd edn., 1968)

Bedoukian, P. Z., *Coinage of Cilician Armenia* (New York, 1982)

Berman, A., 'The Turbulent Events in Syria in 658–9 A.H./1260 A.D. Reflected by Three Hitherto Unpublished Dirhems', *Numismatic Circular*, vol.84 (1976), pp.315–16

Bjorkmann, W., *Beiträge zur Geschichte des Staatskanzlei im Islamischen Ägypten* (Hamburg, 1928)

Bodroglieti, A., 'A Collection of Turkish Poems from the 14th Century', *Acta Orientalia Academia Scientarum Hungarica*, vol.16 (1963), pp.244–311

Boswell, A. B., 'The Kipchak Turks', *Slavonic Review*, vol.6 (1927–8), pp.68–5

Bosworth, C.E. *The Ghaznavids* (Edinburgh, 1963)

——— 'Christian and Jewish Religious Dignitaries in Mamluk Egypt and Syria', *IJMES*, vol.3 (1972), pp.59–74

——— 'The "Protected Peoples" (Christians and Jews) in Medieval Egypt and Syria', *Bulletin of the John Rylands Library*, vol.62 (1979), pp.11–36

Boyle, J. A., 'Turkish and Mongol Shamanism in the Middle Ages', *Folklore*, vol.8 (1972), pp.177–93

Brinner, W. M., 'The Significance of the Harafish and their "Sultan" ', *JESHO*, vol.6 (1963), pp.190–215

Cahen, C., 'Les Chroniques Arabes concernant la Syrie, l'Égypte et la Mesopatamie de la conquête Arabe à la conquête Ottoman dans les bibliothéques d'Istanbul', *Revue des Études Islamiques*, vol.10 (1936), pp.332–62

——— *La Syrie du Nord* (Paris, 1940)

——— 'Notes pour l'histoire de la himaya', in *Mélanges Louis Massignon*, vol.1 (Damascus, 1956), pp.287–303

——— 'Editing Arab Chronicles: A Few Suggestions', *Islamic Studies*, vol.1 (1962), pp.1–25

——— *Pre-Ottoman Turkey* (London, 1968)

——— 'Le Testament d'al-Malik as-Salih Ayyub', *BEO*, vol.29 (1977), pp.97–114

——— 'Une Source pour l'histoire des Croisades: les mémoires de Sa'd ad-Din ibn Hamawiya Djuwaini', in Cahen, *Les Peuples Musulmans dans l'histoire médiévale* (Damascus, 1977), pp.457–82

——— 'Mamluks bahrites en Asie Mineure?' in *Quand le Crible était la paille: Homage à Pertev N. Boratav* (Paris, 1978), pp.149–23

The Cambridge History of Iran, vol.5, The Saljuq and Mongol Periods (ed. J. A. Boyle) (Cambridge, 1968)

The Cambridge Medieval History, vol.4, The Byzantine Empire, part 1 (ed. J. M. Hussey) (Cambridge, 1966)

Canard, M., 'Le Traité de 1281 entre Michel Paléologue et le Sultan Qala'un', *Byzantion*, vol.10 (1935), pp.669–80

——— 'Le Royaume d'Armenie-Cilicie et les Mamelouks jusqu'au traité de 1285', *Revue des Études Armeniennes* (n.s.), vol.4 (1967), pp.217–59

Chambers, J., *The Devil's Horsemen* (London, 1978)

Chapoutot-Remadi, M., 'Une Institution mal connue: le Khalifat abbaside du Caire', *Cahiers de Tunisie*, vol.20 (1972), pp.11–23

——— 'Le Vizirat sous les premiers Mamluks', in *Actes du XXIX Congrès international des orientalistes* (1975), vol.1, pt 2, pp.58–62

——— 'Une Grande Crise à la fin du XIIIe siècle en Egypte', *JESHO*, vol.26 (1983), pp.217–45

Crone, P., *Slaves on Horses* (Cambridge, 1980)

Digby, S., 'The Broach Coin-Hoard as Evidence of the Import of Valuta across the Arabian Sea during the 13th and 14th Centuries', *JRAS* (1980), pp.129–38

——— 'The Maritime Trade of India, in T. Raychaudhuri and I. Habib (eds), *The Cambridge Economic History of India* (Cambridge, 1982)

Dols, M. W., *The Black Death in the Middle East* (Princeton, 1977)

—— 'The Second Plague Pandemic and Its Recurrences in the Middle East', *JESHO*, vol.22 (1979), pp.162–89

Douglas, F. M., 'Dreams: The Blind and the Semiotics of the Biographical Notice', *Studia Islamica*, vol.51 (1980), pp.137–62

Eckman, J., 'The Mamluk Kipchak Literature', *Central Asiatic Journal*, vol.8 (1963), pp.303–6

Ehrenkreutz, A., 'Strategic Implications of the Slave Trade between Genoa and Mamluk Egypt in the Second Half of the Thirteenth Century', A. L. Udovitch (ed.), *The Islamic Middle East* (Princeton, 1981)

Elham, S. M., *Kitbuga und Lagin. Studien zur Mamluken-Geschichte nach Baibars al-Mansuri und an-Nuwairi* (Freiburg, 1977)

Eliade, M., *Shamanism: Archaic Techniques of Ecstasy* (London, 1964)

Escovitz, J. H. 'Vocational Patterns of the Scribes of the Mamluk Chancery', *Arabica*, vol.23 (1976), pp.42–62

—— 'The Office of Qadi al-Qudat in Cairo under the Bahri Mamluks', unpublished PhD thesis, Institute of Islamic Studies, McGill University, 1978

—— 'The Establishment of Four Chief Judgeships in the Mamluk Empire', *JAOS*, vol.102 (1982), pp.529–31

Flemming, B., *Landschaftsgeschichte von Pamphylien, Psidien und Lykien* (Wiesbaden, 1964)

Forand, P. G., 'The Relation of the Slave and the Client to the Master or Patron in Medieval Islam', *IJMES*, vol.2 (1971), pp.59–61

Gabrieli, F., 'Venezia e i Mamelucchi', in A. Pertusi (ed.), *Venezia e l'Oriente fra tardo Medioevo e Rinascimento* (Venice, 1966)

—— *Arab Historians of the Crusades* (London, 1969)

Garcin, J. -C. 'Histoire, opposition politique et pietisme traditionaliste', *Annales Islamologiques*, vol.7 (1967), pp.33–89

—— 'Le Caire et la province: constructions au Caire et à Qus sous les Mameluks Bahrides', *Annales Islamologiques*, vol.8 (1969), pp.47–62

—— *Un Centre Musulman de la Haute-Égypte Médiévale: Qus* (Cairo, 1976)

Gaudefroy-Demombynes, M., *La Syrie à l'epoque des Mamelouks d'après les auteurs arabes* (Paris, 1923)

Gibb, H. A. R., *Studies on the Civilization of Islam* (Boston, 1962)

Glubb, J.B. *Soldiers of Fortune* (London, 1973)

Grekov, B. and Yakoubovski, M., *La Horde d'Or* (Paris, 1939)

Grousset, R., *'L'Empire des steppes* (Paris, 1948)

Haarmann, U., *Quellenstudien zür fruhen Mamlukenzeit* (Freiburg, 1970)

—— 'Auflösung und Bewahrung der klassischen Formen arabischer Geschichtsschreibung in der Zeit der Mamluken', *Zeitschrift der Deutschen Morgenlandischen Gesellschaft*, vol.121 (1971), pp.46–60

—— 'Altun Han und Cingiz Han bei den agyptischen Mamluken', *Der Islam*, vol.51 (1974), pp.1–36

al-Hajji, H. N., *The Internal Affairs in Egypt during the Third Reign of Sultan al-Nasir Muhammad b. Qalawun 709–741/1309–41* (Kuwait, 1978)

Halm, H., *Ägypten nach den mamlukischen Lehensregistern. I. Oberägypten und das Fayyum* (Wiesbaden, 1979)

Hambis, L., 'La Lettre mongole du gouverneur de Karak', *Acta Orientalia Academia scientarum Hungarica*, vol.15 (1962), pp.143–6

Hambly, G. (ed.), *Central Asia* (London, 1966)

Hasan, Y. F., *The Arabs and the Sudan* (Edinburgh, 1967)

Heissig, W., *The Religions of Mongolia* (London, 1980)

Heyd, W., *Histoire du commerce du Levant au moyen age*, 2 vols (Leipzig, 1923)

Hill, G., *A History of Cyprus*, vol.2. *The Frankish Period, 1192–1432* (Cambridge, 1948)

Hiyari, M. A., 'The Origins and Development of the Amirate of the Arabs during the Seventh/Thirteenth and Eighth/Fourteenth Centuries', *BSOAS*, vol.38 (1975), pp.509–24

Holt, P.M. 'The Sultanate of Lajin (696–8/1286–9)', *BSOAS*, vol.36 (1973), pp.521–32

—— 'The Position and Power of the Mamluk Sultan', *BSOAS*, vol.38 (1975), pp.237–49

—— 'Qalawun's Treaty with Acre in 1283', *English Historical Review*, vol.91 (1976), pp.802–12

—— 'The Structure of Government in the Mamluk Sultanate', in P. M. Holt (ed.), *The Eastern Mediterranean Lands in the Period of the Crusades* (Warminster, 1977)

—— 'Qalawun's Treaty with Genoa in 1290', *Der Islam*, vol.57 (1980), pp.101–8

—— 'The Treaties of the Early Mamluk Sultans with the Frankish States', *BSOAS*, vol.43 (1980), pp.67–70

—— 'An Early Source on Shaykh Khadir al-Mihrani', *BSOAS*, vol.46 (1983), pp.33–9

—— 'Some Observations on the Abbasid Caliphate of Cairo, *BSOAS*, vol.43 (1984), pp.501–7

Horst, H., 'Eine Gesandschaft des Mamluken al-Malik al-Nasir am Ilhan-Hof in Persien', in W. Hoernbach (ed.), *Der Orient in der Forschung, Festschrift fur Otto Spies* (Wiesbaden, 1967), pp.348–70

Humphreys, R. S., 'The Emergence of the Mamluk Army', *Studia Islamica*, vol.45 (1977), pp.67–91 (part 1); vol.46 (1977), pp.147–82 (part 2)

—— *From Saladin to the Mongols* (Albany, 1977)

Ibrahim, L. A., 'The Great Hanqah of the Amir Qawsun in Cairo', *Mitteilung des Deutschen Archäologischen Instituts*, vol.30 (1974), pp.37–64

Irwin, R., 'Iqta' and the End of the Crusader States', in P. M. Holt (ed.), *The Eastern Mediterranean Lands in the Period of the Crusades* (Warminster, 1977), pp.62–77

—— 'The Supply of Money and the Direction of Trade in Thirteenth Century Syria', in P. W. Edbury and W. M. Metcalf (eds), *Coinage in the Latin East: The Fourth Oxford Symposium on Coinage and Monetary History*, British Archaeological Reports, International Series, vol.77 (1980), pp.74–104

Jackson, P., 'The Crisis in the Holy Land in 1260', *English Historical Review*, vol.95 (1980), pp.481–513

James D., 'Mamluke Painting at the Time of the Lusignan Crusade, 1365–70: A Study of the Chester Beatty Nihayat al-su'l wa'l-umniya', *Humaniora Islamica*, vol.2 (1974), pp.73–88

Jomier, J., *Le Mahmal et la caravane des pelerins de la Mecque XIII-XX siécles* (Cairo, 1953)

Khowaiter, A. A., *Baibars the First, His Endeavours and Achievements* (London, 1978)

Kortantamer, S., *Ägypten und Syrien zwischen 1317 und 1341 in der Chronik des Mufaddal b. Abi l-Fada'il* (Freiburg, 1973)

Labib, S. Y., *Handelsgeschichte Ägyptens im Spätmittelalter* (Wiesbaden, 1964)

Lambton, A. K. S., *Landlord and Peasant in Persia* (Oxford, 1953)

Laoust, H., *Essai sur les doctrines sociales et politiques de Taki-d-Din Ahmad b. Taimiya (1262–1328)* (Cairo, 1939)

—— 'Le Hanbalisme sous les Mamlouks Bahrides (658–784/1260–1382)', *REI*, vol.28 (1960), pp.1–71

Lapidus, I. M., *Muslim Cities in the Later Middle Ages* (Cambridge, Massachusetts, 1967)

Latham, J. D. and Paterson, W. F., *Saracen Archery: An English Version and Exposition of a Mamluke work on Archery (ca. AD 1368)* (London, 1970)

Levi della Vida, G., 'L'Invasione dei Tartari in Siria nel 1260 nei ricordi di un testimone occulare', *Orientalia* (n.s.), vol.4, (1935), pp.353–76

Lewis, B., *The Assassins* (London, 1967)

Ligeti, L., 'Prolegomena to the Codex Cumanicus', *Acta Orientalia Academia Scientarum Hungarica*, vol.35 (1981), pp.1–54

Little, D. P., *An Introduction to Mamluk Historiography* (Wiesbaden, 1970)

—— 'An Analysis of the Relation between Four Mamluk Chronicles', *Journal of Semitic Studies*, vol.19 (1974), pp.252–68

—— 'The Recovery of a Lost Source for Bahri Mamluk History: al-Yusufi's Nuzhat al-Nasir fi Sirat al-Malik al-Nasir', *JAOS*, vol.94 (1974), pp.42–54

—— 'Did Ibn Taymiyya Have a Screw Loose?', *SI*, vol.41 (1978), pp.93–112

—— 'Coptic Conversion to Islam under the Bahri Mamluks 692–755/1293–1354', *BSOAS*, vol.39 (1976), pp.552–69

—— 'Al-Safadi as Biographer of his Contemporaries', in D. P. Little (ed.), *Essays on Islamic Civilization: Presented to Niyazi Berkes* (Leiden, 1976), pp.190–211

—— 'The Founding of Sultaniyya: A Mamluk Version', *Iran*, vol.16 (1978), pp.170–5

—— 'The History of Arabia during the Bahri Mamluk Period According to Three Mamluk Historians', in *Studies in the History of Arabia, vol.1, Sources for the History of Arabia*, part 2 (Riyad, 1979), pp.17–23

—— 'Notes on Aitamis, a Mongol Mamluk', in U. Haarmann and P. Bachmann (eds), *Die Islamische Welt zwischen Mittelalter und Neuzeit: Festschrift fur Hans Robert Roemer zum 65 Geburstag* (Beirut, 1979), pp.387–401

—— 'The Significance of the Haram Documents for the Study of Medieval Islamic History', *Der Islam*, vol.57 (1980), pp.189–219

—— 'Religion under the Mamluks', *Muslim World*, vol.73 (1983), pp.165–81

Lyons, M. C. and Jackson, D. E. P., *Saladin* (Cambridge, 1982)

Makdisi, G., 'Ibn Taymiya: a Sufi of the Qadiriya Order', *American Journal of Arabic Studies*, vol.1 (1973), pp.118–29

Martin, H. D., 'The Mongol Army', *JRAS* (1943–4), pp.46–85

Mayer, L. A., *Saracenic Heraldry* (Oxford, 1933)

Meinecke-Berg, V., 'Quellen zu Topographie und Baugeschichte in Kairo unter Sultan an-Nasir b. Qala'un', *ZDMG*, supp.3 (1977), pp.538–50

Memon, M. U., *Ibn Taymiya's Struggle against Popular Religion* (Hague, 1976)

Moberg, A., 'Regierungspromemoria eines egyptischen Sultans', in G. Weil (ed.), *Festschrift Eduard Sachau* (Berlin, 1915), pp.406–21

Morgan, D. O., 'Cassiodorus and Rashid al-Din on Barbarian Rule in Italy and Persia', *BSOAS*, vol.40 (1977), pp.302–20

—— 'The Mongol Armies in Persia', *Der Islam*, vol.56 (1979), pp.81–96

Mottahedeh, R. P., *Loyalty and Leadership in an Early Islamic Society* (Princeton, 1980)

Muir, W., *The Mamluke or Slave Dynasty of Egypt* (London, 1896)

Musallam, B. F., *Sex and Society in Islam* (Cambridge, 1983)

Nielsen, J. S., 'Mazalim and Dar al-'Adl under the Early Mamluks', *Muslim World*, vol.66 (1976), pp.114–32

Paterson, W. F., 'The Archers of Islam', *JEHSO*, vol.9 (1969), pp.69–87

Pipes, D., *Slave Soldiers and Islam: the Genesis of a Military System* (New Haven and London, 1981)

Poliak, A. N., 'Les Revoltes Populaires en Egypte à l'epoque des Mameloukes et leur causes economiques', *REI*, vol.8 (1934), pp.251–73

—— *Feudalism in Egypt, Syria, Palestine and the Lebanon, 1250–1900* (London, 1939)

Pouzet, L., 'Hadir Ibn Abi Bakr al-Mihrani (m. 7 muh. 676/11 juin 1277), sayh du sultan mamelouk Al-Malik az-Zahir Baibars', *BEO*, vol.0 (1978), pp.173–83

Prawer, J., *Histoire du Royaume Latin de Jérusalem*, vol.2 (Paris, 1970)

Pritsak, O., 'Mamluk-Kiptschakisch', in J. Deny *et al.* (eds), *Philologiae Turcicae Fundamenta*, vol.1 (Wiesbaden, 1959)

Rabie, H., *The Financial System of Egypt, A. H. 564–741/A.D. 1169–1341* (London, 1972)

——— 'Some Technical Aspects of Agriculture in Medieval Egypt', in A. L. Udovitch (ed.), *The Islamic Middle East, 700–1900: Studies in Economic and Social History* (Princeton, 1981), pp.59–90

Richard, J., 'Isol, le Pisan: Un Aventurier franc gouverneur d'une province mongole?', *Central Asiatic Journal*, vol.14 (1970), pp.186–94

Richards, D. S., 'The Coptic Bureaucracy under the Mamluks', in *Colloque International sur l'Histoire du Caire* (Cairo, 1969), pp.373–81

Rogers, J. M., 'Evidence for Mamluk-Mongol Relations 1260–1360', in *Colloque International sur l'Histoire du Caire* (Cairo, 1974), pp.385–404

——— *The Spread of Islam* (Oxford, 1976)

Runciman, S., *A History of the Crusades*, vol.3 (Cambridge, 1955)

Saleh, A. H., 'Les Relations entre les Mamluks et les Bedouins d'Égypte', *Annali Istituto orientale di Napoli* (n.s.), vol.30 (1980), pp.365–93

Salibi, K. S., *Maronite Historians of Mediaeval Lebanon* (Beirut, 1959)

Salim, A., *Tarikh al-Iskandariyya wa hadarataha* (Alexandria, 1982)

Sato, T., 'Irrigation in Rural Egypt from the 12th to 14th Centuries', *Orient*, vol.8 (1972), pp.81–92

Saunders, J. J., *The History of the Mongol Conquests* (London, 1971)

Sauvaget, J., *La Poste aux chevaux dans l'Empire des Mamelouks* (Paris, 1941)

——— *Introduction to the History of the Muslim East* (2nd edn by C. Cahen) (Berkeley and Los Angeles, 1965)

Schein, S., 'Gesta Dei per Mongolos 1300. The Genesis of a Non-event', *English Historical Review*, vol.94 (1979), pp.805–19

Schimmel, A., 'Kalif und Kadi im Spätmittelalterlichen Ägypten', *Die Welt des Islams*, vol.24 (1942), pp.1–26

Schregle, G., *Die Sultanin von Ägypten. Sagarat ad-Durr in der arabischen Geschichtsschreibung und Literatur* (Wiesbaden, 1961)

Sinor, D., *Inner Asia, History — Civilization — Languages* (Bloomington, 1969)

——— *Inner Asia and its Contacts with Medieval Europe* (London, 1977)

Sivan, E., *L'Islam et la Croisade. Idéologie et propagande dans les reactions Musulmans aux croisades* (Paris, 1968)

——— 'Ibn Taymiyya: Father of the Islamic Revolution. Medieval Theology and Modern Politics', *Encounter* (May, 1983), pp.41–50

Somogyi, J. de, 'Adh-Dhahabi's Record of the Destruction of Damascus by the Mongols in 699–700/1299-1301', in S. Lowinger and J. de Somogyi (eds), *Ignace Goldziher Memorial Volume* (Budapest, 1948), pp.353–86

Stern, S. M., 'Petitions from the Ayyubid Period', *BSOAS*, vol.27 (1964), pp.1–32

——— 'Petitions from the Mamluk Period', *BSOAS*, vol.29 (1966), pp.233–76

Tritton, A. S., 'Tribes of Syria in the Fourteenth and Fifteenth Centuries', *BSOAS*, vol.12 (1948), pp.567–74

Tyan, E., *Histoire de l'organisation judiciare en pays de l'Islam*, 2 vols (Paris, 1938–43)

Udovitch, A., 'England to Egypt, 1300–1500: Long-term Trends and Long-distance Trade', in M. A. Cook (ed.), *Studies in the Economic History of the Middle East* (London, 1970), pp.115–28

Vermeulen, U., 'Some Remarks on a Rescript of an-Nasir Muhammad B. Qala' un on the Abolition of Taxes and the Nusayris (Mamlaka of Tripoli, 717/1317), *Orientalia Lovanensia Periodica*, vol.1 (1970), pp.195–201

——— 'The Rescript of al-Malik as-Salih Salih against the Dhimmis (755

A.H./1345)', *Orientalia Lovanensia Periodica*, vol.9 (1978), pp.175–84

Walls, A. G., 'The Turbat Barakat Khan or Khalidi Library', *Levant*, vol.6 (1974), pp.25–50

Weil, G., *Geschichte des Abbasidenchalifats in Egypten*, 2 vols (Stuttgart, 1860–2)

Wiet, G., *L'Egypte arabe* (vol.4 of G. Hanotaux (ed.), *Histoire de la nation égyptienne*) (Paris, 1937)

Wolff, R. L., 'The Second Bulgarian Empire. Its Origin and History to 1204', *Speculum*, vol.24 (1949), pp.167–206

Ziada, M. M., 'The Mamluk Sultans to 1293', in R. L. Wolff and H. W. Hazard (eds), *A History of the Crusades*, vol.2 (Wisconsin, 1969), pp.735–58

——— 'The Mamluk Sultans, 1291–1517', in H. W. Hazard (ed.), *A History of the Crusades*, vol.3 (Wisconsin, 1975), pp.486–512

INDEX

Although transcription marks are not given in the text, they are given here. The system of transliteration for Arabic words is essentially that of the Cambridge History of Islam.